Awaken the Doctor Within

See Pages:
76 - 79

Awaken the Doctor Within

The body is its own best physician!

A low cost, natural healthcare solution
to
Unlock the Secret of Optimal Healing

Raymond Augustyniak, Ph.D.

Notice

This book is intended as a reference volume only, not as a medical manual. The information written within this book is designed to help you make informed decisions about your health and healing. It is not intended as a substitute for any treatment that may have been prescribed by your doctor. If you suspect that you have a medical condition or problem, we urge you to seek competent medical help. This publication is designed to provide accurate and authoritative information with regard to the subject matter covered. It is sold with the understanding that the publisher, copyright owner and author are not engaged in rendering legal, accounting, or other professional or medical advice. If legal or medical advice or other expert assistance or emergency assistance is required, the services of a competent professional should be sought.

Additional copies of this book are available by mail or internet.
Send $32.88 US each (includes tax and postage) to:

Style States Publishing LLC
1000 East William Street Suite 204
Carson City, Nevada 89701

or visit
www.bowenhealingsystem.com

ISBN 0-9717742-0-X

Printed in the United States of America

In support of

BOWTECH

The Original Bowen Technique®

and

Bowen around the world

This book is dedicated to:

Tom Bowen

The founder and originator of this profound, miraculous, and life changing work ~ a wholistic visionary, _well_ ahead of his time.

Oswald and Elaine Rentsch

For their dedication and devotion to teaching and openly sharing Mr. Bowen's original work; and keeping their promise to present this legacy of healing to the world.

Milton Albrecht

The man who brought Bowen to the United States from its Australian seclusion, and worked with great diligence to use and perfect this work until his passing in 2003.

All Bowen Instructors

Who have shown me how to use and teach this therapy that enables me to make **the** difference in the lives of countless others.

Students

Who arrive with eager hearts and open minds to learn Bowen and in course, experience the life-changing effects of

"As the healer heals, the healer is healed."

while bringing to pass…

"As the teacher teaches, the teacher is taught."

and

Raymond and Winston

My two precious sons ~ my most treasured gifts and greatest teachers!

I Love You!

Acknowledgements

I give thanks to those who have assisted me through this laborious book-writing adventure. I thank editors, John Gray, Lisa Behrmann, Duane Newcomb, and Carla Johansen, for their editing gifts. Without their talents and abilities this book would have been a mind-numbing and long-winded dissertation, with only one paragraph and three <u>very</u> long sentences. I thank proofreaders, Barbara Hatch and Doug Straight for their sharp eyes and attention to detail.

I thank the students of Bowen, for their well thought out questions that added to the straightforwardness of this book.

I thank Carol Bennett for contributing portions of the "Bowen for Animals" chapter in this book. Thank you for all the work you do for all kinds of adorable and loving pets and animals in need.

I acknowledge the necessity for all Western medical and alternative healthcare methods, as they all exist to play their role in health and healing. I thank all healthcare professionals who diligently strive to enhance the health and lives of people everywhere. To you I owe much of my knowledge and understanding. I take this opportunity to thank all those who have assisted me and encouraged me in this endeavor, by sharing their gifts, talents, examples, voices and written words. You have taught me well.

To my parents, brothers and sisters, sons and dear friends, who have been with me through the many challenges in this Life - I give thanks for your insights, support, and love. I give thanks to my sons for understanding when I wanted to write instead of play.

I thank my former mother-in-law, Darlyne Andrus, who has always been very kind and loving, who introduced me to Bowen and has always supported me as a caring friend.

I also want to thank all the extensive research contributions of numerous others in Western medical, alternative, and holistic fields.

To each and every one who has touched my life in their own special way, and to God, the Divine Source, from which all healing comes, I thank you.

Namaste'

Mr. Bowen, a native Australian, was a soft-spoken man who became interested in finding ways to alleviate pain and human suffering.

He was self-taught, intuitive and a very gifted man who devoted his entire life to the development of the Bowen Technique.

As a pioneer, Tom Bowen developed this original, brilliantly simple, and truly wholistic therapy without any prior training in any medical or therapeutic discipline. He began to notice when he made certain "Moves" in specific areas on the body that particular and consistent effects took place, which unlocked and re-initiated the healing mechanisms and responses within the body. Over a period of several years he developed the original system as it is used today.

Mr. Bowen frequently stated that he had the ability to sense energy changes in the body and that the work he did was simply "a gift from God."

This ingenious and profound work grants freedom to other compassionate hearts and gifted hands. It richly blesses and changes the lives of many by repeatedly and often miraculously eliminating pain and rapidly restoring health.

Bowen Therapy is unveiling a very significant new era in the healing of humankind.

Thomas Ambrose Bowen, your legacy of healing lives on...revolutionizing healthcare worldwide.

From our hearts we thank you.

~ *Raymond Augustyniak* ~

Foreword

by Oswald and Elaine Rentsch

Oswald "Ossie" has been asked by many people around the world to write a book to further explain what Bowen does to the body and how it actually works. We have both been deeply moved and honored by such requests. In traveling the world sharing the knowledge that has been given to us by Tom Bowen, we have realized that our strengths and talents are in teaching Tom Bowen's original technique to the world. Our dedication is to bring Bowen to as many parts of the world as we are able.

As we both read a manuscript of this book, we were both taken aback by the way that it was so brilliantly written. We both remarked to each other that this book is written as though we had written it with our own hands.

We thank Raymond Augustyniak, for his wholehearted dedication to the work. His commitment to use his God-given gifts and abilities for the purpose of furthering Tom Bowen's work to new levels is warmly welcomed as he, as well as many other dedicated individuals, help pioneer the next chapter in the advancement of Bowen around the world.

About the Author

In the early 1990's, Raymond Augustyniak received a near lethal exposure to toxic chemicals, which took a major toll on his health and life. His former mother-in-law recommended and paid for his first two Bowen sessions. His initial experiences with Bowen not only saved his life, it also brought about such tremendous changes and profound healing in so many areas of his life that he initially chose to learn this technique for the use on just family and friends. Little did he know at that time how a few Bowen sessions would completely transform him and alter the entire course of his life, in such a blessed and unimaginable way.

Since 1994, Raymond has rigorously and intensely studied numerous aspects of the human body and its relationship to injury and healing on various levels. He has implemented his findings with the theory, principles, and philosophy of Bowen into his work to address a wide variety of conditions and pain that many tens of thousands of people have presented him. His enhanced insight of this marvelous work and how it works *with* the body to help it heal multi-dimensionally on very core levels has significantly expanded and advanced the understanding of Bowen, especially for those who desire to gain further insight into these very healing principles initially used and taught by Tom Bowen himself. Over the years, Raymond has developed an extensive array of other Bowen related Moves and Procedures which he has found to be useful and highly successful in addressing very particular issues or for the occasional rare pain or condition that doesn't readily respond to commonly established Bowen Moves or Procedures.

By performing Bowen for very complex cases on nearly a daily basis since 1994, Raymond has keenly observed what works for the human body and what doesn't. He has seen countless times where Bowen works miraculously and he has also seen the very, very rare instances where Bowen itself has not fully worked. He has discovered that physical trauma and injury include deep-seated mental and emotional elements as well as their direct physical consequences. These discoveries have lead him to further investigate the effects of emotional and mental trauma and their direct influence on one's health. The investigation of the effects of emotional and mental trauma has revealed a direct connection to very specific physical manifestations occurring in precise locations and/or as specific conditions that appear in the body.

Ongoing discoveries continually reveal how Bowen repeatedly assists the body to heal these areas while helping to reverse and disappear the effects of the experienced trauma(s) as well. This knowledge, that trauma and injury and their long- lasting effects on the body really are multi-dimensional, has revealed that truly healing the body on all levels _is_ definitely possible. For this to happen, the methods used to facilitate healing on all levels simultaneously must indisputably include an approach that encompasses healing on multiple levels.

The extraordinary multi-dimensional healing capacity of Bowen to consistently address common health and pain-related issues and heal the body in such a gentle, simple, straightforward and superior manner, has made it Raymond's premier choice. Its effectiveness in drastically reducing and, in most cases, eliminating pain in all areas of the body no matter how long a person has had it, while simultaneously addressing the entire body as a whole to rapidly assist its healing, truly makes it second to none.

Raymond is the founder of **Bowen Healing System**™ Centers. His passion for Bowen extends well beyond clinical work into educating professionals and laypersons worldwide. He commonly uses a variety of written and verbal media to share this work. These include writing books, manuals, articles, teaching and demonstrating Bowen in conferences, seminars, and workshops internationally, as well as television and radio appearances and internet coverage. His work includes increasing public education and awareness of this brilliantly simple and phenomenal work. When asked why he does so much for Bowen, he simply answers without hesitation, "I am just passing on the gift of life and health that was given to me."

As an accredited senior instructor for **Bowtech**® (the worldwide teaching organization for Bowen practitioners) Raymond shares the art of Bowen using a very simple, down-to-earth, easy-to-learn approach, which features segments on refining the technique and its application in addressing difficult cases and specific conditions in the body.

Additionally, Raymond has developed unique Bowen protocols and procedures specifically to significantly enhance athletic performance in a natural way. Many professional, Olympic and collegiate athletes have quickly benefited from Bowen after they have suffered from a "game or event time" injury, which would normally take them out of competition for many weeks. After a "quick fix" with Bowen, most athletes are able to return to competition at 80 -100% in as little as just 2-5 minutes.

Currently, Raymond resides just outside Sacramento, California.

Introduction

Welcome to the World of Bowen

At the dawning of the 21st century when many individuals are searching for natural healthcare methods, Bowen is unveiling new discoveries into how the body heals. It leads natural alternative healthcare technology by presenting profound multi-dimensional healing, using a single approach. It commonly addresses the underlying causes of pain and ill health, making it far more effective in addressing the body as a whole.

Bowen offers solutions for many vexing and complex pain and health-related issues. It has been found to work especially well for those individuals who have exhausted the options that conventional Western and alternative medicine have offered, and also for those who have heard their doctor say, "There is nothing more I can do for you; you'll just have to learn to live with the pain and what you have."

If Bowen only worked a handful of times, one could chalk it up to luck. If it only worked for a couple of hundred people, or even a few thousand, it might be considered a statistical coincidence. The fact that it has worked on an estimated one million people over the course of almost fifty years is unassailable proof that it has the power to produce results.

This gentle, non-invasive therapeutic approach to optimum health and healing often works when other traditional and well-known alternative therapies, or more invasive approaches to health, fall short or fail altogether. It is an all-natural, phenomenal, and often miraculous remedial therapy that is literally revolutionizing the healthcare industry worldwide--not because it is something new, necessarily, but because it *works*. And because it works, it is quickly becoming the number one preferred alternative healthcare method around the world. It is a direct, yet gentle, approach to the body that can be used on anyone, from newborn infants to the elderly, from world-class athletes to the physically impaired.

As an all-encompassing healthcare approach, it is one that works *with* the body and enhances its own healing system to do the work. It assists many people plagued by a myriad of health issues and concerns that seem to elude even the most modern medical and alternative methods.

This book will reveal some of the inner-workings of a relatively unknown therapy which is life-changing and truly life-saving, as in cases such as mine. It can make the difference in the level of health of yourself and loved ones. Even many veteran Bowen Practitioners still do not understand how or why Bowen works. What they do know for sure is that it ***does*** work and those who receive Bowen will attest to that fact.

This Australian approach to extraordinary health and healing is relatively new to the United States *and* the rest of the world. Though new to many, it is an exceptionally effective, economical, and brilliantly simple therapy that is extremely results-oriented by nature. It assists individuals to gain "Maximum Health for the Minimum Price™".

Understanding this unfamiliar non-medical discipline might seem difficult at first, because of the lack of previously-written material on the subject and because of its pure and simple approach. However, by breaking Bowen down into straightforward and simple components, this book will offer a greater level of understanding and comprehension of the work as a whole.

Often, for those who have comprehensive medical training, or possess a greater understanding of the body, its inner workings, and intricacies, Bowen can prove to be even more difficult to understand primarily because of its extreme simplicity. It is a discipline that cannot be easily described using well-known traditional, modern, or alternative views or terms. The fundamental nature of this work challenges individuals of all levels of knowledge, giving them an opportunity to empty their mental cup of what they think they know. With an open mind, these people are given an opportunity to gain a magnificently greater insight and understanding of what they have often sensed or just knew is actually happening or *could* take place in the body, if the body was just given the correct information to work with.

This book presents an in-depth look into the fastest growing, best-kept secret in natural and alternative healthcare available today. Included in this book are a variety of examples which give definition to what Bowen is, some explanations into how it works and why it causes the body to respond often immediately, *and* at times, in miraculous ways. A list of the many ailments, conditions, disorders, and dysfunctions that Bowen has become renowned for addressing is also included. Insights into what Bowen consistently offers the body in a very non-invasive and natural way as a whole, several testimonies of those who have received the results Bowen *freely* gives, and a few brief cases are also shared within these pages. The testimony of numerous individuals, in their own words, illustrates the significance of the profound and lasting impact Bowen has on their own health and lives of their families and friends who have received Bowen.

The explanations, theories, and interpretations contained within this book are founded on personal knowledge gained through learning and using the original technique as taught by Bowen Therapy Academy of Australia (BTAA) accredited instructors, and my own personal continual in-depth study, observation, experience, and research into how the body works with and readily responds to Bowen in various ways and on multiple levels. They are also founded on what I see is taking place in the body based on my background and experience in mechanical design and fabrication; seeing the body as mechanical, chemical, electric, and hydraulic in nature, at its basic form.

Many years of experience treating countless numbers of people using Bowen also greatly contributed to the inquiry that was the foundation of this book. Witnessing Bowen's far-reaching results on a daily basis and teaching and lecturing in a variety of settings has contributed enormous insight and discovery into much of this work. Constant personal refining of the work in order to address very specific, unusual and difficult cases has exponentially added to the advancement of this work. Continual discovery and development of new Bowen procedures which produce consistent and profound changes in the body, resulting in enhanced well-being and more rapid restoration of health and healing, are relentlessly being explored ad infinitum.

Although Bowen is in its infancy and currently is still in the process of compiling reliable comprehensive statistical, historical, qualitative, and quantitative clinical scientific analysis, it stands in the forefront as a results-oriented remedial healing system by those who perform the work and have witnessed its capacity to induce healing and rapidly restore health.

The work contained in this book is by no means all-inclusive. Details of how Bowen works in restoring health and healing to the body is constantly being discovered. Greater insights that unlock the unidentified realms of how the body functions are constantly being revealed through this work as well. The mysteries of the inner workings of the body, mind, and spirit continually unveil themselves on all levels through this simple, yet miraculous work. The vast research contributions of numerous others in traditional, medical, alternative, and holistic fields also greatly broaden the understanding of this work.

The information in this book will introduce you to a simple, very effective, and innovative approach to health that many millions of people have been searching for. Although the information you will read may be new to you, it will be worth every bit of your time and effort to acquaint yourself with it so you can use it for your benefit.

Many individuals and healthcare organizations are searching for alternative methods for healing the body that are gentle, cost-effective, non-invasive, *and* drug-free. They are intensely searching for ways to greatly reduce or eliminate pain, stress, tension, disorder, dysfunction, and disease in the body. They are also searching for a *simple alternative solution* that can *directly address a wide range of conditions* that the human body commonly presents.

They are looking for methods that contribute to greater health, longer life-expectancy, and enhanced overall total body wellness, while retaining youthfulness. They also desire to find a method that will work for the whole family, from newborn infants to great-grandparents, which can achieve optimum <u>and</u> consistent results using only a few sessions.

My experience is that Bowen is very consistent in showing that it can often surpass all other methods in addressing and eliminating pain and suffering. To me it has proven time and time again that it can exceed the criteria these people and organizations are looking for. It is an extremely effective therapeutic approach to restore health and healing to the body that is seemingly simple, yet it produces extraordinarily profound effects that help the body to heal rapidly. While doing so, Bowen has its unique way of also helping clear the mind and awaken the spirit simultaneously, at a speed that the body itself can handle.

Often, it defies logic and reasoning by producing marvelous, and as stated by many, "miraculous" results when other avenues, both traditional and alternative, have fallen short or failed altogether. Many who have received this unfamiliar approach share the belief that they have witnessed results that are, in their words, "nothing short of a miracle."

Skeptics have visited the Bowen Healing System® Center and other competent Bowen Practitioners throughout the world. They followed the advice of a trusted neighbor, friend, or colleague. They have walked away astounded at the results they have received after just a few minor sessions.

I ask that you read this book carefully as it contains information that is <u>not</u> known to most people and has not been shared to this magnitude until this time. Though the information in this book may be new to you and you may have some reservations, please understand that...the action and <u>results</u> Bowen achieves speak **much** louder than any words which can be written about it.

If you are skeptical, GREAT! I ask you to receive a minimum of 3-5 sessions from an experienced *and* qualified Bowen Practitioner and prove to yourself what it can do.

Chapter 1
Bowen

A Lifesaving, Life Transforming Therapy

I had suffered from poor health throughout much of my life. Within two weeks of my birth in 1960, doctors gave me only minutes to live as they were injecting me full of penicillin in order to keep me alive. They told my parents to kiss me goodnight for the last time, because I would be gone by morning. A nurse's sharp fingernail had penetrated my skin moments after I was born, causing a severe life-threatening and life-altering Staph infection. I survived, but maintaining my health after that was next to impossible.

At nine months old, another severe illness struck and nearly took my life again as doctors struggled to find any cause.

At 13, I was given a 20% chance to live. My appendix had unknowingly been ruptured for two weeks and spewed gangrene into my body. Doctors from the Mayo Clinic examined and analyzed the remains of my appendix and told the surgeon that I couldn't possibly have lived. They told the surgeon that in cases only half as bad as mine, the patients had all died. After many days in intensive care, the surgeon came to tell me that it was truly a miracle that I was alive.

At 33, the employer I worked for as a mechanical designer and fabricator lied about exposing employees to highly toxic airborne substances. After working there for nearly six months, I woke up one morning, extremely sick. My eyes were nearly swollen shut, my nose was bright red and severely irritated. My ears were dark red and had the texture of beef jerky. I looked like a heavy long-time cocaine user from some movie, although I had never used drugs in my life. I had a rash over my entire body. I had difficulty breathing and I could hardly move. Something was drastically wrong!

I talked to the plant manager and the main supervisor about the problem I was having and told them that I needed to see a doctor. They said, "Ah, don't worry about it. It's just something that is going around the plant. It's nothing serious. You'll get over it."

I told them, "This is serious." I demanded to see the company doctor threatening to go elsewhere. Very reluctantly they sent me to a physician.

The doctor took one look at me and said, "Topical dermatitis. You must have gotten into something. I'll give you some *prednisone* and you'll be just fine." I took the prescription as directed and my condition looked like it started to clear up. Then two days after taking the final dose, all the prior symptoms came back with vengeance and my tongue started bleeding.

Immediately I called the doctor at home, as it was a Saturday. He asked me to meet him at his office. He took one look at me and said, "I have *never* seen anything like this. I'll have to send you to some specialists."

Following his advice I went to various specialists that came highly recommended. They did their checks, prods and multiple tests. In the end they said there was nothing wrong with me. I was adamant and demanded a diagnosis.

After many months of going to doctors without a trace of knowing what was going on, I visited one specialist who decided to look up my nose with a nasal scope. He nearly dropped the scope when he saw what was happening inside my sinus cavities. He said, "It looks like a war zone in there. There is massive hemorrhaging and pieces hanging down. It looks like a bomb went off. Whatever you are exposed to around your work is killing you. Sorry, you no longer work there."

Doctors gave me medication after medication. They sent me to other specialists but my health continued to go downhill. One day, they finally explained that I was dying and that there was nothing else they could do.

Within a few days, I barely had enough energy to get out of bed. Day-to-day tasks seemed insurmountable and working to support a family took everything I had. Even though I needed to and did go back to work (at a different place of employment), I slept every spare moment. When I had a fifteen or thirty minute break at work, I slept for all but five. When I returned home I would shower, eat and go to sleep. On weekends all I wanted to do was sleep. Participating in any activities other than work was impossible.

The medication I took did nothing good for me; it only made me extremely tired, very irritable and left me in a stupor. During this time, I also suffered extreme mood swings which came without notice. Someone turning on the TV, closing a door too hard, or talking loudly would often instantly set me off. It seemed to come from nowhere. The rage would arrive suddenly and depart just as quickly as it came. I *knew* there was something terribly wrong.

One day, Darlyne Andrus, my former mother-in-law, recommended Bowen and paid for my first two visits. I traveled to Auburn, California to visit Milton Albrecht, a Bowen Practitioner.

The first session did not seem to have any impact on me and I clearly didn't feel anything, as far as I was concerned. The second, however, put me in an extremely deep state of relaxation and created an intense heat from within my body. By the end of the Bowen session my clothes were completely soaked with perspiration. My clothes literally dripped like I had just gotten out of a pool as I strolled around the room at the conclusion of the session.

Much to my amazement, my body and brain felt centered and balanced for the first time ever. My body was tingling and for once I felt truly alive. The severe brain fog I had for 30+ years of my life completely vanished. I really felt *GREAT* for the first time in my life. As a result, I did not continue with the Bowen sessions until three months later when some of the conditions started to return.

I went back to Milton for another session, as he was the only one who had been able to make any noticeable difference. The Bowen session Milton gave me that day took all of ten, *maybe* fifteen minutes – I felt very apprehensive because it was so short. Milton did not seem to do anything. After he finished, I didn't experience the impressive heating up, tingling or sweating of the previous visit. As far as I was concerned, I wasn't even given time for relaxation. I was just agitated. I thought, this guy didn't do a damn thing for me today; I'm not coming back to him anymore, he just ripped me off. He just did a couple of touches on my body and then took my money…*so I thought!*

On the way home, though, I started coughing. I coughed the rest of the evening and throughout the entire night. The more I coughed, the more irritated my lungs became. The more irritated my lungs became, the worse it got. I thought my lungs were going to turn inside out and I was going to die.

When it was finally over, I had discharged nearly 40 ounces of the nastiest looking and smelling phlegm and debris from my lungs that I had ever seen. My sinuses were draining like someone had hooked a water hose to them. My chest felt open and free.

I said to myself, "There is nothing in Western medicine that can do this. Milton hardly even touched me." Immediately after this coughing bout, my energy increased, I felt on top of the world. My healing had definitely begun.

Bowen did more for me in three simple sessions than what the medical community was able to do in well over a year. A few weeks later I asked myself, "If Bowen could do this for me, what could it do for my family and friends? Could I learn to do Bowen? Milton didn't seem to need to know much or how to do much. How could *I* learn it, knowing nothing about the body?"

THE DECISION

I called Milton one day and asked, "What does it take to learn Bowen?" He asked me one question. "Do you have a desire to learn?" "Yes, of course." I replied. "That's all you need. The rest you can learn over time with *much* study and practice," he emphasized. "I'll do whatever it takes." I replied. "And…when can I start?" I eagerly asked.

Having been healed through this seemingly illusory and unexplainable therapy, I desired to somehow help others to do the same. I wanted to learn Bowen *just to help out a few family members and friends*…so I thought.

After making the decision to learn Bowen, I quickly found that learning and mastering Bowen was far more challenging than I could ever imagine. I struggled severely from the beginning. I was anatomically and physiologically illiterate; knowing only head, shoulders, knees and toes. I had no real knowledge of the body or any experience working with it either. Learning just the basic Bowen Moves and Procedures took everything I had.

Many of the people advancing in the Bowen classes I registered in were already healthcare professionals; doctors, nurses, physical therapists, chiropractors, naturopaths, along with other alternative healthcare practitioners. I was petrified being in classes with others who were more experienced than I was.

My deep fears of making mistakes and having to touch another person erupted to the surface and my brain froze. I had great difficulty in remembering what to do and where to do it – hand placement -- how much pressure to use -- how little pressure to use -- when the person was supposed to breathe, when to turn them over and scores of other protocol and specific details. After a short time, I was overwhelmed and thoroughly mystified. Not familiar with terminology associated with the body, I constantly asked for help throughout the entire course. Not fully knowing what I was doing, not having a clue what I was looking for, I asked for anyone to show me how to do the Moves and explain the concepts in terms and in ways that I could understand.

However, somehow I knew from deep within, without a doubt, that I could do something with Bowen to help others *if* I could only learn it. My fears caused me to make *countless* missteps.

After each course, I rigorously studied about the body and repeatedly sought further instruction and guidance to deepen my understanding of the body and what Bowen was doing to cause such huge changes releasing people from the bondage and agony of years of pain and suffering. I called or visited many Bowen instructors, assistants and other experienced Bowen practitioners asking question after question. I sought out doctors, physical therapists, chiropractors, massage instructors and other Western and healthcare practitioners to gain greater insight into how the body works and what makes it heal.

FIRST TEST

The day after finishing the initial Bowen course, a gentleman, referred to me by his daughter, came for a Bowen session. His right leg was crippled and pushed way out to the side, causing him to rely heavily on two canes to walk.

He explained that eleven years ago, he had 750 pounds of material fall off a forklift onto his head and shoulders. Doctors fused his neck and low back and used metal rods in order to help him. Unfortunately, this left him totally disabled, in constant extreme pain and unable to get around very well.

He was taking very heavy doses of multiple, very powerful, pain medications on a daily basis since the accident. Doctors told him that he had to learn to live with the pain. He was actually 6' 4" but now stood at a height of 4' 6". Because of his crippled condition, he was on full disability and he hated being seen in public.

I told him "I don't think I can do anything for you. I will gladly give you Bowen sessions at no charge and use any results as personal research." Even though I was walking proof myself of Bowen's ability to help the body to miraculously heal itself, I previously had only heard about the results Bowen had been able to achieve in more complex and chronic cases such as his.

I performed Bowen on him using only basic Bowen Relaxation Moves (BRM's) and what Bowen Practitioners call the Ankle Procedure. I took my time (nearly two hours) insuring that I did every procedure correctly and to the best of my knowledge and ability (although in class we were told that a normal Bowen session can regularly take only 20-45 minutes).

As I performed Bowen on this man, remarkable changes took place in his body. The severe muscle tension and the pain/spasm cycles that had been torturing his body for nearly eleven years gradually released. By the end of the session, his body was calm and relaxed, his breathing smooth and deep. The gripping tension that shrouded his face upon his arrival had disappeared.

After he sat up, I instructed him, *just as I was taught in class*, to "place both feet evenly on the floor and take a stroll around the room." His first response was "I need my canes." I replied, "I don't think so." He stepped onto the floor and began to take small, yet confident steps for the first time in eleven years without the use of his canes.

He left with a huge smile on his face using only one cane for balance. Six days later he called and said, "I don't know what you did, but 80% of my pain is gone and my right foot works better than it ever has, thank you so much!"

After the second session he said, "The two Bowen sessions have done more for me than over eleven years of extensive medical treatments, physical therapy, massage, and any other conventional or alternative therapy I could find, combined." His daughter later told me her dad was going back to work again.

After performing Bowen on that first person and personally observing the extraordinary and miraculous changes that took place in a *very* short amount of time, Bowen became the passion that created a powerful drive from deep within me. ***Bowen not only saved my life, it also transformed my entire life and way of being from the inside out.***

Bowen consistently initiates such profound transformations in the bodies, minds, and lives of individuals I have cared for, that I passionately continue to pass on the gift of health and healing that was given to me.

Since my first training with Milton, the majority of my Bowen training and study has been completed under Oswald and Elaine Rentsch and other senior **Bowtech**[R] instructors around the world. Today, I instruct doctors, nurses, physical therapists, chiropractors, massage therapists and laypersons how to properly use Bowen to help others liberate themselves from illness, pain and suffering.

My intent in writing this book is:

1. To provoke a deeper understanding of HOW the body is designed to work

2. To explain how *Bowen makes nothing but sense*, as it works wholistically (as a whole) with the body to simultaneously address the entire body and mind, in order to facilitate completion of unfinished "healing," while eliminating the body of unnecessary and obsolete patterns and cycles

3. Offer a very effective and advanced alternative healthcare solution to those who are committed to using natural sources of healing

My desire is that this book is one of my contributions to health and healing for everyone world-wide.

Chapter 2

Thomas A. Bowen

The Man and His Legacy

Thomas Ambrose Bowen
(1916-1982)

Thomas Ambrose Bowen was born April 18, 1916, in Melbourne, Victoria, Australia and died September 6, 1982. He was the only son and third child of William and Norma Bowen who emigrated from England to Australia.

Tom's father was a carpenter who believed his children should receive only enough education to get a good job. His mother was straightforward and strict, but the couple was hospitable and often helped people who were down and out.

Tom married Jessie MacLean in 1941, and soon after moved to Geelong, Australia. The couple had three children, two daughters, Pam (Trigg) and Heather (Edmonds), who currently live in Australia with their families, and a son, Barry (who lives in the United States). Tom's first job was as a milk carrier, followed by a job as a general hand at a woolen mill. He then worked as a carpenter on the Geelong wharves, which lead him to the Geelong Cement plant where he was an industrial chemist.

At the cement plant in 1958, Tom saw a man fall from a thirty-foot scaffold. A voice from within said, "Go over there, you can help this man." Tom hesitated, and started to turn away. The voice within repeated, "Go over there, you can help this man." Upon hearing this he approached the seriously injured man, laid his hand on his back as directed by an inner guidance, and performed the first two "Bowen Moves," ever. The injured man immediately told others that surrounded them that he didn't know what Tom just did, but his excruciating pain left almost immediately. The man never went into shock and recovered very quickly from his injuries.

The knowledge of Tom's ability to rid people of pain and suffering spread quickly. At work people would stop and ask him if he could work on their arm, or hand, wrist or ankle, or could he address the nagging back ache they were suffering from. Before long, people began showing up at his house at all hours to ask him to help relieve the pain in their neck, hand, shoulder, knee or muscle ache or some other pain. Or they would ask if he could relieve some other ailment they had, or the ailment of a family member or friend.

Stan Horwood, a friend from the cement plant, invited Tom to use his home in the evenings as a clinic to perform what became known as Bowen Therapy.

The following year, in 1959, he finally quit his job and opened a full-time clinic. It was from this point forward that Tom began to more fully develop his skills. Stan's wife, Rene, was a successful business owner and offered to help Tom run his business. His business relied purely on word-of-mouth promotion. People traveled from all across the country to receive Bowen from him.

At his peak, he was seeing 100 people a day. Tom also made evening house calls to help those unable to come to his clinic. He helped children, doctors, nurses, and police officers free of charge because they were "doing right" by serving others. On the third Saturday morning of each month, Tom would help those who were in wheelchairs at no charge. At least once a month on a Sunday morning, he helped prisoners at the Geelong Prison. Tom was awarded a medal from the Victorian Police Board in appreciation of his efforts.

Tom Bowen's formal education extended through the eighth grade. He lacked any recognizable medical training or other medical qualifications, except for his first-aid skills which he acquired in the army as a medic. Most believe that his intense desire to find a way to help alleviate human pain and suffering came through his military experiences during wartime. This intensity multiplied when his granddaughter was born with Cerebral Palsy.

In Practice

In his practice, Tom identified problems quickly and knew instantly what was happening in a person's body. He could often take just one look and readily "see" what was wrong with a particular individual. Often he did this by recognizing specific tension and pain patterns in the body referenced by how the individual held themselves as they sat, stood, or how they moved, coupled with the level of vitality they exhibited. How quickly the body responded to the work that he did was used as another indicator. These and other markers were used as a guide to then perform a few specific "Moves" to *enable the body to quickly remove unnecessary patterns of pain and tension* -- ***no matter how long they had been held in the body***, in nearly every case.

Tom said that "the body will tell you everything *if* you know what to look for and it *will* respond if you know what to do to address the cause." Most healthcare professionals - even now, rely primarily on *many* years of study and training *plus* extensive testing in many cases, just to give a diagnosis that is not always accurate. Tom counseled his students to look at the body very carefully. "Look at the whole story, not just part of it," he would say. "Study what the body is or isn't doing, find where it is resisting or protecting itself and learn to read it like a book. It tells you a story, it's just in code." "Getting it right the first time," while valuing people's time, seemed to be a familiar underlying theme in his work.

It is after understanding how the body is designed to work and function on many levels, that one can begin to see that every clue is given as to what is happening in the body on much deeper levels *and* in areas other than the obvious ones. Honing these assessment skills and then combining them with the correct "Moves" or sequences of "Moves" then allows the Bowen Practitioner to give the body the correct signal(s) to begin addressing and correcting the problem on its own.

Tom claimed that he could sense energetic changes in the body through his fingers. He could feel nerve or muscle pulses that were discharged as the "Moves" were performed indicating that a particular "Move" was performed successfully. Successful "Moves" trigger the body to "let go" of whatever it is holding on to and begins to help it relax and respond in a healing manner from foundational core levels.

Tension and release of a muscle or specific muscle groups also helped Tom find the correct locations to perform the "Moves" while he worked. In this way, the body "told" him what to do. It told him what *it* needed, not what anyone "thought" should be done. From his findings of what the body consistently told him what to do, he was able to adapt various "Moves" or combinations of "Moves" (procedures) to trigger a specific, consistent and predictable response in the body.

"Where the spirit does not work with the hand there is no art."

-Leonardo da Vinci-

1452 - 1519

Tom used only a few simple Moves, and then waited a few moments to give the body time to receive and decipher the information. Tom found that this waiting period also allowed the body time to respond and make necessary changes. When Tom sensed or observed changes beginning to take place, he ended the session to allow the body to follow its natural healing course.

Tom sent some cases home for a week before they returned for the next session. For others, the pain disappeared after one session, and their health was fully restored after a few days.

In working with the body, Tom found that by performing a series of precisely-located yet gentle movements over muscles, tendons, nerve intersections, or soft tissue, and by using precisely the correct amount of pressure and tempo for performing the Move, the body would immediately begin to intensify and redirect its own energy and stimulate healing *throughout the entire body*. He quickly observed in his work that once the healing processes are properly stimulated in the body, the restoration back to optimal health would soon follow.

Tom based his work purely on common sense. He addressed what was there directly in front of him, nothing more; knowing there was always a reason for what was happening in the body. He initially used his work to address only pain, tension and musculo-skeletal disorders. However, the more he performed his work, the more he discovered that certain Bowen Moves or Procedures often improved or eliminated more serious health conditions, such as asthma, as well. In developing this system of healing, his aim was to assist the person's body to heal by addressing the cause and correcting the problem, while at the same time encouraging them to be responsible for their own health.

On rare occasions when the body would not respond, Tom would re-assess and take another approach…that of intuition. He would "ask the body" what it needed and what Moves, if any, needed to be performed. Using his perceptive abilities along with his knowledge and experience, he discovered many new "Moves" and Procedures which advanced his healing system even more. Tom knew that it was the system that he used to address the body, *combined with* the body's ability to heal itself, which did the healing. He was always saying that the work he did "had nothing to do with him or any ability that he may have had". He *always* insisted his abilities were "a gift from God."

Frequently his Bowen Procedures required only one or two Moves to initiate the changes in the body that were necessary to eliminate pain and restore optimal health. In some cases, he found that combining one or two Moves of one Procedure with one or two Moves of another Procedure would produce a completely different, yet predictable outcome. Over time, Tom refined these new Moves or Procedures and linked their application to address a specific region or condition of the body. He also developed protocols and timing for each Move or Procedure to standardize their purpose and application.

Unfortunately, Tom did all his work from memory and never documented any of his work. A small card was used to keep each person's information and track past visits. A code on this card informed his office staff when the person needed to return or what they needed to do to assist their return to optimal health.

In his later years, Tom wore a hearing aid and turned it off while performing Bowen on people to keep conversation in the clinic to a minimum. Instead of talking, he devised a system of finger clicks to direct his staff.

Tom also observed relationships between ailments and certain foods and/or beverages. When people didn't respond to his work, Tom often found that he obtained unparalleled results by asking them to refrain from consuming specific foods or beverages. Coffee, he discovered, was the main cause of migraines.

Tom often had people remove specific foods from their diet such as: sago (a food thickening agent), rice, spaghetti, fried foods, potatoes, onions, white flour, milk and *all* dairy products. This list also included chocolate, pastry, peanuts, strawberries, and passion fruit. When he had people refrain from eating specific foods he found that their health would dramatically improve.

By combining refined Moves with simple dietary changes, including removing all dairy products, Tom found with these Moves that, 90% of *all* asthmatics are cleared of respiratory congestion. The other 10%, who did not fully respond, received enough relief *to bring their asthma under control without the use of any medication.*

In 1972, the Australian College of Osteopaths and the South Pacific Osteopaths invited Tom to become a member of their associations.

In 1973, the Osteopathy, Chiropractic, and Naturopathy Committee of Australia conducted an inquiry into his operation as a natural therapist. This investigation revealed that Tom was self-taught and that he studied from a few books that he found helpful.

In 1975, a Victorian Government study of Alternative Healthcare Professionals revealed that Tom treated nearly 13,000 people a year with an extremely high success rate of 88%.

Many in the healthcare industry believed that Tom Bowen had deciphered much of the cryptic code of health and healing that has eluded leading healthcare professionals for thousands of years. He broke this code by developing an extraordinarily unique system of purely soft-tissue Moves that are ever-so-gentle on the body, which stimulates and activates foundational core healing responses from deep within the body.

Tom loved to play many sports and regularly shared time with what he called his "footballers", treating them for their injuries and keeping them well, to play another day. In the words of Rene Horwood: "Tom was involved with and played all sports, except wrestling. He loved swimming, umpiring cricket on Saturday afternoons, and in his later years he played lawn bowling. Tom also ran a very successful Boys Club with the Salvation Army."

Tom did have a family. Although the demands of his busy clinic were great, Tom did share many wonderful times with them when he could. Not much else is known about Tom or discussed about him by any of his surviving family members or relatives; except that he was a *very* kind, giving and loving man who had very large hands with long, soft fingers.

TOM BOWEN'S PHILOSOPHY

Tom Bowen was confident that the body ultimately has an innate ability to quickly restore health when given the correct information in a suitable setting. He was sure that there was little that the body could not heal. According to Tom, there was "no need to *make it happen* by using forceful manipulations or therapies. The body just needed coaxing in the proper direction." Tom realized that one of the main keys existed in opening up the body's resources and clearing its energy pathways, making the body its own best physician. *It knows what to do.*

Tom believed in using the least amount of intervention to cause the greatest measure of healing. "Less is best with Bowen" was commonly heard from him. "You don't make anything happen. You just set the body up with the right Moves, then you just walk away and let the *body* do all the work," was commonly heard by those who learned from him. The goal being "*to influence the body in such a way that the dynamic healing system of the body is brought back to life.*"

A state of imbalance within one system or organ will directly affect other systems and organs as well. Our bodies perform best when there is balance within the body as a whole, meaning that the systems and organs are correctly communicating and synchronized. This balance is also tied into various forms and levels of body energy and chemical balance as well. Individuals who are balanced in these areas have more stamina and will heal at a *much* faster rate. They are also better able to focus and more readily recognize what their body needs and what is required to release stress and tension.

> Tom believed that once the body is solidly put on its path of healing using his approach, it would deliberately begin to heal on its own.

This unique kind of stimulation generated by Bowen Moves, using pauses or waits in-between certain numbers of activation points, very often results in proper re-balancing and restoration of each system and organ down to the cellular level.

Using and perfecting his approach, Tom became aware that the body would restore itself back to optimum health after only a few sessions in most cases. Tom also found that too much of his work performed on the body in one session would somehow overload the body and hamper the body's work as a whole. He found that the body would always work within the boundaries of its own present state of health, its ability to heal, and its available energy and resources.

Tom recognized that for some people, their body occasionally needed a bit more coaxing to get and keep it healing. He found that this was usually the case in deep-seated pains or long-term chronic conditions.

Many of Tom's clients commented on the superior results they received with his system of healing, even over many other traditional and Western methods.

Tom also noticed that many methods of treating the body, especially chiropractic, physical therapy, massage, and other methods which use manipulative intervention and multiple long-course treatments, often produced very mixed results. He also found that mixing Bowen with any other treatment that is more invasive than Bowen was counterproductive and severely compromised the outcome of his work. Mixing other therapies with his work had a tendency to cancel out the work he had done.

He discovered that these other therapies often triggered the body back into protecting itself, counteracting the body's ability to heal. Because of his discoveries, Tom *always* instructed his clients to discontinue all forms of therapy during the course of Bowen sessions. Tom could always tell if a person had received another form of therapy or treatment during the week, as the body would not present its normal consistent and predictable response to his work. He would tell them that if they continued to mix *any* other therapy with his work, that he would ask them to leave without receiving a session. He was very unyielding about this.

Over time, Tom mastered reading a person's body by seeing, feeling and sensing specific patterns, it became second nature to him. He knew the solution to healing a problem in the body was always subject to returning the proper balance and functioning to interconnected systems, rather than just treating a specific symptom, condition, or disease after it revealed itself in the body long after it first began.

In many cases, the condition that the body is displaying has only a partial relation to the cause, and is not the cause itself. It is the cause that needs to be addressed and corrected to allow the body the freedom to do away with the condition on its own without outside intervention, if it is able.

Tom also believed that at times when the body was unable to right itself on its own that, *then and only then*, should a more aggressive or invasive approach be taken, and not before.

Honesty was his policy. He always told potential recipients of his work that if they did not begin to see results after just a few sessions that they were wasting their money and they were to seek help elsewhere. Tom also respected the expertise of doctors and the abilities of modern medicine, especially in emergency situations.

He very successfully demonstrated the effectiveness of his technique to assist the body to relieve and eliminate all kinds of acute and chronic muscular, skeletal or nerve imbalances and injuries for a very wide variety of conditions. Over a 30-year period Tom helped hundreds of thousands of people. In that 30-year period, from the time the first Bowen Moves were performed until a day or two before his passing, Tom Bowen continually developed new Moves and Procedures, while continually re-examining his philosophy of how the body works.

Tom Bowen never explained specifically why he did what he did, to anyone. He viewed the Practitioner only as a facilitator. The "Less is More" approach was the foundation of his philosophy.

Before Tom passed away in 1982 from complications after a surgery, he personally trained six people, all men, who possessed some form of professional training in healing the body naturally. These included Osteopaths, Chiropractors, massage, and natural therapists. These men were initially invited to observe Tom work. He was quite selective about whom he trained. He turned down anyone he didn't feel would do well. He also dismissed trainees who he felt weren't learning. As was a very common and customary practice back then, he never accepted a woman as a trainee.

Tom's students were taught in the standard apprenticeship style that involved long periods of observation while being of assistance to the mentor. He combined his teaching with occasional testing to ensure that his students had a firm knowledge and understanding of what he was teaching them, long before he would allow them to perform Bowen on those visiting his clinic.

When a trainee reached a certain level of proficiency, Tom allowed him to work in his clinic while he supervised. He only allowed a select few of this group to work with him after they received their initial training. Tom told his trainees that he had only shared with them about 10% of what he knew and they would have to find the rest.

Within this select group of students that worked with Tom in his clinic was Oswald Rentsch.

OSWALD RENTSCH

Oswald "Ossie" Rentsch was a farmer-turned-alternative-healthcare practitioner. His wife, Elaine, fell out of a car that was traveling 50 miles per hour onto her head when she was just 5 years old. At the time of the accident, her parents assumed she was fine because she quickly got up and ran after the car. Shortly thereafter, they discovered something was wrong and took her to visit many practitioners to get help for her, none of whom could solve the problem. She continued to have chronic neck problems into adulthood.

Years later, after Ossie married Elaine, they continued to look for help for Elaine to find someone who could help her. Because it was expensive and very time-consuming to travel long distances, Ossie decided to study natural techniques himself, including massage, so he could help his wife. Eventually, he became qualified as a Naturopath and Osteopath.

In 1974, through the help of a friend, Ossie was introduced to Tom and asked him to look at Elaine's neck. Tom treated Elaine and said, "We'll get this right. It may take six months, but we'll have you back to where you should be. You must never have your neck manipulated again."

From the beginning of the very first session she felt something different was happening. There were structural and energetic changes taking place in her body that she had never felt before. It didn't take anywhere near six months.

In Ossie's words, "Meeting Tom Bowen was one of the strangest experiences of my life." At the time that they met, Ossie said to Tom that "he would like to learn from him." Tom agreed and invited Ossie to come and observe.

Learning from Tom was very different from any learning that Ossie had received. The whole Bowen process seemed <u>completely contradictory</u> to all the other conventional therapies Ossie had been highly trained to do. Tom worked on people primarily using soft and gentle "Moves."

Most of these were performed on bare skin and sometimes through clothes. He would perform a few Moves on a person, and then leave the room. Ossie found it quite odd that Tom didn't stay with the person and keep doing something. Upon returning a few moments later, Tom would perform a few more Moves, and then leave the room again. This continued throughout the course of the session. This was *exactly opposite* of how the other therapies are performed.

For the first few weeks, Tom asked Ossie to just observe. Tom did not keep any written records of his work, nor keep charts or notes on Moves or procedures he performed. Because most of what Tom did was from memory, it made learning Bowen *much* more difficult for Ossie.

After three weeks observing Tom, Ossie said to Elaine, "This is crazy, I'm not learning anything. I'm giving it up." Before doing so, he talked to Tom. Tom just asked that Ossie take the time to talk to people who came to the clinic before he made his final decision. .

In the waiting room, people willingly shared that whatever Tom was doing made such a tremendous impact on their health and lives that many called his work "truly miraculous." They couldn't, however, explain what Tom did or how it worked. They just <u>knew</u> it worked when many other treatments they had received elsewhere, which cost much more, had failed completely.

Ossie discovered that many of these people had already gone to numerous doctors, chiropractors, physical and physio-therapists, massage therapists and other kinds of alternative practitioners, with little or no results. Most had been told by those who gave them treatment that they would simply have to "learn to live with the pain."

Ossie found that in nearly every case, after receiving only a few Bowen sessions, these people experienced **very** rapid relief from pain and in addition to the elimination of a long list of other ailments they had. Many also shared that they were *definitely* well on their way to a total and complete recovery. Talking to these people firmly convinced Ossie to "make a go of it." Tom then asked Ossie to make charts and take notes to document his work.

Over the next two and one-half years, Ossie studied as an apprentice under the personal direction of Tom.

In the beginning, Ossie would write down and draw what he saw. Sometimes, Tom would look at it and say, "That's not right" and draw a line through it. At other times, Tom would say, "That's right" and they would work together to further refine the specifics of how to correctly perform the Move or sets of Moves. Together they modified, revised, and refined these initial procedures. Ossie meticulously documented each Bowen Move in detail.

> Ossie meticulously documented each Bowen Move in detail...
> He also compiled the assessments and sets of rules that Tom routinely used for each procedure.

Along with the drawings he made, Ossie compiled the common tell-tale signs and assessments Tom used to determine which procedure was indicated to address a specific pain, condition, or region of the body. He compiled vast numbers of thumb and finger combinations that were used to perform each Move, as well as the proper hand placement and positioning for each individual Move.

Ossie also documented the many sets of rules that Tom routinely had for each procedure and the very specific exercises that were used to help strengthen or stretch particular muscles or muscle groups. Additionally, simple home remedies regularly used to enhance the outcome of the work, along with many other lesser-used protocols, were included in this record in order to help standardize the work as a whole.

Eventually, both Tom and Ossie assigned numbers for each individual Move. In time, each procedure was also given a specific name identifying it with the area of the body it was addressing or the common ailment it consistently resolved.

"With Bowen, the practitioner doesn't make anything happen. You perform the correct procedure on the body based on what the body is telling you, and *if* you have chosen the correct Procedure the body **will** respond," Tom always said.

It took a while for Ossie to really comprehend the depth of these innovative concepts that Tom was teaching him. Over time, Ossie came to the realization that Tom had created an original and brilliantly simple technique which addressed the entire body *as a whole*. Ossie also discovered that Bowen is the only therapeutic system available in the world today which entirely addresses every system and organ in the body down to the cellular level.

After Tom's tutelage, Ossie operated his own clinic in Hamilton, Australia. Ossie would often call Tom with questions. He also regularly visited him every 4-6 weeks to continually refine the work he had already learned, and to be trained in some of the new work Tom was developing. Sometimes, Tom and Ossie worked together developing new Moves and Procedures to address rare or complex issues that known Bowen Procedures didn't address.

Prior to his passing away in 1982, Tom requested that Ossie not teach his work to anyone until *after* he had gone.

Elaine shared with me: "On Tom's deathbed, Ossie took hold of Tom's hand - Tom never let his hand go again. Ossie said, 'Tom, I PROMISE YOU, I'll make your name known around the world.' With tears welling up in his eyes, Tom squeezed Ossie's hand and said, 'Thank you, son.'"

In 1986, Ossie began teaching his interpretation of Tom Bowen's work, in Perth, Australia. With his wife Elaine by his side. They began teaching Bowen to students in its "original" form using the principles and high standards learned from Tom, making Tom's name legendary for healing around the world. Even to this day, they use a clear and straightforward approach, in order to retain its purity and simplicity.

Initially, they called the work, "Bowen Therapy, The Bowen Technique, or The Bowen Therapeutic Technique."

Ultimately, they agreed to call the work:

"BOWTECH" ~ *The Original Bowen Technique*

They use this abbreviated version of Bowen Technique in order to distinguish their high standard of teaching from the other small offshoot groups that began to form after their students deviated from the original teachings taught to them by the Rentschs. **Bowenwork**™ is used as their trademarked name for Bowen in the United States.

Ossie and Elaine's primary focus has emphatically been to teach Bowen (Bowtech®) to students in its original form.

Ossie and Elaine Rentsch

In 1989, Ossie and Elaine introduced this phenomenal therapy outside Australia for the first time, taking it to the United States with the help of Milton Albrecht.

By 1990, teaching Bowen became the Rentschs' fulltime passion – a passion that has empowered and inspired many others to learn and use this remarkable work. The Rentschs have personally introduced Bowen to many thousands of people worldwide. They have taught individuals from all walks of life, from medical doctors to mechanics, from the highly educated to those with little or no formal education. As of 2006 they have been instrumental in introducing Bowen to 31 countries throughout the world.

Currently, Ossie and Elaine are only teaching refresher and advanced level courses, leaving the basics to be taught by hand-selected instructors around the world. Today, there are 70 Bowtech® accredited instructors. As of April, 2006, the number of people who have taken the basic course is well over 17,000 around the world.

Indeed, Ossie and Elaine are one of the most delightful couples one could ever meet. Without these two determined individuals, the work that Tom Bowen began would not be known or available to the world.

The names Ossie and Elaine are synonymous with Bowen and **Bowtech**®. Together they have created the Bowen Therapy Academy of Australia (BTAA), the Australian Academy, and **BOWTECH**® ~ *The Original Bowen Technique*, the worldwide instructional entity.

The rising worldwide popularity of Bowen in recent years has been extraordinary, especially since it is relatively new and is still virtually unknown to most healthcare professionals.

MILTON ALBRECHT

Milton and his wife, Deni Larimore Albrecht were first introduced to Bowen in January 1989, when they visited Australia for Deni's sister's wedding. While visiting Australia, Ossie performed a Bowen session on Deni, who was suffering with Multiple Sclerosis and Lyme's Disease. The relaxation effects were immediately evident. Deni offered to help introduce Bowen to people in the United States.

About four months later, Ossie came to Auburn, California. Milton and Deni introduced him to many people in their small town. That evening, Ossie briefly showed Milton how to perform a very basic Bowen regimen on Deni, so he could continue to help her. Milton gave Deni weekly Bowen sessions, which greatly reduced her pain and frequent spasms.

In September 1989, Ossie and Elaine held the first Bowen training in the United States for five interested, yet skeptical, body workers.

Milton zealously went to work performing Bowen on anyone he could. In due course, Milton qualified as the first certified Bowen Practitioner outside Australia and New Zealand. The elementary level classes which Milton taught in the United States created an opening of interest for the global expansion of Bowen. Milton also began organizing other classes for Ossie and Elaine to teach.

Around 1995, Milton and Ossie parted ways surrounding differences of opinions.

Anyone who ever received Bowen from Milton knows that he was a gifted man. Until his sudden death on January 14, 2003, he practiced his own interpretation of Tom Bowen's work from his home, helping many thousands of people.

Through the love he gave to his family and those he both taught and treated, Milton helped to heal and transform the community where he lived in ways too numerous to mention. He was known to many simply as "Milt."

He had very unorthodox views, and his love for laughter often brought many a serious soul to their knees, in gut-wrenching disbelief and hair-raising laughter. At his memorial service, many shared of Milt's light-hearted and very untraditional ways, his humming a tune while he worked from room to room, and his ability to "get to the point," whether with Bowen or as a friend. They spoke of the great love they had for "Uncle Milty" and how their life was more complete and forever blessed because of him.

Milt's example of freely being who you are, loving your family, and sharing the gifts you possess...*no matter what*...is forever ingrained deep within the hearts of those he touched. One of his mantras which came passionately from his heart was, "No one should live with pain."

On first meeting Milt, many doubted he could do anything for them, as he had a very rough earthly appearance. His "beer in one hand - cigarette in the other" habits were the exact opposite of the ideal "healer" people often picture in their minds. However, once they were touched by his loving hands, their doubts and fears about his abilities quickly disappeared.

Milton had the uncanny ability to intuitively read the body. He combined this with his understanding of how the body can heal itself. Through this he was able to see or sense many inner struggles an individual was experiencing on several levels.

Milt's view of Bowen included a very unorthodox firm and heavy-handed version - his own interpretation of the original technique - very different from the concepts and principles he learned from Ossie and Elaine Rentsch. His view encompassed using much deeper *and* sharper Bowen-style moves on the body. In many cases, he used movements on the body using a very firm touch that often inflicted some level of discomfort to the recipient. Milt shared that he did Bowen in this way "in order to antagonize and irritate the body, to *make it fight back*."

This approach <u>was exactly the opposite</u> of what Tom taught Ossie and what Ossie taught Milton. The results he (Milton) commonly obtained through his own unique approach to Tom Bowen's work speak volumes and Milton did help to change and save many lives, including mine, using his own interpretation.

Many of Milt's students, who have chosen to attempt to match and use Milt's heavy-hand, firmer-touch, approach, have found it very difficult to obtain the level of results that he did, because Bowen performed in this way usually inflicts more discomfort than healing to the recipient.

Most people who use "Milt's way" to address the body, although they *call* it Bowen Therapy, the Bowen Method, The Bowen Technique, or by some other name related to or used in conjunction with the name Bowen, find that their results are nowhere near as consistent, predictable, or profound as using the original, lighter-touch approach.

Milton was just one man, but he played a significant role in bringing Bowen out of Australia to the world, and for that, we are *all very grateful*. The lives of many people are far better off because Milton "played his part." The focus of Milton's life, especially after he learned Bowen, was undeniably one of humble service.

Milton Albrecht will forever be in the hearts and minds of those who experienced his heart-filled touch and side-splitting jokes and laughter.

Chapter 3

Body Basics 101

Understanding the body

Things should be made as simple as possible . . . but no simpler than that.

~ Albert Einstein ~

In the next few chapters, I propose to explain in simplified terms, what the body is, what it does, how systems, organs, glands and the brain are designed to interactively function together as a whole. Also, I will include information on how and why the whole body needs to be addressed when it is out of balance (due to injury, trauma, weakness, illness, or other cause). Also included is information on some of the inner workings of what the body *really* needs to heal itself on many levels simultaneously. There is an order to all things in the body.

To understand Bowen thoroughly and the unique and extraordinary way that it works *with* the entire body and mind to (1) activate the healing mechanisms, (2) accelerate healing and (3) rapidly restore optimal health, it is important to first have a basic understanding how some of the *systems, organs, and glands in the body work synchronistically and synergistically as a whole, and together with the mind* (one directly affecting the other). It is also very important to understand that the body is undeniably designed to heal itself; especially when given the correct information in the way that the body can receive it.

> The body is undeniably designed to heal itself; especially when given the correct information.

The blueprint for the existence and continuance of optimal health is already there. It just needs to be properly stimulated to be re-activated or revived – in other words, brought back to life.

The body is a finely-tuned balance of multiple systems, glands, organs, tissues, fibers, and muscles, etc., which employ and move a vast array of chemical compounds and fluids, using a very complex web of electro-chemical stimuli in order to communicate. Unfortunately, sometimes it can take very little to disturb this delicate balance and just a little more to throw it off course. In many instances, we take our own good health for granted until something goes wrong, and then regaining our health becomes a top priority.

First, let's define a few common terms used in association with the body and its physical condition, both for clarity and to make your reading more insightful and meaningful.

Acute: Coming on suddenly and severely; a sharp or severe sudden onset, lasting a short time – as "an acute pain"; it is felt, perceived, or experienced intensely, demanding urgent attention

Ailment: Any combination of symptoms that together signify a named condition or disorder

Chronic: Long duration or frequent occurrence – as "a chronic pain or condition"; always present; constantly vexing, weakening, nagging, or troubling

Condition: A general term for the state of a patient. A health disorder: an abnormal state. A reaction or response that usually typifies a defect, deficiency or imbalance – whether serious or otherwise

Disease or Dis-ease: An advanced and critical stage of sickness or illness; impairment of health or condition of abnormal or weakened functioning. An advanced stage of a named disorder, condition or ailment with recognizable symptoms, warning signs or indicators that result from infection, improper diet or some *other cause*.

KEY NOTE: Disease can only develop if all three of the following three basic conditions are present:

   1. The proper environment
   2. The presence of an active pathogen
   3. A susceptible host

If one of these three conditions is absent, then disease cannot exist.

Pathogen: A specific disease agent (as a bacterium or virus)

Disorder: An abnormal or troubled physical or mental condition; an ailment

Dysfunction: An impaired or abnormal functioning; a state in which the proper response or activity of a part (muscle, nerve, organ, system, etc.) is weak, absent, or otherwise abnormal

Health: Soundness of physical or mental condition

Rest: Freedom from disturbance of body, mind, or spirit; tranquility; a regenerating interval of silence or peace

Restore: To give back; to reinstate; to bring back to health or a normal or original condition; to reestablish; to reclaim

Sign: A mark used to identify a disturbance. Evidence or trace of dis-ease, more evident than a symptom

Symptom: Evidence of dis-ease or physical or chemical disturbance; something that indicates the presence of a bodily disorder. A reaction to a pathogen

Syndrome: A complex of signs and symptoms presenting a clinical picture of a dis-ease or disorder.

The body is a fascinating labyrinth of multiple systems and organs, most of which go through various complex use, resting, and cleansing cycles at different times of every day. Research shows that the brain takes in nearly 500 billion units of information per second, yet a healthy body is only capable of deciphering and using around 2000 units.

Most of the information is cast off as unnecessary to survival or insignificant. There are ninety miles of flexible electro-chemically charged sets of wiring we call "nerves."

Nerves make up the electrical wiring system that allows the brain to telegraph messages to and from organs and muscles. The brain uses a specialized chemical-electrical code to communicate to and receive messages from various parts of the body. These chemical-electrical communications are responsible for coordinating and synchronizing every system and organ, and many hundreds of thousands of other things which take place in the body at the same time, from cell creation to a person recalling something that happened decades ago.

These nerve connections also transmit messages to and from the heart and brain. For example, the heart speeds up or slows down depending on physical and mental demands and our emotional reactions. Our emotions strongly influence the activity of the heart and body through messages sent over this nerve network.

Nerve connections are also responsible for converting thoughts into action. This process is at work even during mental rehearsal or imaging.

There are two kinds of nerves: motor, which help you move, and sensory, those that send sensory messages, i.e. sight, sound, smell, taste and touch.

The brain controls over 100 billion nerve cells and generates more electrical impulses in one day than all the telephones in the world put together. These impulses take place at speeds somewhere between 150 and 250 miles per hour. There are over 100,000 different chemical reactions which take place in the brain.

The brain can efficiently store and recall around 10,000 different odors and distinguish between around 8,000,000 colors and up to 500 different shades of gray.

The human body has 634 muscles accounting for nearly 40% of the body weight. The average human flexes their finger joints over 25 million times over the course of their life. The body has 206-208 bones (depending on the person – some people have 2 extra bones) with over 100 joints, and the average skeleton weighs somewhere around 29-30 pounds. The body has about 60 trillion cells in all, with 300 million dying and being replaced every minute.

The eyes move back and forth up to 100 times per second while the retina performs 10 billion calculations in the same time frame. The muscles in the eyes move some 100,000 times a day, while sight accounts for 90-95% of all of our sensory perceptions, except in those individuals who are visually impaired, where their sensory perceptions of sound, touch, and smell are drastically increased to compensate for not being able to see.

The ears distinguish between hundreds of thousands of different sounds. The nose can smell *and* classify over 10,000 different odors. The mouth has around 10,000 taste buds that detect sweet, bitter, salty, or sour. It takes the use of around 72 muscles to speak a single word.

The heart beats an average 70-80 beats per minute, 100,000 times a day, 40 million times a year. It efficiently circulates up to 1.6 million gallons of blood a year; which is 50 million gallons over the course of a normal life.

Red blood cells only live an average of four months and are replaced at between 2-3 million a second. There are around 100,000 miles of blood vessels contained within the body that play their part to nourish every system, organ, gland, muscle, and cell.

With all these virtually incomprehensible amounts of activity taking place simultaneously in the body, twenty-four hours a day for a lifetime, it's no wonder that the synchronicity of the body needs to be in balance or it can all come to a halt quickly.

If you think of the human body as a modern cruise ship of sorts, it may make more sense. Cruise ships are self-contained vessels that have all the basics that they need. It takes a concerted effort to maintain a ship. Ships are very high maintenance and require many man-hours, tons of supplies, and lots of fuel to work properly. The human body is also high maintenance and uses food and oxygen as its primary needs. The body continually functions and maintains *itself* with little help from us.

Each system is interconnected through a vast system of nerves, arteries, veins, fascia tissue, and muscular support, many of the primary conduits through which Bowen produces its results. Even though many of these parts work independently, each also has a separate responsibility to each other and to the body as a whole. Each must play its part to help provide adequate supplies, communication, protection or support to some degree for the entire body, down to the cellular level. This enables the body to maintain itself, uphold overall balance, maintain and also restore optimal health, and provide proper healing to the body as a whole when needed.

Understanding the body is quite simple when you realize that the body basically works in five primary areas.

- Mechanical
- Electrical
- Chemical
- Hydraulic
- Energetic

MECHANICAL

Muscles connect bones across joints. They are contracted and released in precision timing by the brain to operate and stabilize the speed, direction, and amount of bone movement. Utilizing precision muscular contraction, the body moves and can also stay erect. Tendons are tough bands of fibrous tissue connecting a muscle to a bone or some other part of the body. Ligaments, on the other hand, are bands of fibrous tissue which connect the ends of bones (at the joint) or hold an organ in place. Both tendons and ligaments can either be cable-like or flat.

TENSEGRITY

To further understand the mechanical action that happens in the body using muscles, you must have at least a basic understanding of "Tensegrity" or integrity of tension. Tensegrity is the pattern which results with synchronistic push and pull movements. The pull is continuous and regular. The push is discontinuous, considered alternating or irregular. The continuous pull is balanced by the discontinuous push – Tensegrity keeps the body either upright, in motion, or at rest.

The push and pull *are not opposites*. They are complements that work together. Muscles can only pull and not push. As the muscles pull the bones, the bones contribute to a pushing action. The combined pulling (tensioning) then releasing of various muscles simultaneously, all organized and directed by the brain assists the body in movement. This system of Tensegrity offers the maximum amount of strength possible, using the smallest amount of tension.

With muscles of the body, tensional forces are transmitted over the shortest distance between two points. The muscles are positioned in such a brilliant way so as to withstand the greatest amount of stress or "tension" on them, using the least amount of muscle tissue. The body is truly an ingeniously designed mechanical marvel.

Another example of a different kind of Tensegrity exists in the eyes, tongue, and skin. In these cases, the discontinuous fluids push against the pulling tissues causing fluid movement, to move a vast array of fluids *into* the body and waste *out from* the body, as well, using and having hydraulic-like properties and principles. To learn more about Tensegrity, visit our website-www.bowenhealingsystem.com

It is through Tensegrity that the body can stay erect, move, keep itself together, and move some fluids in the body.

ELECTRICAL

The body is electrically "wired" through the central, peripheral, and autonomic nervous systems. These systems are a "network of wiring," so to speak, which interconnects and integrates all parts of the body together, either directly or indirectly. This network sends and receives ELECTRO-CHEMICAL signals to and from the bio-computer (brain).

The brain works to maintain order and give direction, all the while maintaining an organized balance throughout the entire body on many levels at the same time. Millions of small electro-chemical interactions occur so quickly in the brain that modern technology perceives them like rapid-fire lightning storms. This "brain storm" is generated as the brain sorts, deciphers, and responds to the complex stimuli and response dynamics (loops or cycles) which occur simultaneously in the body as an effort to maintain an overall optimal state of health and balance.

These nerve systems are actually more than just wiring (neuropathways) that send information back and forth. These neuropathways are actually micro-miniaturized electro-chemical plants which create, adjust, re-generate, and re-create chemicals as they send and receive the constantly changing impulses, which are modified thousands of times as they travel from one part of the body to another, and back again.

When the body is healthy, the rapidly-fired series of the multiple electro-chemical stimuli which are sent from the brain to the muscles and from the muscles back to the brain, or visa versa, cause muscular contractions and releases to occur at very precisely-timed intervals, causing accurately calculated movements. The impulses are also simultaneously sent to other systems and organs associated with the muscles that are being used. These impulses are also precisely timed, to keep the entire body properly "in tune" and "up to speed" with what the body needs for proper synchronization and functioning under any level of use, from one where the body is completely in a deeply relaxed state, to one of high intensity or high stress, as well.

When a muscle, system, organ or other part of the body is injured, tense (at tension), or unhealthy, the capacity for it to function properly is reduced, causing irregular highs and lows in its functioning. This causes compensation to occur in other systems and organs to one degree or another in order to attempt to rebalance the body.

The skin, for example, senses varying degrees of pressure, sensation or pain caused by contact, or from the radiation of a source of heat or cold. This sensation stimulates activators that lie beneath the skin to produce what are called "piezo-electric currents."

These piezo-electric currents instantly transfer the signal from the skin to the brain via the nervous systems, while also producing other forms of minute energy and electro-magnetic currents which radiate out into more distant parts of the body, affecting the body to a very minor degree. At the same time, while all this is happening within the body, the brain sends numerous signals to *many* other parts of the body, setting off a series of physical, mental, emotional and chemical changes and compensatory reactions, attempting to counteract whatever it was that activated the skin sensors. All this happens routinely in the body around 30 times or cycles per second.

If a *critical event* occurs where the body receives a severe injury, for example, other deeper, more intense alert and response systems designed specifically for an "emergency use only" mode are automatically set off. The processing within the brain instantly changes to completely focus *all* the body's resources on critical lifesaving requirements.

The mass number of physical, mental, chemical, compensatory, and energetic processes that instantly occur throughout the body to make this happen is so huge it is unbelievable. To go into detail and map out all the intricate and micro-processes and changes and re-processing which take place simultaneously in the body throughout the neuropathic network, just in response to a moderate or severe injury to the body during the first minute after the injury occurs, would actually take hundreds of volumes of books to explain.

CHEMICAL

In a healthy body, all systems and organs live in a chemically stabilized, synchronistic, and balanced way for the greater good of the whole body. Chemically, the systems and organs play a vital role in producing enzymes, amino acids and myriads of other chemicals necessary to keep the body in a state of chemical, physical, mental, and emotional balance, again, all organized and maintained by the brain.

The processes of breaking down foods and nutrients into usable fluids small enough to penetrate the cell walls is also part of one of many thousands of these chemical processes.

Chemical imbalances can often occur when the body is "not full of health" (unhealthy) or when it has been physically, mentally or emotionally traumatized (whether perceived or otherwise), automatically putting the body out of perfect chemical balance, leading also to physical and mental imbalances. Ordinarily, extremes cause a state of crisis to occur in the body and can lead to the body warring with itself.

Take for example, when someone says "NO" to us. However we took that "NO", and what we made it mean, causes the body to immediately mechanically, electrically and chemically react to what we think the other person meant by the "NO!" (i.e. they don't like me, I'm not good enough, etc..) This one event causes a whole array of forceful and concentrated disruptions and imbalances in the entire body, causing it to go immediately into survival mode, sometimes having lasting results for decades or, in some cases, an entire lifetime. All that the person said was *one single word*, no. Nothing more, nothing less, with no other meaning behind it...except the one WE gave to it.

In many cases of trauma, primarily those physical in nature, the intensity and severity of the reaction which is provoked in the body can become so extreme that it can cause the body's individual systems and organs to "fend for their life," causing a desperate state of self-survival chaos throughout the entire body.

This troubled state that the body *automatically* goes into in order to protect itself is commonly called "shock". Normally, shock rapidly causes severe physiological reactions and chemical imbalances as the body torques around the source of pain and, at the same time, attempts to splint the injured area, for survival and safety measures.

Mental and emotional trauma commonly provokes the same kinds of intense physiological reactions and chemical imbalances in the body as well.

This desperate state of chaos, or "shock," that the body goes into kills more people than the actual injury itself. In a desperate fight for survival, each system or organ will rob whatever it needs in an attempt to remain alive and functioning.

After the body has had an experience of "going into shock" the first time, the reactionary response pattern is firmly imprinted into the brain and set in place. Once in place, this pattern can instantly be recalled and the body will react, already knowing what and how to react to a shock-like or shock mimicking event. It is much easier for the body to automatically go back into some level of shock to protect the body when another injury of almost any degree occurs. The same can happen at merely the sign of any threat or possibility of danger, whether actual or perceived, and can cause people to "freeze" instead of fighting or fleeing.

This is why some people get "shocky" by even thinking about the possibility of experiencing a traumatic event, such as receiving a "shot" at a doctor's office, or a near miss incident where they *almost* got into a car accident, or even worrying that they may get laid off, for example.

The actual state of shock causes a *huge* "shock-wave" to radiate throughout the entire body. This shock-wave triggers various instantaneous chemical, neuropathic, physiological, and psychological, reactionary responses and changes throughout the entire body. These changes can and regularly do alter the course of a person's entire life from that moment or event forward.

For example, at ten years old, a friend of mine had what he called a near-drowning incident, where his arm was momentarily caught in the water intake and he was sure he was going to drown. When this happened, severe panic set in. He was momentarily unable to breathe as his head was barely above water. He struggled and fought fiercely to free his arm, but to no avail. He tried to scream to get someone's attention, but he was so overtaken with panic and fear, that he couldn't. Desperately, he fought to free himself. Finally, he gave his arm one big jerk, and out it came.

He is now in his mid-forties, and to this day he WILL NOT get into a pool for fear that he may get his arm stuck and *really* drown this time! Just talking about it puts him into a full sweat and he begins to violently shake. This experience happened over thirty years ago and his body still recalls it as though it is happening to him right now! His episode of severe panic and fear was deeply imprinted into his brain.

This one episode put his body into such a deep state of emergency, for survival of the body, that the brain re-routed neuronal patterns in order to "save the body". When a severe accident happens where a part of the body is amputated from the whole, the state of survival becomes one to "save what is left". Even when a near-tragic event is over, the body is still neuro-chemically "programmed" to continue in this highly altered state of functioning for survival.

Very frequently, fire fighters, police officers, emergency personnel, people returning from a war-time experience, and especially members of S.W.A.T. teams comment that they have been taught to "turn this ultra-high state of awareness of their surroundings on, but they have not been taught how to turn it off." Being in this "emergency high-alert mode" for years or decades, in some cases, it is extremely difficult for them, if not next to impossible, to let go and relax. Many comment that "It is as though, the body will not let them relax."

During this time, such as that just described, the body makes massive amounts of changes and imprints as it attempts to reroute and re-pattern itself for survival. This state, this new imprint, now becomes the "status quo" or normal state of affairs for the body and the brain to work and function with.

Caught in this short-circuited or mis-imprinted patterning, the body must continually labor in an attempt to restore some kind of sub-par level of balance and stability (health). Prior functioning levels of systems and organs are altered, also contributing to altered chemical levels throughout the entire body, as well.

When these deep-level changes happen, the body is in need of an influence stronger than itself and that of what is happening inside, in order to correct itself. It is as though the body has to be influenced in such a way that it is "told" what it needs to do to, in order for it to fully reset and restore itself back to a state of balance. This is the unique gift that Bowen can provide the body, a way out of this short-circuit.

To properly function and maintain optimal chemical balance, proper water and nutritional requirements are also crucial, and a necessary part as well of the hydraulic system of the body.

HYDRAULIC

The body has many pumping systems. Three of these pumps are:

1. The heart
2. The muscles
3. The alimentary canal

The heart keeps the life-sustaining nutrients and oxygen moving to all parts of the body. The action of the muscles, when we move or breathe deeply, pumps fluids and semi-solids to the body, supplies hydrating liquids and nutrients to nourish and replace organic cellular components, and also removes the "lymph" or waste products from the body.

The alimentary canal is the tube-like tract through which food is conveyed, broken down into usable components, assimilated, and the remnant solid waste is removed. It extends from the mouth to the anus. The alimentary canal uses wavelike muscular contractions that propel its contents onward. This muscular contraction is called "Peristalsis".

Well-timed cyclic peristalsis also helps to move food and fluids from the stomach to the small intestine, to the large intestine, to the colon, and then eventually, out of the body.

For the body to function properly, the hydraulics of the body must be working to keep fluids and waste flowing.

ENERGETIC

The body also works on another much deeper and subtler levels. This level is called energetic or vital life-force (energy). Energy (energetic) flow or lack thereof in the body significantly affects and directly impacts the physical, mental, and psychological state and well-being of the body.

Ancient Asian forms of medicine inform us that a subtle energy called Chi, Ki, or Life-Force energy circulates throughout the entire body in a highly complex invisible network. This life-giving vital force is what separates the living from the dead. Its balanced and unobstructed flow is critical to sound health.

The life-force energy is meant to flow throughout the whole body, encouraging all parts to function with each other in a natural and harmonious way. When any blockage or unnatural flow of this energy occurs, it diminishes the energy to some part of the body. This blockage or energy deficiency eventually manifests itself as a symptom or disorder. A blockage in one area creates an overflow of energy to the rest of the body, sending too much energy into an organ, system, or area. Too much energy can almost be as detrimental to the body as a deficiency. Because the excess energy has to go somewhere, it goes to other areas that are receptive and causes other systems or organs to become over stimulated, and overworked.

The body then becomes fragmented through energy blockages and creates disharmony between various systems, organs and the body as a whole. To return the body back to good health, the energy blockage must be removed *and* the energy must be re-distributed to fulfill the needs of the body.

The body has its own unique pattern and order for clearing, re-opening and reorganizing the body's energy, depending on prior injury or trauma and the severity. This clearing or re-opening process within the body must be accomplished in phases. Each phase must build upon another, so one part does not interfere with the completion of other phases.

Energetic repairs, in contrast to physical ones, are much more subtle, yet the repairs, or restoration of proper energy flows throughout the body, *are just as crucial* as physical repairs, especially in the long-run.

Energy healing or energetic repairs are well beyond the scope of most Western-medical-related healthcare professionals. Energetic repairs are triggered in a very subtle manner and are repairs the body is programmed to do on its own when properly triggered to do so. Energetic repair of the body is primarily controlled by the autonomic nervous system.

Physical, mental, and emotional traumas contribute to energetic dysfunction. Trauma to the body in any way, shape, or form sends a violent shock wave throughout the whole body which disrupts the neuro-processing of the normal body-brain loop, and therefore affects the natural energy flow.

Energy is a particular form of power, strength, or spirit shown in words or action. It has its root in the mind, and is the power that produces an effect, whether exerted or not. The body *creates* its own energy, though invisible to the naked eye. This energy is created and then used or given off in various ways.

Some of the ways energy is created in the body are through friction during movement of the body, the flow of blood, movement of other fluids, or semi-solids, the generation of electrical currents again through touch, movement and friction, and also through countless complex chemical reactions which occur throughout the body and brain. The energy created *by* the body helps keep us alive. The mere presence of this energy in the body separates the living from the dead.

Vigor, another form of power, is the fresh quality of mind and body that has its roots in health. The amount of energy the body has and the amount of vigor it displays go hand in hand.

Energy plays a very crucial natural and harmonizing role that circulates to all parts of the body, even the most remote cells. Its strength and natural unimpeded flow is *critical* to optimal health.

Any blockage, restriction, deviation, or disturbance of the amount, flow, or balance of energy in the body can be directly linked to, and often also results in, tension, pain, dysfunction, a weakened immune system, over-worked systems or organs, and poor health. Reduced energy in any one part, system, or organ of the body can also cause an excessive surge of energy in another, which throws the entire balance of the body off as well.

On the other hand, any system, organ, or gland which requires an abnormally high amount of energy for any reason, systematically deprives the rest of the body of what it needs. This leaves the body in a reactive state as it attempts to counterbalance the rest of the body with whatever energy remains. This invariably leaves the body lacking in one or more areas, causing it to be in less-than-optimal health.

In other words, a balanced distribution of energy is a key element in optimal health. It is governed by the mind, and the body *depends* on it.

This energy that is being described directly influences the systems, organs and cells of the body: endocrine (glands), urinary, respiratory, reproductive, nervous, skeletal, digestive, muscular, and circulatory. Each of these is interrelated *and* interdependent upon each other for proper functioning and survival.

When the energy in the body is at an optimal level and is distributed freely, everything in the body and mind flows freely, and tension, stress, and anxiety are virtually non-existent. We feel good about ourselves and life is flowing. We feel whole and healthy, having a sense of inner-connectedness, wellness, and calmness.

The energy in the body is intended to flow freely. Any sustained blockage, deviation, or disruption of a balanced distribution or flow of the energy directly affects the body as a whole causing abnormal (sub-par) functioning to occur throughout, greatly affecting the health of the body.

Energy can also be stored as reserve for future use in different forms and in various tissues and organs in the body, somewhat like electricity is stored in a battery. The body stores energy for use in times of need or crisis.

Because the body is so interconnected and reliant upon the proper functioning of all its parts, a malfunctioning part forces other parts to act in response to the malfunctioning part. This directly impacts the natural flow of the body, causing energetic disturbances throughout.

One source of energy that the body produces is displayed as radiating heat. An increase in heat radiating from a certain part or organ reveals that that part of the body is being affected somehow and that it is calling for and using more energy than normal and needs to be cared for.

On the opposite end of the spectrum, a decrease in heat, appearing as a body part that is cold, shows a lack or suppression of adequate energy (life force) to the particular area. It also indicates an impediment or blockage within the energy flow to this area causing among other things, a lack of nutrients to this area and directly cause compensation in other parts of the body which is actually traceable. The coldness is not necessarily a lack of blood circulation to the area as previously thought, although it can be. All organs and cells in the body have a very specific and individual frequency which can be directly affected by many forms of energy from both external and internal sources.

Chemical energy, for example, is produced from the food we eat, which converts into metabolic energy and provides raw building blocks for repairing and regenerating aging cells, as well as the creation of new cells to take the place of those that have died off and have been removed.

To understand this better, you must begin to recognize that the body has a detectable, measurable, and visible energy field that surrounds the body. This energy field emanates out from the body to a distance of 18 – 24 inches for most people. It also emerges from the body's core near the navel. This field can be detected in a variety of ways and it can be measured in Hertz (Hz) using highly specialized equipment. It can also be seen in its varying strengths, degrees, shades, and colors throughout the body or emanating out from it, using instruments such as Magnetic Resonance Imaging (MRI), CAT or PET scans, Thermo-scanners, and Kirilian photography, to name just a few.

Highly sensitive individuals can actually feel the energy produced by the body as heat or an energy force that can be subtly felt as a form of resistance, somewhat like pressing on an inflated balloon, or like moving your hand through the air, verses through water. Some people who have refined their ability to see energy can actually see this energy as a radiating wave or as a vast array of colors. They can also see immediate changes taking place within the energy field as they occur.

Unconsciously or instinctively, everyone can detect this field to some degree. To experience the energy field, I invite you to perform this experiment: The next time you are standing in line at a grocery store move *very slowly* toward the person standing in front of you. When your own

18–to-24 inch energy field comes in contact with theirs, most people will reflexively move or lean away so your field doesn't touch theirs. Next, back up slightly and notice what they do. You'll become more aware of this energy field and how you respond when someone whom you do not know "gets too close to you."

Some people's energy fields are considerably stronger and some are weaker than others. Refining this energy awareness tool can be very beneficial in your health and life. Any imbalance, depletion, or blockage within a person's energy field blocks clear and direct communication and signaling between systems, organs, cells, and the brain, leading to the portrayal of signs, symptoms, disorders, dysfunction, and disease.

Various types of energy exist within the body. Each type of energy plays a role in strengthening and supporting various body parts, such as the brain, systems and organs and the body as a whole. Research reveals that cells emit small bursts of ultraviolet light that appears as a kind of control system the cells use to communicate with each other.

There are various kinds of energy that are part of the energetic make-up of the body, which I will *very* briefly describe.

Proximate Energy is the energy field that surrounds our entire body. We use this one mainly for self-protection and self-preservation. Most people are unaware of it, though it is always there and is easy to feel or sense from others.

Within this Proximate Energy are two, possibly three, different kinds of energy that exist simultaneously. Electrostatic wave energy can be observed and measured by EEG and EMG. "Copper wall" experiments carried out by Elmer Green have consistently shown that healers produce voltages as high as 190 volts. This is over 100,000 times greater than EEG voltages. Another kind of energy that exists within the Proximate Energy is Magnetic.

Using super-conducting magnetometers, the magnetic field that surrounds the organs in the body can be measured. The human brain commonly produces signals in the 9-10 Gauss range. The heart, on the other hand, produces signals that are over 1000 times stronger than those of the brain. The signals from the hands of healers have been found to be as high as 1000 times stronger than those of the heart.

Another energy awaiting further scientific confirmation is that of the energy produced by mental activity, measurable as a form of gravity generated by human activity, within the gravitational field of the earth.

Chakra Energy consists of seven energy centers that exist in the body, as per Eastern Culture. Each plays a vital role in our body *and* our lives. When the Chakras are working properly our life has a tendency to flow freely and naturally. When an individual Chakra is not functioning properly, we may feel weak, vulnerable and hampered in that area of our body. Each individual Chakra also has a direct correlation to a specific area of your life.

Here are the seven energy centers, what they influence, and their locations

1st or Governing Chakra

Creative Influence

Lower Abdominal Region

2nd or Emotional Chakra

Emotional Stability

Naval Region – central abdominal

3rd or Life Chakra

Life Participation

Solar Plexus Region – upper abdominal
(the soft spot just below the sternum or breast bone)

4th or Heart Chakra

Loving Expression – Connectedness

Heart Region

5th or Truth Chakra

Speaking One's Truth – what is true for them

Throat Region

6th or Intuitive Chakra

Meaningful Discernment

Forehead Region

7th or Crown Chakra

Power and Influence

Crown of the Head – top

Restrictions in these centers often impede proper functioning of the body, causing sluggishness of specific systems, organs or glands that are related to the areas surrounding these centers.

One of the ways that energy flows within the body is through *Energy Meridians*. Energy Meridians are actual energy pathways that exist throughout the body. They are like small interconnected streams that run lengthwise through the entire body allowing the natural movement or flow of energy from one system, organ or gland to another

Any restriction or blockage of energy along any of these energy meridians quickly causes malfunctioning somewhere else that seems unrelated, because of the direct link the meridians have to other parts of the body. Any restriction or blockage in the meridian causes the body to act like a wire that has short-circuited in your house.

Acupuncture is usually performed along these energy meridians at specific points. Acupuncturists use a needle to insert a temporary physical blockage along a meridian directly connected to a specific system, organ or gland. This temporarily dams up the energy. When released, the dammed energy commonly causes the entire or partial removal of a restriction or blockage that has adversely affected the body in some way or form. However, the insertion of needles can cause the body to protect itself as the needle penetrates the skin. This can be counterproductive to some degree, especially at times when the acupuncturists use larger needles, as the body will automatically defend itself from outside intrusion, first.

Proper functioning each of these energies is equally important to assist the body in maintaining and restoring good health and for proper healing. *One kind is just as important as another.*

There are many different kinds of energy that the body produces in order for it to truly function at optimal levels. I suggest that you investigate the many books, tapes, videoes, and DVDs on the subject of energy and the body. They will give you further insight into how energy and the body work together. Additional discovery and inquiry on your part may be necessary in order for you to further understand how the body works on these levels. Search for the latest up-to-date information on meridians, chakras, body energy fields and forces, etc. Your findings will also greatly assist you in understanding what is going on in your body from time to time.

The science and study of how and where the body's energy flows is well documented, and this knowledge has been used very successfully for many thousands of years by many Eastern cultures for preventing, diagnosing, and treating the *cause* of illness and pain.

Modern (Western) medicine commonly does not recognize the "energetics" in and of the body as being one part of the whole, as do the Eastern cultures. Western medicine, it seems, segments the body into parts and falls short in recognizing that one part of the body commonly does affect other parts (If someone intentionally hit your toe with a hammer, there is a VERY high probability that you will scream AND your fist will be coming at them – it is connected). Western Medicine, for the most part, shows no interest at all in understanding how the body works on this very fundamental, yet vital, energetic level that *gives life to, and sustains the life of* the body.

Although Western medicine does not readily recognize energy and its degree of existence in the body as necessary or useful in prevention, Western medical "technology" is beginning to find it useful, to some degree, for primarily diagnostic reasons. They are beginning to discover that the body *has* an energy field and that each organ and system does have its own definite energy signature when healthy, and another one when it is not functioning properly. The latest technological advances in Western medicine using highly specialized instruments are just beginning to be used to detect subtle disturbances and abnormalities in the body to diagnose, or "tell" what is happening in the body. These new tools are wonderful for early disease detection as they can help reveal issues long before any sign of the condition appears or even before it can be felt by an individual.

3.1 Systems

Each system plays a specific vital role in maintaining Life. When a system becomes unbalanced, it directly affects the entire body.

Muscular System Interactions

Muscular tension, strain, spasm, imbalance and injury greatly affect each system. By addressing these muscular issues Bowen can significantly facilitate the body's ability to make sweeping and lasting adjustments.

MUSCULAR SYSTEM SUPPORT

To better understand what takes place in the body on the physical level, let's briefly look at basic *Muscular System* interactions which occur. You may discover that muscles play a more major role in maintaining and restoring optimal health than you have ever realized. The muscles are interconnected to almost everything that takes place in the body. Understand that there is a complete loop of interactive give and take between the muscles, systems, organs, and the rest of the body. Something else that is very notable and vital to gain a greater understanding of how the body interacts within itself is that muscles are unique in their design because they must work in pairs to balance the body. This physical balancing leads to chemical balancing, and therefore mental and emotional balancing as well. Within the proper inner workings of muscles lie key elements of optimal health.

Over 634 muscles play an important part interacting with the body. Muscles use an electro-chemical stimulus to convert chemical energy into mechanical movement. Muscles can only pull, they cannot push.

Three different types of muscles in the body each perform specific tasks: Cardiac, Smooth, and Skeletal. Powerful "Cardiac" or heart muscles produce the action necessary to pump blood throughout the entire body. "Smooth" muscles assist internal organs in performing specific functions. Cardiac and smooth muscles are commonly called involuntary muscles, since we cannot consciously control them. "Skeletal" muscles carry out voluntary movements and are the most abundant tissue in the body, comprising about 23% of a woman's body weight and about 40% of a man's. Their smooth and uninhibited operation is crucial to maintenance and restoration of optimal body health.

Muscles do more for the body than just supply movement. The muscles also directly affect the body physically, mentally, emotionally and energetically. They play a role in providing balance and they also assist in synchronizing the systems. Movement of the muscles produces hydrostatic and hydraulic effects to assist the movement of fluids, which also creates friction that produces electrical charges that recharge and strengthen the body's life force energy field.

Within the muscular system, just like in many of the other systems discussed in this part of the book, mechanical, electrical, chemical, hydraulic, and energetic factors are directly influenced. The muscles play their vital role to provide movement, facial expressions, support, *and* produce heat.

The contractions of skeletal muscles are controlled by the nervous system. In stimulated muscles, tension is held so that a muscle cannot shorten. All motor neurons leading to skeletal muscles have branching axons, each of which terminates in a neuromuscular junction with a single muscle fiber. Nerve impulses that are passed down through a single motor neuron will trigger the contraction in all the muscle fibers where the branches of that neuron terminate. This minimum unit of contraction is called the motor unit.

The size of the motor unit depends on the precision required for control and the size of the muscle. For small muscles that control precision eye movement, for example, a single motor neuron triggers fewer than 10 muscle fibers. In comparison, in larger muscles, such as the gastrocnemius (calf) muscle, a single motor unit may include as many as 1000 – 2000 fibers that are uniformly spread throughout the muscle.

Even though the response of a certain motor unit is all-or-none (on or off), the strength of the response of the entire muscle as a whole is determined by the number of motor units that are activated simultaneously. While our bodies are at rest, most of our skeletal muscles are in a state of at least partial contraction to one degree or another, caused by the activation of just a few motor units that are stimulated at all times. When one set of motor units relax, an entirely different set takes over.

The process of contracting a muscle takes around 50 milliseconds, while the relaxation of the same fiber takes around 50 – 100 milliseconds. Because it takes longer for muscle fibers to relax than it does to stimulate them, *they can be held in contraction as long as they remain stimulated.* I believe this is a crucial element in understanding how the body works and what it needs to reset and heal itself.

An injury triggers various sensors in the body to acknowledge the existence of the injury and pain is felt in the body. The sensation of pain triggers the accumulation of inflammation or fluid to an area and also causes muscular contraction or spasm (to some degree or another) in order to help the body protect itself in that specific area. High concentrations of inflammatory fluids repeatedly re-trigger muscular contraction attributing to more pain. High-level-pain immediately sets off muscular contractions that in turn set off a myriad of other reactive compensatory controls throughout the entire body. This initiates large scale modifications to take place in the body in order for it to maintain some form of order and control.

The *Integumentary System*, otherwise known as the skin, is the largest organ in the body. It sloughs off over one million skin cells per hour and forms an entirely new outer skin every 27 days. One square inch of skin contains 3 million cells, 1,300 nerve cells, 12 feet of nerve fibers, 100 sweat glands, 36 heat sensors, 600 pain sensors, and 75 pressure sensors. The skin is so sensitive that the weight of a gnat (1/1600 of a gram) can be felt on the skin. This system produces Vitamin D, a precursor which increases calcium absorption for muscle contraction, and protects muscles and other tissues against abrasion and UV light. The skin rapidly performs self-repair when injured and helps regulate body temperature and prevent water and fluid loss.

The *Circulatory System* is a kind of delivery service that runs throughout your entire body. It delivers everything the cells need and removes what is no longer needed. As the heart beats, it carries oxygen and nutrient-rich blood, white blood cells (which fight infection, bacteria and disease), platelets (which help clot blood) and other chemicals and liquids. The oxygen and nutrient-depleted blood returns to the heart through veins, to become oxygenated and replenished again.

The *Digestive System* uses many muscles for the digestion *and* elimination processes. Some are responsible for chewing food and for swallowing, others protect the abdominal organs and still others are used for controlling voluntary defecation. As food passes through the body, it is blended with chemicals, which break it down into smaller components of solid and liquid foods, creating usable nutrients (cellular fuel) that can be absorbed to generate energy while also eliminating solid wastes from the body.

The digestive system provides the initial breakdown arena for nutrients, water, chemical, and cellular fuel for the entire body. It also uses various mechanical, electrical, chemical, and hydraulic components that are related to mental/emotional and energetic reactions in the body that can have life altering repercussions. Emotions can disturb and upset digestive functioning. The digestive system, though tough comparatively speaking, can be disturbed by cold drinks and food that slows down the entire system.

The digestive system actually begins in the mouth where food is chewed into small particles. Saliva mixes with both food and fluids to begin the digestive processes. The body uses about two quarts of saliva daily to process and digest food. When we swallow, this seeming insignificant event sets off a myriad of precisely timed reactions that move and sort fluids, air, and solids and sends them to their proper place. The throat produces a wave-like motion that moves the food and fluids to the stomach.

Although the stomach is primarily a food reservoir, it has about a two quart capacity and performs second stage digestive processes where it thoroughly mixes foods and digestive juices to continue the digestive process.

The stomach can be easily irritated by the increased acid needed to digest sugars, starches, caffeine, alcohol, and nicotine. Eating moderate small meals more often, limiting white flour consumption, and drinking water instead of other liquids or beverages tends to assist in rebalancing the stomach by bringing excess acid back into control.

It can also be irritated by outside factors that are happening in a person's life which affect the emotional state or well being. Emotional energy is also stored in this area of the body when the body is uneasy. An upset stomach commonly occurs when emotional triggers caused by stress or other factors, which puts the body in an initial protective mode when a person does not feel safe. In other words, the stomach reflects emotions or moods.

Fear, panic, and anxiety cause the face *and* the stomach to turn "pale." Anger turns both the face and the stomach hot and red. Stressful situations cause elevated acid production in the stomach which commonly causes mucus depletion, leading to stomach lining deterioration and leading to ulcers and more serious diseases such as cancer. Very deep-seated emotions cause the stomach to expel excess acid through vomiting, a kind of natural emotional housecleaning. Vomiting is also the body's natural process of ridding the body of harmful toxins.

The stomach secretes about three quarts of digestive juices daily from approximately 35 million digestive glands. These digestive glands primarily produce:

Pepsin – an enzyme for protein digestion

Hydrochloric acid – to assist the breakdown of foods for digestion

Many other enzymes – further assist in food breakdown for digestion

Actually, the consumption of some kind of hot, spicy food during a meal – in moderation, of course – assists the stomach mucus lining to recoat itself. A relaxing walk *after* a meal also encourages the stomach to calm down.

Part of the digestive tract includes the intestines. The intestinal tract is around 26 feet long. It is an intricate food-processing plant which actually feeds the entire body by breaking down the food into very small particles that can be assimilated. The intestines are primarily made up of the small intestine, large intestine, and colon. The small intestine consists of the duodenum, jejunum and approximately 12 feet of ileum. The large intestine is about 5 feet long, containing around 50 different microbes which are beneficial in maintaining optimal health.

Outside bacterial infestation, as well as medication, nervousness, extended periods of high stress, insufficient water intake, poor diet and emotional distress interfere with proper intestinal function. Ample water and adequate fiber intake greatly assist the digestive system and intestines in functioning properly. The book, "The Body's Many Cries for Water", by Dr. F. Batmanghelidj, explains how much water we really need.

Constant or long-term use of medicines and acid neutralizers has been found to be detrimental to the digestive system. Taken too often, many medicines and acid neutralizers can lead to alkalosis, which is much more severe than acidosis. Alkalosis is a condition where the pH of the body is too alkaline. Alkalosis causes an *enormous* burden on the kidneys, which can quickly lead to harmful body disorders and disease. You never want to assist the body in fighting one condition or disease only to create another that may be more serious.

The *Urinary System* is the liquid filtering system of the body. The muscular walls in the ureters (the long tubes that connect the kidneys to the bladder) contract, making wavelike movements forcing the urine into the bladder. The muscular walls also close the openings into the ureters so the urine cannot backflow into the kidneys. The urinary system is like a plumbing system that allows water and salts to flow through. It is also the liquid waste removal system.

The kidneys--the blood pressure regulators--are two blood filters that remove waste products from the circulatory system while regulating blood pH, ion and water balance. Both kidneys play a role in this filtering process. The left kidney filters out acids while the right kidney filters out alkalines.

The kidneys reabsorb almost 99% of the fluid in the blood while sending only two to four pints of waste (urine) to the bladder for storage before removal. Urine is produced in the kidneys twenty-four hours a day while the kidneys allow the blood to retain glucose, minerals and salts.

The *Lymphatic System* uses muscles to provide the skeletal muscle "pump" that helps move lymph through the lymphatic system and moves fluid waste out. It is one of the body's waste removal systems. It helps filter out and remove foreign substances from the blood and lymph. It absorbs fat from the intestines and eliminates the by-products of cellular breakdown and bacterial invasion. It removes waste produced by live cells, and unnecessary fluids which cause swelling. It also removes excess interstitial fluid or fluid that exists in spaces within the body.

The lymphatic system provides immune cells which provide protection against microorganisms and toxins by releasing chemical mediators. It produces certain white blood cells and generates antibodies to combat disease while promoting tissue repair. Because of these actions, the body is able to fight infection and ward off foreign invasion. The movement of the fluid produces small electrical charges that help strengthen the body's life-force energy field. This system plays an important part in the body's internal defense mechanism. To function properly the lymphatic system needs exercise and proper water intake.

The *Respiratory System* uses many muscles surrounding the thoracic region (chest) to change thoracic volume during breathing. Other muscles used in conjunction with the respiratory system control vocal cord tension for tone modulation when talking, humming or singing. The respiratory system also provides oxygen and removes carbon dioxide. It can be viewed as an O_2 and CO_2 gas mover.

The respiratory system helps supply a constant oxygen supply and removes carbon dioxide, which is vital for proper maintenance, restoration and healing. It also supplies oxygen and other gases to the blood, thereby oxygenating the entire body while removing carbon dioxide and other harmful gases. Respiration is an automatic function controlled by the brain. Although breathing is an obvious part of respiration, respiration also includes sneezing, yawning, hiccupping, and coughing, and works with the body, to a small degree, to assist our sense of smell. The respiratory system also helps to produce energy and is also a major energy mover for the body. It assists other organs and systems to maintain adequate hydration levels in the body, playing a vital role in helping maintain proper blood pH balance.

Muscles also play a major role in the *Cardiovascular System*. The cardiovascular system is made up of the heart, blood vessels and blood. The heart, the blood pump, transports nutrients, gases, hormones and other chemicals throughout the entire body while also removing waste products. This system also plays a role in the immune system response and the regulation of body temperature as well.

The *Skeletal System* utilizes muscles to move bones, resulting in body movements and maintaining body posture. The bones form a system of levers which facilitate body movements while providing a calcium reservoir necessary for smooth and proper muscle contraction. Muscular contraction places tension on bones which promotes bone growth, strength and maintenance.

Bones also assist in blood cell production by producing red blood cells from the bone marrow of certain bones and white blood cells from the marrow of others. Bones of the skeletal system also support and protect the internal body organs.

The average human adult skeleton has 206 to 208 bones joined by ligaments and tendons to form a supportive and protective framework for connecting muscles and soft tissue. Babies are born with 270 soft bones. Many of these bones fuse together between ages 20 and 25 to form the permanent skeletal structure.

The *Nervous System* is the body's immediate internal and external information collector and disseminator. It uses high-speed electro-chemical impulses which travel through neuro-pathways which are hard-wired, so to speak, directly to the brain. The neuropath ways are made up of cells which process information and initiate an action or reaction within milliseconds. These impulses travel at speeds up to 250 miles per hour. Systems other than the nervous system, such as the lymphatic system, are nowhere near as instantaneous and can take hours to respond.

The nervous system also acts as a storage center and control system for every muscle, system, organ and response in and of the body. This system detects sensation and controls movement while also controlling physiological *and* intellectual functions.

The nerves within the nervous system form several interrelated systems. Parts of these systems are physically separate, while other parts are separated by function only. The primary purpose of the nervous system is to analyse external and internal information and initiate responses in order of survival needs. The secondary function of the nervous system is to keep the body together, repaired and maintained. Other subsystems also work within the frame of the nervous system as well.

The nervous system extensively utilizes the strategically placed sensory receptors within the muscles and tendons (i.e. muscle spindles and Golgi tendon organs), as well as in organs and glands, in order to gather and distribute useful information throughout the body's neuropathic network at lightning speeds to help the brain control the entire body's functioning. The nervous system plays its part to provide the wiring and electro-chemical modifications needed to stimulate muscular contractions. It helps in maintaining muscle tone and it assists the body in relaying the necessary information which controls a wide variety of system, organ and gland functions. It also relays information throughout the body to help maintain delicate chemical balances.

Lack of muscular exercise or muscular movement greatly contributes to psychological fatigue. This is due to many factors, such as a decrease in repetitive firing of nerves in the body and brain, as well as a decrease in energy production and movement within the body, decreased blood movement creating an inadequate exchange of oxygen and carbon dioxide, and lack of specific chemical production and availability.

The nervous system is divided into the *central* and *peripheral* nervous systems. Together they produce opposing actions to keep each other in check and to provide balance. The entire nervous system exerts a profound influence on all digestive processes.

42

The central nervous system is comprised of the brain and spinal cord, and can also be considered to include the peripheral nervous system. The central nervous system controls voluntary movements, while the peripheral nervous system is responsible for involuntary body functions such as breathing, the heart rate and the digestive system.

A part of the peripheral nervous system is the Autonomic Nervous System (ANS) which is divided into three parts:

- The sympathetic nervous system
- The parasympathetic nervous system
- The enteric or intrinsic nervous system

The sympathetic and parasympathetic nervous systems also oppose each other and provide a check and balance. The sympathetic accelerates body and brain functions and controls the fight or flight response, and the parasympathetic slows the body and brain functions and induces the relaxation response throughout the body *and* brain. The enteric nervous system is actually a local nervous system which works only with the digestive system and is controlled from connections between the digestive system and the central nervous system. The enteric nervous system can and does function autonomously, although normal digestion does require sympathetic and parasympathetic links for communication between this system and the central nervous system.

The ANS is responsible for controlling nearly 90% of all body functioning. It primarily governs digestion, respiration, heart and circulatory function, blood pressure, muscles, glands, chemical balance, immune function, as well as the energetic levels and repair and healing aspects of the body.

Stimulating the sympathetic system immediately throws the body into protective mode and puts the body and brain on alert and on the defensive. It also reduces non-essential activities, such as digestion, salivation, and urine production while simultaneously increasing survival activities, i.e. fight or flight responses. The sympathetic system's primary function is to gear up the body to achieve a certain task or produce a state of fear, anxiety, or panic--a highly reactionary state--throughout the entire body, causing it to react. Stimulation of this part of the nervous system immediately launches physiological changes such as an increase in heart and breathing rates, increased blood supply to the muscles, and dilation of the pupils of the eyes. It also radically increases energy levels in the body.

The parasympathetic system helps the body to *conserve energy*. It does this through inducing relaxation, providing an inner calmness which helps the body in maintaining and restoring the balance needed to aid in restoration of health and healing. Proper stimulation of the parasympathetic system leads to widespread physiological relaxation throughout the *entire* body *and* mind. A few of these observable and easily measurable changes are constricted pupils, improved digestion, and reduced heart and breathing rates. In a healthy person, the sympathetic and parasympathetic systems work together well and compliment one another.

Western medicine displays an understanding of how the sympathetic and parasympathetic responses work in the body, commonly using Beta-blocking medicines to artificially decrease the sympathetic response, thereby decreasing the heart rate and blood pressure. Sometimes, athletes and people with high stress or highly competitive jobs use Beta-blockers to create a sense of calmness when they need peak physical or mental performance. With some people, however, Beta-blockers produce the opposite effect and have detrimental affects.

The ANS can be effectively assessed for proper and normal functioning. Heart Rate Variability (HRV) is one way that can be used for assessment. HRV is a simple measure of the evenness of the time interval between consecutive heartbeats. Because the HRV actually shows variations between the heartbeats, it can also be used as a predictive indicator of risk associated with a variety of behavioral disorders, including chronic diseases, aging, etc.

HRV is measured with an Electro-Cardio-Graph (ECG). The ECG is a machine that is used to trace revealing heart function abnormalities by showing the differences in electric potential produced by heart action. HRV is a non-invasive method of testing that is useful in evaluating the autonomic nervous system and cardiac function at the same time. The HRV can also show an increase in the total energy of the body and greater balance between the sympathetic and parasympathetic nervous systems as they begin to work together again and compliment each other when parasympathetic response is triggered in the body.

Abnormal ANS functioning can usually be diagnosed in people who are always tired, fatigued, or exhausted and complain of "not being able to sleep" although they are *very* tired. In these people it is common that the parasympathetic activity in their bodies is extremely low or virtually non-existent, resulting in an overall reduction in energy. It has *taken many of these people years to get to this point* of exhaustion. Often, many seemingly "healthy" individuals do not have a balanced ANS. They are not experiencing the level of optimal health that they could, although they feel "OK." For these people, a "tune-up" would provide a much-needed boost for both their body and mind to quickly bring them into prime condition again.

Taking a deeper look into the importance of the muscular system and its direct connection with the nervous system and its inner workings, it is essential to understand that the muscles are interconnected to almost every system, organ, and gland in the body and these are interwoven neuropathically as well. The nerves transmit vital information to and from every part of the body to the brain. Muscles provide information, including body position, through sensory receptors in the muscles and tendons.

The brain stimulates muscle contractions by way of the nervous system for normal muscular activity. Movement (use of muscles) and good nervous system communication help to maintain muscle tone. Movement stimulates the nervous system, which stimulates functioning of other systems, organs and glands as well, assisting in maintaining a balance of every one of them. Good nervous system communication and good muscle tone go hand in hand and vice-versa.

When a muscle is stretched past its normal resting length, the muscle spindle fibers cause a reflex contraction of the muscle called the "stretch reflex." The stretch reflex is, in very simple terms, a biological feedback control system in the body, used to control the amount of tension on muscles and tendons. It is a kind of overload protection system.

When passive tension is applied to the muscle (tension that occurred without the active support of action potentials causing an increase in the tension of a muscle without normal signals stimulated *from* the brain), the passive tension together with the increasing length of the muscle over stimulate the receptors of the spindle organ. The excitation of the receptors from the spindle organ in exact reverse of their normal operation, i.e from the inside out, cause the sensory nerve fibers to send a signal back to the spine and to the brain. This in turn cause the brain to send a stimulus to cause a series of very minute muscular contractions in opposing muscle groups as a "reflex," or kind of balancing, in order to maintain muscular balance.

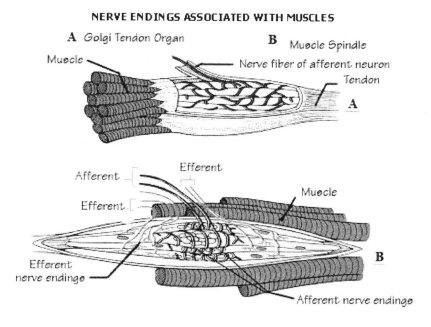

NERVE ENDINGS ASSOCIATED WITH MUSCLES

A Golgi Tendon Organ   **B** Muscle Spindle

Afferent nerves carry signals from the muscles or tendons to the brain
Efferent nerves carry signals from the brain to the muscles

When the spindle organ is stretched as the tension is increased, (the muscle is getting longer rather than shorter), the spindle organs send a series of signals through the spine to the brain. The brain sends back a signal back to the surrounding muscle stimulating or "telling it" to contract. As the surrounding muscle tissue contracts, the spindle organ is no longer stretched, inhibiting the activity of the spindle organ. This causes another set of responses which shuts off the spindle organ, causing the immediate release of muscle tension.

When a tendon organ is stretched, they respond to the stretch in a similar manner to the spindle organ, except they only contain nerve fibers that send information to the brain. Because of this, the tendons themselves cannot respond to nervous system stimulus that causes action potential. When tendon organs are suddenly passively stretched, a set of signals are sent to the spinal cord and brain which sends a signal back "telling" the attached muscle to contract. Because of the minuteness of the signal that was actually sent, and there was no inherent danger of damage or injury to the muscle or the body detected, the Golgi tendon is triggered to immediately send out signals to inhibitory neurons in the spine which suddenly "shut off" muscular contraction, causing the muscle to instantly release.

Psychological fatigue (both mental and emotional) often restricts muscular movement causing weakened connections and communications between the systems, organs, glands and the muscles. Similarly, it weakens the connections and communications between the muscles and the systems, organs and glands in the reverse as well.

Excessive muscular movement (use), without proper rest and nutrition for the restoration of the muscles and their function contributes greatly to psychological fatigue. This is because of the amount of cellular breakdown and dehydration which occurs as well as many other chemical factors. Muscles under tension (stress) over extended periods of time can cause psychological fatigue and greatly reduce body efficiency and function, causing the increase of stressors

45

throughout the body leading to improper overall body function. This can be readily observed in marathon runners who "hit the wall, hard" and are basically unable to continue to move. They have become so fatigued that the body's functions become unable to manage in a normal way, and the runner becomes confused and delirium/disorientation set in, which has a significant impact on their health for some time, often many weeks, after the race.

On a smaller scale, people who continue to keep going and going without resting, because "they have things that just have to get done," can experience the same kind of body breakdown, confusion and disorientation, to some degree, as their bodies go beyond the point of fatigue, exponentially magnifying the amount stress their bodies and minds are going through. Their body says "STOP" and they just keep going. In these cases, their physical, mental and emotional health becomes affected, and if not reversed, ill health can and usually does follow. This is because the stress level increases to such a degree that their body can no longer function and something is triggered in their body to get them to stop.

The body _needs_ time to stop, time to rest and "re-create" itself, sufficient for _its_ needs. Just one day or two days a week off is not sufficient in some cases. Most people are busier on the weekends or on their vacations that when they actually work. The body needs _rest_. Rest is crucial for proper and efficient nervous system functioning _and_ overall body functioning for good health.

3.2 Organs

KIDNEY

The kidneys filter the blood and regulate blood pressure. They have the ability to self-repair (to some degree) when injured. Acid-producing substances cause the kidneys to overexert themselves in an effort to balance the overall pH of the body. This especially affects the left kidney because it filters acids out of the blood, while the right kidney filters alkalis. Overworking the kidneys reduces their effectiveness in removing toxins and impurities from the blood and body, as they are designed to do. Over time they become unable to keep up with removing large quantities over a long period of time. When the kidneys cannot expel toxins fast enough because the filters are "dirty" and do not receive proper flushing, kidney stones begin to form.

When the kidney filters are "too dirty" some of the blood bypasses the filters. The heavy particulates in the blood need to go somewhere. The body puts them "somewhere", usually in an opening or gap between bones that is abnormally large. Bunions often form on the toes because tight-fitting shoes open the gap on the outer portion of the big toe and the body gives the brain a signal that the gap is too wide. Arthritis is a sign and the result of a kidney-related disorder, not necessarily kidney malfunction.

The kidneys are very proficient and work very efficiently. When working properly, they multi-task extremely well. The kidneys:

- Work as the Master chemist of the body
- Help produce red blood cells
- Oversee proper levels of potassium, sodium chloride and other substances in the blood
- Control vital water balance by removing excess water
- Control blood pH
- Assist in regulating blood pressure
- Filter 25% of your entire blood supply every minute
- Keep blood composition constant
- Remove excess nitrogen, salts, acids, and alkalis
- Contain over 70 miles of tubules

When the blood flowing through the kidneys back to the heart drops below a normal pressure, the kidneys signal the heart to pump harder. This increases the blood pressure. The same cycle occurs when the blood flowing through the arteries is restricted due to hardening of the arteries or a restriction of the kidneys' ability to filter blood. When one kidney becomes sluggish because of impurities, for example, it reduces the flow of blood back to the heart and starts the cycle of increasing blood pressure to compensate. Hardening of the arteries also reduces the blood flow through the kidneys and causes the heart to pump harder and sometimes faster in order to increase blood pressure and blood flow.

When the blood going through the kidneys does not have enough pressure, the kidneys once again signal the heart to "pump harder". This occurs over and over again while minimally increasing blood pressure, slightly signaling the heart to pump harder until it achieves the proper pressure. Over time, this has a tendency to overwork the heart. Many researchers say that it isn't the condition of the heart which causes disease; it is the condition of the arteries and/or improper kidney function, along with other factors, which leads to overworking the heart, causing heart disease and failure.

When the blood flow rises above what the brain perceives as normal, the kidneys signal the heart, through the brain, to slow down and to pump lighter and less. This reduces the blood pressure and decreases the blood flow to normalize the system.

Kidney stones occur partly because of improper hydration of the body, causing a very slight thickening of the blood. The thickened blood has impurities (particulates) in it which the kidneys filter out. When there is not enough water to keep flushing the kidneys properly, the impurities are not able to flush out, and collect in the kidneys. The accumulation of the impurities over time forms a "stone," which the kidneys will attempt to pass out of the body, just as it is designed to do. This accumulation of stones can be avoided in most cases. You can avoid getting kidney stones by maintaining adequate fluid intake (just water is by far the best). Experts state that we should drink enough water to equal ½ of your body weight in ounces on a daily basis (i.e. 150 lbs ÷ 2 = 75 ounces) or just under 2 ½ quarts [if you are able, as some people unable to do so for various medical reasons]. When working in hotter temperatures or exercising, this amount may need to be increased, even significantly, to balance out any losses caused by perspiration and respiration.

Alcohol and caffeinated products can and often do cause severe dehydration of the body and kidneys, leading to dehydration of the body as a whole. This dehydration causes the kidneys to shrink slightly, causing the kidneys to become loose in the sack-like enclosures that protects them. In order to protect the kidneys from being bruised or damaged, the body naturally increases muscular tension (spasms) in the region surrounding the kidneys, causing the area to shrink just enough to hold the kidneys in place. I have also discovered that the common factor for those who have kidney pain, problems, or kidney stones on the left side (left kidney) consume excessive amounts of caffeine in its various forms.

3.3 Glands

The *Endocrine System* is comprised of a group of glands which produces chemical messengers called "hormones." These hormones regulate growth, sexual development and metabolism. The glands--the pituitary, adrenal, pancreas, thyroid and parathyroid--release hormones directly into the blood stream.

The glands work in the body to help balance energy, resources, and chemicals to one degree or another. There are, of course, many glands in the body that assist the body to function at its optimal level. How these glands work and what they affect in the body is very complex.

Other glands perform wonderful and beneficial tasks, however there is so little information available on what they actually do or how they work that little meaning would be gained from any information that I could produce for this book, at the present time. I have mainly included the glands that are commonly known.

The *adrenal glands* are primarily responsible for offsetting the negative effects of physical, mental, and emotional stresses on the body. The adrenal glands are a pair of 1-2 inch-long glands situated above the kidneys, weighing only a fraction of an ounce each. The adrenals, as they are commonly known:

- Take instruction from the pituitary gland
- Have effects on development, growth and physical characteristics
- Secrete more than three dozen hormones directly into the bloodstream

The adrenals can be divided into two distinct parts:

• The outer region

- Takes instructions from the pituitary hormone ACTH
- Secretes hormones which affect energy storage, food use, blood chemical composition, and a variety of body characteristics. These hormones also influence body shape and the amount and thickness of body hair
- Secretes three major types of hormones called "steroids", which control sodium and potassium balance, increase sugar levels in the blood and control the sex hormones

• The inner region

- Receives all commands from the nervous system
- Is comparatively smaller than the outer region
- Is a part of the sympathetic nervous system
- Is the first line of the defense mechanism of the body, triggering defense/reaction mechanisms to physical, mental and emotional stressors
- Produces two types of hormones
- Produces chemicals which cause the body to instinctively react to danger, threat, anger and fear (causing fight-or-flight response)

48

Adrenal hormones, and the biochemical support system within the body, work together to achieve and maintain cardiovascular health, proper pH balance, sex-drive, energy levels, skin conditions, disposition, optimal health, and overall psychological and physiological processing. The body's ability to sustain proper blood-sugar levels, stamina, peak energy, and muscular strength are dependent upon optimal adrenal function. The adrenals also support the body's ability to regulate and manage environmental stressors.

The adrenal glands produce and regulate certain hormones called "stress hormones." They prime the body by increasing the heart rate, dilating the airway to the lungs, accelerating the respiratory rate and increasing glucose levels. Elevated oxygen and glucose levels in the blood, combined with increased blood flow throughout the entire body, help force extra-ordinary muscular contraction to assist the body in performing supernatural feats (lifting a car off of a person after an accident, for instance.) Poor eating habits (improper nutrition), lack of exercise, lack of sleep and stress have a toxic *and* harmful effect on adrenal function, causing problems in systems, organs, and the entire body.

The *Pituitary Gland* is regulated by the "hypothalamus," a tiny cluster of brain cells just above the pituitary gland. The hypothalamus is commonly called the "master gland," which electro-chemically transmits and sorts out messages to and from the body and the brain. It responds to the body through the pituitary gland by either sending nerve impulses or needed hormones.

The pituitary gland:

- Is subservient to the hypothalamus
- Is an important link between the nervous and endocrine systems
- Produces hormones to answer the body's needs
- Is made up of two lobes: anterior (front) and posterior (back)
- One lobe releases hormones which affect growth, sexual development, metabolism and reproduction
- The other lobe releases hormones which affect bone growth and regulate the activity of other glands
- Hormones produced by the pituitary and sent to other glands and organs stimulate further hormone and chemical production.

The *liver* is a gland, not an organ, and it is commonly called a glandular organ. It performs over 500 functions as the body's top chemical manufacturer and recycling plant. The liver also removes solid waste products from the body and also converts lactic acid returned from the muscles back into glucose for use again, while also storing portions of the glucose for future and emergency use. Alcohol or drug consumption, food additives and preservatives, as well as a poor diet, directly and adversely affect the liver.

Among many other things, the liver:

- Provides fuel for muscular movement
- Manufactures specific vitamins for the body's use
- Assists in digestion
- Produces over 1000 different enzymes to assist the body in performing millions of intricate chemical conversions throughout the body
- Dissolves fats
- Collects nutrients
- Synthesizes important proteins for the blood
- Cleans toxins from the blood
- Removes ammonia from the body
- Manufactures antibodies
- Detoxifies the body by keeping toxic levels to a minimum
- Assists in maintaining proper glucose levels
- Manufactures blood clotting agents in the blood
- Removes excess salts
- Removes damaged red blood cells
- Destroys microbes and cell debris
- Acts as a safety valve for the heart by swelling and soaking up excess blood, then slowly releasing it back into the bloodstream
- Produces over one quart of bile daily – debris filtered from the body
- As much as 80% of the liver can be removed and it will continue working at a normal rate while totally rebuilding itself within a couple of months

One of the least understood facets of the liver is its direct effect upon our overall vitality, moods, and attitudes. An unhealthy liver can create a tremendous amount of physical pain as well as physical, mental and emotional stress. One's level of happiness can often be determined by the condition of the liver itself and can often be a primary indicator of how the body is functioning as a whole.

A congested or improperly functioning liver creates disharmony throughout the entire body. This disharmony can be exhibited as resentment, bitterness, impatience, aggression, or anger. A person can help augment liver function with proper nutrition, vitamins, water, and rest.

The *Pancreas*, a powerful long gland, lies across and behind the stomach and consists of tissues imbedded in nest-like cells which resemble clusters of grapes. These cells secrete digestive enzymes. The pancreas also secretes the hormones insulin and glucagon into the blood. Insulin regulates the use of glucose in all parts of the body except the brain, and glucagon assists in the creation of glucose.

The pancreas:

- Is vital to proper endocrine and exocrine functions
- Secretes digestive juices which assist in breaking down carbohydrates, fats, proteins and acids
- Secretes bicarbonate to neutralize stomach acid as it enters the duodenum
- Produces some cells which secrete hormones to regulate blood glucose levels

Without the enzymes the pancreas produces, the body could consume virtually endless amounts of food and still remain malnourished. The pancreas has the delicate and crucial task of:

- Producing two key hormones, glucose and insulin, that empty into the blood stream to supply cells with energy
- Keeping blood sugar properly regulated
- Producing about two pints of digestive juices (daily)
- Manufacturing alkaline fluids to neutralize acids in the digestive tract
- Working with the liver to enable it to store excess insulin until needed
- Producing three enzymes:

> **Trypsin** – initiates protein breakdown for utilization in the body
> **Amylase** – converts starches to sugar
> **Lipase** – breaks down fat globules into fatty acids and glycerin

You can greatly assist proper pancreas functioning by eating a balanced and nutritious healthy diet and by drinking water instead of alcoholic or sugar filled beverages.

The *Thyroid Gland* weighs less than one ounce and controls the rate at which the body produces energy from nutrients. It needs iodine to produce the proper amount of hormones to assist the body in converting nutrients to energy. The *Parathyroid Glands* are four small oval glands which are seated next to the thyroid and control blood-calcium levels. Calcium is very important for bones, teeth, muscle contractions, blood clotting, nerve functioning, and glandular secretion. Low calcium levels in the blood cause the body to seize calcium from the bones, allowing them to fracture more easily. Low calcium often causes twitching, spasms, convulsions and in extreme cases, even death. Too much calcium, on the other hand, can cause kidney stones and weakened muscle tone.

When imbalances exist in the thyroid or parathyroid, it throws off body functioning. Excessive thyroid gland secretion causes weight loss, nervousness and emotional disturbances. Extremely low secretions on the other hand often produce sluggish bodily functions.

The thyroid gland:

- Secretes hormones which regulate energy for proper emotional balancing
- Regulates body metabolism

3.4 Connective Tissue

On a basic level, there are four different forms of connective tissue. These include:

Fluid connective tissue – obvious in forms of mucous, lymph, and blood

Structural connective tissue – unmistakable in forms of bone and cartilage

Proper connective tissue - both *regular* and *irregular*

> Regular - tendons and ligaments made up of parallel layers of collagenous (collagen) fibers
> Irregular - a fibrous three-dimensional lattice like structure made up of two types
>> 1. *deep* or dense fascia.
>> 2. *superficial* or loose fascia.

Many beneficial effects of healing definitely take place by *properly and directly* stimulating these irregular forms of connective tissue in ways that the body will respond.

The *fascia tissue* (a thin layer of connective tissues) is a strong, opaque membrane-like fibrous connective tissue having a tensile strength of up to 2000 pounds per square inch. It encases and supports muscles, internal organs and nerves, while it also sheaths other structures in the body, much like a latex balloon.

Thomas Atlee, Principal of the College of Cranial-Sacral Therapy in London, believes that every illness, tension and injury, both physical and mental, leave its mark in the body. Researchers find that fascia tissue holds the memory of physical trauma, while conscious and subconscious areas of the mind hold the memory of mental trauma. Each has far-reaching positive, life and health-enhancing effects, as well as negative, life and health-deteriorating effects.

One of the keys to understanding how the body functions is through understanding the impressively profound and crucial role which fascia tissue plays in both illness *and* optimal health. Muscular contraction and the pumping motion of the muscles propels bodily fluids through the fascia tissue both in and out, similar to the way water squishes and sucks back and forth through your socks as you walk around in a wet shoe.

The fascia is the primary regulator of fluids and waste throughout the entire body. It also plays a major role in cellular metabolism and in maintaining proper water levels for the immeasurable amount of chemical reactions which occur throughout the body on a daily basis. It also maintains cellular homeostasis (or balance), tissue repair, growth and immune functions.

The fascia interconnects *all* the muscles and organs in the body - forming a kind of mesh or web around these structures, as a kind of "shrink wrap", so to speak. Fascia sustains life through playing its vital part in helping the body remove waste. However, it can also harbor sickness and disease at the same time, by restraining the removal of wastes as well as the memory of trauma and injury. Because of its unique makeup and design characteristics and how it functions with the body serving it as a whole, the fascia has a great tendency to help the body hold on to old patterns and cycles.

All the fascia tissue for the entire body connects near the knee. This connecting point is unmistakably a *very* key point in the body.

Connective Tissue and its role in disability

The fascia tissue can easily become dehydrated due to low water concentrations in the body. Eventually, this causes unnecessary discomfort and pain throughout the body, as the muscles become resistive to movement due to fascial shrinkage and its adherence to muscle tissue. Adhesion of muscle to fascia limits motion and range of motion, while causing nerve sensors to rapidly and repeatedly fire sending pain signals to the brain, while also generating higher-than-normal piezo-electricity levels, as well. At this point, the body goes into a "protect mode" to help defend itself from itself, once again causing increased levels of fatigue, discomfort and/or pain. Fibromyalgia is one of the magnifying results of this abnormal condition in the body. The medical dictionary defines *Fibromyalgia* as a disorder of unknown origin. It is characterized by muscle pain, stiffness and fatigue.

When water concentrations are low in the body, blood pressure increases dramatically, due to changes in various chemical and hormone secretions. Some of these changes occur because a decrease in water concentration will automatically raise the sodium content in the body.

Movement of the muscles within the encasement of the fascia tissue causes hydrostatic pressure to vary within the enclosure. These changes in pressure cause fluids to move throughout the entire body. The fascia must have freedom of movement to receive *and* remove fluids necessary to maintain proper bodily function. Within the matrix of the fascia, capillaries feed life-supporting nutrients to the muscles and organs, while the lymphatic system removes unwanted fluids and waste.

The release and removal of impurities and poisonous fluids, commonly called toxins, is a vital function. We would quickly die without it. The structure of these fluids or toxins (having the consistency of light syrup) is crystalline in nature--therefore, the more hydrated the body, the more fluid the state of the crystal. The more dehydrated the body, the more solid and rigid the crystal becomes, thus greatly decreasing the natural flow of both nutrients into the body and waste from it through the fascia tissue.

Dehydration of the body can easily provoke malfunctioning of the fascia. This occurs because of the consumption of dehydrating foods or fluids, such as white flour, refined sugars, alcohol, and coffee.

Facts surrounding dehydration are:

- Increases in body temperature, exercise and stress cause dehydration in the body

- Dehydration adversely affects digestion, kidney and heart function

- 75% of all Americans are chronically dehydrated

- In 37% of all Americans, the thirst mechanism is so weak it is commonly mistaken for hunger

- Even mild forms of dehydration will slow the metabolism as much as 3 to 5%

- Lack of water is the number one contributor to daytime fatigue and mental confusion because of the altered neuro-electrical and neuro-chemical effects dehydration has on the central nervous system

- A minor 2% drop in body water-content can trigger short-term memory fatigue, causing individuals to have difficulty performing basic arithmetic or focusing on a printed page or computer screen

Facts about hydration are:

- Water is the universal solvent. It dissolves nearly anything if there is sufficient water supplied or if given enough time to wash/scrub the impurity(ies) away, or by dissolving it through friction

- A University of Washington study revealed that one glass of water will shut down midnight hunger pangs for nearly 100% of all dieters.

- Drinking just five glasses of water a day decreases the risk of colon cancer an average of 45%, reduces the risk of breast cancer by an average 79%, and makes a person 50% less likely to develop cancer of the bladder

- Higher concentrations of water in the body produces large decreases in blood pressure

Stress-related trauma or injury (physical, mental, or emotional), stress, tension, anxiety, constipation, excessive non-food consumption, lack of sufficient water intake, improper digestion, laxatives, malnutrition, over-medication, extended periods in dry environments excessive exposure to the sun, insufficient exercise, and lack of rest also contribute to the causes of dehydration.

When the body is dehydrated the matrix, the passageways for both nutrients and waste, become clogged. The fluids, which are syrupy and crystalline in nature, do not flow well in either direction and in extreme cases they stop flowing altogether. The fascia tissue begins to dry up and rapidly shrink. When this happens, it wrinkles, causing cavity-like crevasses or pockets to form within the shrunken fibers.

During extended periods of dehydration, the syrupy crystalline-compound within the crevasses dries up. These dried masses adhere to the fascia causing even more dehydration, leading to the formation of many more crystalline-filled cavities.

When a series of other processes take place in the body and when the number of these cavities reaches a critical stage, they begin to group together because of the energetic/magnetic attraction which takes place within the crystals that are formed. These larger groupings then begin to interrupt and destabilize the natural and fundamental energetic flows within the body, causing the initial stages of dysfunction and dis-ease.

A bonding or gluing effect also occurs. When adhesion of these fibers takes place at this advanced stage, tension, discomfort and pain is a natural result, as tissues within the fascia become inflamed. When this occurs, it is more difficult to bring the tissue back to normal. This fascia must first be re-hydrated to reduce shrinkage of the fascia *and* to disperse the impurities.

Excessive inflammation causes the fluid which remains trapped inside the fascia wall to stagnate. This stagnation begins to break down the cellular structure causing tissue damage or dis-ease (rotting) of the tissue. When the damaged tissue and stagnating fluids reach critical levels, extreme dis-eases as severe as cancer naturally occur.

This reduction in flow both in and out of the fascia tissue could assuredly account for many dis-eases of the body which are caused by the impairment of lymphatic movement and drainage, a suppressed immune system, reduced gland and organ function, and restricted neuropathic flows to and from the brain.

I highly suspect that the occurrence of dehydration and the accumulation of adhesions of the fascia tissue is the main cause of Fibromyalgia. Nearly 3 million people in the United States alone are affected by Fibromyalgia. I see Fibromyalgia as a disorder in the body which occurs when the elasticity of the fascia tissue becomes stagnant, almost brittle-like in nature, causing adhesions to form between muscles, organs, tissues, and the skin, causing discomfort and pain.

Dehydration could also be the cause of the "brain fog" that many people experience from time to time. It may also be one of the main causes for immune system disorders such as chronic fatigue syndrome, Epstein Barr, M.S., and the like. I believe that this also applies to arthritis; where deposits not removed from the body are held on to, then deposited somewhere else in the body.

The fascia has the capacity to re-hydrate and return to normal, if given proper recourse. I have seen it happen rapidly time and time again.

Chapter 4

Body Basics 102

The body and how it is designed to work

The body tells a complete story. It is an open book that tells an entire story of what is happening from deep within itself. The story is illustrated throughout the body in multiple, yet simple ways; skin tone, color, tension or sag, levels of pain tolerance (too high *or* too low – neither is good), eye color and movement, eyelid tone, fluidity of movement and range of motion are just a few. Where the body has tension or lack of proper tension, how it supports itself, and where it is protecting itself are a few hints the body gives as it illustrates its story.

For those who can examine it for what is really there, it is as though the body is being displayed on a "big screen" monitor. Seemingly insignificant details such as breathing, attentiveness, peacefulness, ability to rest, proportional strength, clarity of mind, etc., are pieces of the puzzle that truly add up to make the complete picture.

The strength or weakness displayed in any area of the body, for example, can be seen as indicators of how the entire being is doing as a whole. Learning to first see and then read the entire story of the body, seeing where it is *at the present time*, and what IT is trying to show you, are crucial to gaining the necessary insight and understanding of what it would possibly take to return or restore it back to a state of optimal health. It is in taking a much closer detailed look, and examining the pieces that are first obviously out of place or out of normal parameters, *then* searching for those that are just slightly askew, that are the key elements to seeing what the body is saying.

Self-examination and self-assessment, though it may seem difficult for some people to do in the beginning, is crucial to understanding where YOUR body is and what IT is telling you. The problem, however, is that most people are not familiar enough with how the body *should* work, and the even greater piece of the mystery, how the body is actually designed to work.

You have lived in your body your whole lifetime. What is or has become "normal" to you may not actually be a normal and optimal way that the human body functions at all. What may be normal to you, a nagging stiffness, constant headaches or migraines, or a bout with acid-reflux, carpal tunnel, fatigue, fibromyalgia, or asthma, etc., is not "normal" <u>at all</u>. What has happened is that you have become used to the body being a certain way. In many instances it came on gradually, you thought nothing of it at all, until it became such a part of your health that you considered it to be normal, for some reason.

For example, when I was learning to read, I was labeled by my teachers as a "non-reader" – someone who couldn't read or had much difficulty in learning to read. I struggled severely through grade school. My mother often asked me why I "made faces", or why I closed one eye, while studying or reading schoolwork, or she commented, "How come you are making those funny faces – you have to stop that!"

Well, the bottom line was that I didn't even know that I was making "faces." All I knew was that it was very hard to study or read. I didn't know any different. How could I, I had done this my "entire life" up to that point, and knew nothing else.

One day, my mother said, "There must be something wrong with your eyes. It's not normal for anyone to be making faces like that."

It was some time after that, just before I became a freshman in high school, that my parents took me to get my eyes checked, again. They had been told previously that I had perfect, 20/20 vision by another optometrist.

My parents explained to the ophthalmologist what they thought the problem was and what they saw going on. He performed many series of tests. My five other brothers and sisters were also being tested that day and he kept bringing me in and out of the examination room between the various tests he did on me, giving my eyes a rest.

After nearly four hours of testing, he came to my parents and said, "I am unable to find anything." He looked very puzzled as he slowly began walking back to the examination room. About halfway down the hall, he stopped, turned around, and said to my parents, "I'm going to do one more test. What I will be testing for is so extremely rare that it took me a while to think of it."

A few minutes later, he returned to my parents and said, "I found the problem. Your son *has* perfect 20/20 vision. However he also has double vision, in other words, he sees two of everything, especially when he is tired. It could have been caused by a fall or accident, I don't know for sure. It is clear, though, that he needs glasses with specially cut prisms in them to help him to see properly. The problem your son was having wasn't that he couldn't read. The problem is that he couldn't *see* to read. What happens with double vision, in his case, is that the page splits in half, so to speak, he actually sees two pages. One is up and out here, and the other is way down and out there" He gestured. "So he _had_ to close one eye, sometimes physically, in order to see. By the way, how long has he had this problem?" the doctor asked. "As far as we know, *his entire life*," my parents answered.

> Tension *also* indicates that something is awry in the body and *it needs to be addressed* – sooner than later.

For me, having double vision was normal. I had never seen in any other way. I didn't even have a clue how I was supposed to see, what other people saw (I, of course, wasn't in their bodies), or what was *supposed* to be normal. It was the only thing that I knew. I didn't know better vision was even available. How could I, that's all I had ever known...until I had my first pair of glasses. Wearing glasses drastically changed my life and my outlook on life as well - no pun intended.

Just as I thought double-vision was normal, most people think that having stress, pain, and tension is "normal." Being tired all the time, chronic sinus problems, allergies, ear infections, arthritis, Alzheimer's, Parkinson's, or any other kind of disorder of the body *is not normal*! Having <u>any</u> kind of disorder or dysfunction of the body is definitely NOT the way the body is designed to be. It is not supposed to work that hard.

When the body is in a state of optimal health it is in balance and in an "at ease" state – a place where everything "fits". When the body is in an "at ease" state, it takes minimal resources and energy to keep it strong, vibrant and healthy. Everything works together, in cooperation, for the good and betterment of the whole.

When the body is in a state of weakened or ill health, it is in a state of tension or "at tension." When "at tension" the body will tend to primarily concentrate significant amounts of resources and energy to a particular area or level of the body to enable it to keep functioning. The levels consist of the physical, mental or emotional. The body keeps itself tense in an attempt to counter-balance tension or imbalance which is taking place somewhere else in the body. Usually, this tension is *opposite* of where other tension or imbalance exists in the body, in order to keep the head level and erect, while keeping the body in an aligned, upright position. Tension *also* indicates that something is awry in the body and *it needs to be addressed* – sooner than later. That is simply what the body does.

When the body focuses its resources primarily on one area or level struggling to return to an "at ease" state, it often causes the other areas or levels to slip into a weakened state, due to undersupplied resources and reduced energy supply which is needed to keep these other areas or levels in the body healthy and resilient. When the body remains "at tension" for a prolonged period of time it can stealthily digress to a stage where it becomes very difficult for it to clear the problem and return to an "at ease" state on its own. When this "ill-at-ease" or "dis-eased' stage exists, the body becomes *very* unbalanced and unstable in other areas or levels, and other symptoms, signs or conditions appear, clearly indicating that something is not quite right. Many health disorders are the direct result of internal organs not functioning properly.

Symptoms are simply the body's way of displaying a reaction to what is happening within the body. In other words, symptoms are the body's way of displaying that it can no longer handle what is happening, on its own.

> When this "ill-at-ease" or "dis-eased' stage exists, the body becomes *very* unbalanced and unstable in other areas or levels, and other symptoms, signs or conditions appear, clearly indicating that something is not quite right.

In most cases, the body *will* begin to show evident signs or conditions of being in a state of "dis-ease" or in a condition where the body is "ill at ease."

Fatigue, exhaustion, stress, inflammation and pain are just a few of the many indicators the body clearly gives to us. The return to balance and an "at ease" state is clearly necessary. It is going to take some work to bring the body back into balance. It also shows that what is happening is becoming critical, and that making a change has become very urgent.

Designed for survival, the body will throw itself into a state of emergency in a ferocious attempt to rebalance itself, if and when necessary. Left unchecked, the dis-eased (ill-at-ease) condition begins to destabilize other parts of the body as well, including the systems and organs designed to keep the body healthy and well. This destabilization of other parts of the body also has physical, mental, and emotional consequences.

The underlying systems, organs and principles which govern the operations of the body are fundamentally simple. The complexities of the entire body and how it has to operate simply arise out of the necessity of each individual part needing to function freely on its own, as well as synchronistically with all the other individual parts, with ease.

PROTECTION AND HEALING ASPECTS OF THE HUMAN BODY

The body has internal and external automatic mechanisms designed strictly for protection; to preserve the survival of the body. These mechanisms are *always* actively on guard, standing by to jump at the chance to go to work. Along with the protection mechanisms, the body also has automatic maintenance, repair, and healing mechanisms designed to give support and strengthen the body on many levels.

The body is designed primarily to protect and heal itself.

The body is designed to:

> **First and foremost – protect itself**
>
> **Secondarily – repair major injuries to itself in stages**
>
> **Third – self-maintain/survive at predetermined minimal levels**
>
> **Fourth – heal itself**

By obtaining a basic understanding of two of the primary designs of the body, protection and healing, distinctions are brought forth into what it takes to truly assist the body to heal itself and to restore *optimal* health. Through these distinctions, associations can be made which will assist you in understanding the active role you must take to further assist and elevate your own body's health *and* healing.

A body which has been forced to protect itself for a period of time will begin to display a variety of ailments to get our attention. In the beginning, these attention-getting ailments may be an occasional ache or pain, muscle stiffness, aching joints, tension or stress. When first ignored, these nagging factors often join with numerous other factors in an attempt to get your attention, letting you know that something is out of line and needs tending. If left unattended for a period of time, the imbalance becomes more severe and other parts of the body become involved. Conditions worsen and become increasingly difficult to ignore, making life uncomfortable and at times miserable. When something in the body is out of balance, abnormal, or out of place, it will naturally give you signs to get you to slow down, make a change, or stop, before it stops you.

When having to make a choice between protecting, repairing, maintaining, or healing itself, the body is designed and programmed to *always* choose the protecting mechanisms first, the repair mechanisms second, the maintenance mechanisms third, and lastly, if there are enough resources and energy to activate them, and when everything else is being taken care of, the healing mechanisms.

The body *protects* itself, using what is called the fight or flight response or mode. This is the highly defensive and protective state, which the entire body automatically goes into when there is a threat of harm, whether the threat is actual *or perceived*. The body will also go into a state of shock when necessary, in order to protect its survival at much deeper levels. A state of shock causes a state of emergency to occur within the body, which then causes each system and organ to begin fending for itself, to some degree, causing a separation from the whole.

When in the *repair* mode, especially after an injury, the body begins to make essential life-saving external and internal *physical* repairs first, to keep the body surviving and functioning to whatever degree it is able. As the repairs progress, the body then activates repairs for areas that are less vital. Full repair on the physical level takes time, in most instances, where tissue or bone is severed or damaged. However, acceleration of repair of the body and mind *is* possible. Proper rest, exercise, hydration *and* nutrition also contribute their part in accelerated healing as well.

When in *maintenance* mode, the body will be maintained at some minimal status quo/sub par level to conserve energy and resources within the means it has, keeping the systems and organs functioning to some degree. During maintenance mode, the body can and will perform its regularly scheduled tasks on a timely basis, as it is designed to do. As we sleep, for example, many of the organs of the body actually perform "scheduled maintenance": the liver, gallbladder, spleen, and pancreas, for example go through a nightly routine to flush themselves, getting ready for their respective "responsibilities" of the next day.

When the systems and organs are less able to do their own maintenance due to overwork, injury, dis-ease or some lack of resources or energy in the body that is normally available, then other systems and organs automatically begin to take over, stepping in to help with the needs that exist to keep the body functioning at some level. However, these other systems and organs *are not* designed to take on the task and do it <u>as</u> efficiently as the affected system or organ, nor are they designed to perform the task for an extended period of time, or take over the entire task, either.

Fourth and last, the body is designed to *heal itself.* Here the body does <u>much</u> more than just perform maintenance. It uses the complex arrangement of systems and organs along with a vast array of enzymes, acids, chemicals, and electro-chemical components and stimuli, working in unison to automatically *repair, regenerate and re-create* itself. In some cases, after a particular area of the body has sustained damage and has gone through and completed the repair *and* healing processes, it is actually stronger than before the injury. The re-creation of specific cells, tissues and some organs and how this healing can and does happen is truly miraculous.

The *healing* mode or response is activated in the body primarily when and *if* the body is given the correct information to go into a state of rest *and* to turn on the deeper-level healing responses. The healing response then starts the finalizing sequences to properly reset the physical <u>and</u> mental <u>and</u> emotional <u>and</u> energetic aspects of the body which were affected, back to where they were designed to be, according to the original blueprint and programming already in the body.

When reset into its healing mode, the body has the ability to make impressive (near instantaneous and miraculous) transformations on all levels, by clearing mental, emotional, chemical, neuropathic, physical and energetic interferences, as well as the deletion or removal of unneeded neuronal (brain) patterns.

Simply stated, these neuronal patterns are brain cell configured and stored neurological patterns which are interconnected in a complex way to the body's vast and intricate electro-chemical/neurological network which connects every part of the body to every other part of the body to some degree or another, keeping it functioning and in communication.

These modes are all a part of the human body's microprogramming which is encoded in the vast and complex network of our DNA. (Scientists estimate that the DNA, if placed end-to-end and stretched out, would reach to the sun and back over 400 times. They also believe the DNA coded instructions *for just one single cell*, if it translated into English, could fill over 1,000 books the size of a 750 page encyclopedia.)

In our initial programming, the body's first and foremost function is survival!

After initial repairs have begun to ensure the body's survival, deeper level and less crucial repairs begin. The work of repair uses substantially more energy than is needed for the mere maintenance of the body. As an individual begins to feel better after an injury, trauma, illness, or surgery, many believe that they are 100% healed, and they overexert themselves while the body is still in the middle of its repair and healing modes.

Overexertion during this crucial time of repair and healing robs vital energy and resources which are critical for completion of the repairs and finalization of healing. The body will attempt to reset during this time and also attempt to increase its available energy and resources. When a lack of energy and resources exists for an extended period of time during the repair phase, the brain establishes a new neuronal pattern, producing a new status quo or way of being for the body reflecting this lack of energy and resources. What was once foreign to the body becomes familiar, then eventually habitual.

Neuronal patterns run the body. After an injury or trauma, the patterns for the body which are set up are stored as neuronal patterns in the brain. These new patterns are imprinted as acceptable patterns of functioning and reaction or response for the entire body. The power and magnitude of these neuronal patterns in shaping how the body functions, reacts or responds physically, mentally and emotionally to similar stimuli in regards to future events, either real or perceived, is truly mind boggling. How the brain works to trigger chemical addictions we have to situations, the ways we react, and to trauma and injury based on the neuronal patterning can be seen in the highly-recommended movie "What the Bleep Do We Know." Truly fascinating! Definitely - a must-see.

These *new and set* patterns alter other patterns or cycles in the body to some degree, allowing the new patterns to give support to structure and organization, just as they are designed to do.

Because these newly established neuronal patterns are so powerful; they almost instantly become accepted patterns. These patterns, however, are only patterns of *partial* completion of the actual repairs and healing that needs to take place. These patterns contain revised blueprints for body functioning which include partial energy requirements for a particular area of the body, fractional repair, as well as pain, tension, spasm, and stress, and consequently sub-par or ill health. These new patterns now become the dominant patterns for the body and are the new "status quo" for body and mind functioning, even though they allow the body to function at sub-par levels.

Eventually these new patterns form cycles which recur in the body as it attempts to automatically reset itself, just as it is designed to do. Because these newly established neuronal patterns are now the dominant ones, and are very powerful, they change the way that the body must function as a whole and to varying degrees they form an entirely new program within the body and brain. This new program changes the body's vitality and functioning, which can be completely different from what would be optimal. Some of this new programming is so minute that it may be virtually undetectable. The grip and influence the new program has on the body also firmly holds it in altered physical, mental, emotional or energetic patterns and/or cycles as well. Some of these altered patterns are a result of the body compensating for what has happened and what is happening.

It is through the implementation of these neuronal patterns, physically, mentally, emotionally and energetically, that we bring about giving some sort of meaning to and derive meaning from events in life. After time, a level of conditioning occurs because of these patterns and our way of being is molded. It's the patterns, conditioning, learning and exposure, and experiences we have in life that eventually evolve into our own "truths," points-of-view, and expectations about life and how it is for us, and how it "should be" for others as well.

These patterns are stored in very specific areas of the brain as memory (so we don't have to relearn "how to's," such as relearning to walk each and every time we go to walk, or how to reach for and turn a door handle, for example). The memories and references are, in most cases, readily accessed by the brain using lightning speed or *instant recall*.

When an event happens, or one is perceived or anticipated, our brain searches for the known outcomes of past events which appear similar or seemingly interrelated to what is occurring to us or is around us at the time of the event. The similarity of the current event to one that is stored in the brain automatically triggers a recall of "memory." The brain automatically and instantly, on its own, goes through millions of stored "files" to find one, just one, that has some similarity to what is happening now, in order to calculate and anticipate all the possible and probable outcomes pertaining to this one event – based primarily on previous neuronal imprints, patterns, or stored memory.

When the brain finds a file that *appears* to be similar to the experience that is happening now, the possible and probable outcomes are "made known" to us and we begin reacting to what we "think" will happen in this experience, even though this new event and its outcome may be entirely different, in the end. The left side of the brain does this, *doing exactly what it was designed to do*, to help keep us "safe." However, the "file" that was recalled may only include something that is similar to a very minute and insignificant part of the current event or experience, primarily due to the absence of an actual event that is *exactly* like the one that is happening now. The similarity found in the file may only include a very tiny portion of the insignificant part of the actual event. That very tiny part of the insignificant part of the actual event may only as infinitesimal as a specific color, fragrance, sound, temperature, amount of sunlight or darkness, etc., really having nothing to do with any other part of the actual and current event, although the brain thought it was somewhat the same. This causes us to actually act or react in a certain manner, based on what we "think" is going to happen. The mind games we actually play with ourselves--how absurd! We do it to ourselves! Life is a do-it-to-yourself project, if you really want to know.

All along, we play this "game" with our self, or our mind does with us, and subconsciously we think we know what is going to happen. And because we "think" that we know, and it doesn't happen *exactly* the way we "thought" it should, we get bent out of shape, upset and even enraged! Parts of our body go into pain, spasm, stress, tension, illness, etc., all because we think we know what "should" be, when in actuality, we don't know – from our mind's narrow perspective anyway. This happens to us all the time. It's part of the human experience.

When an anticipated event doesn't happen, and this is *always* a shocker to us, such as a book falling to the floor and you think it is going to strike your toe and it doesn't, your body actually responds *as though* your toe were actually struck. Physiologically, your body gets warm or hot, you begin sweating, and your heartbeat and breathing accelerates, just because "nothing" happened. You just thought it was going to, and it didn't. This happens because the brain triggered multiple responses to multiple recalls of countless files it has compiled of how it is to respond when something had fallen and actually hit you. It has already calculated what the body needs to instantly begin the repair processes and has triggered the body to send what it "thought" might be needed in anticipation of an actual blow to the body. Again, this happens because the brain is always calculating and anticipating possible and probable outcomes on every event that is happening in our lives; physical, mental, emotional, etc., all based primarily on previous neuronal imprints, patterns, or memory, based on one of its blueprint designs to "protect and/or heal" us.

This situation can often be very familar to individuals who experience recurring or cyclical pains, illnesses, physical, mental, or emotional states that do not seem to ever go away or just keep showing up from time to time "for no apparent reason," or "at certain times of the year," or "when the weather changes," etc. Firmly held neuronal patterns trigger the body to instantly begin processes or patterns that the brain thinks that the body *will* need, "just in case" a similar injury, illness, or trauma, etc. may occur similar to the one that happened when, "winter came that one year, decades ago" or "when the car accident happened and I was laid up for 3 months," or "when I slipped and fell 5 years ago when it was raining out and couldn't walk for a week," or "when I went to <u>that</u> high school with my girlfriend for a basketball game, and they sat with someone else," etc... And all kinds of physiological responses occur, just because the brain thinks something "might" happen similar to what happened before.

The brain, sending out its protective signals, naturally puts the body back into a fight or flight response mode. Back in this mode, disruption and interference occurs within an otherwise normal neurological communication from the brain to the body, dampening the body's ability to clearly communicate with its various systems, organs and glands. This triggers widespread modifications to occur by the "re-triggering" which occurred in the body due to a present stimulus which resembles (even remotely) an original event. Even though the event may just be perceived to be a reflection of a stimulus which was part of the original event *that caused the neuronal patterning to be established in the first place*, a very specific stimulus resembling just a very small portion of an original event can cause re-triggering of old cycles and patterns in the body and brain as though the injury or trauma *just happened*. I also believe that this can be due, in part, to any significance or meaning we gave to the event that occurred, (i.e. what we made the event mean to us, or for us, or for our life or the life of a loved one or friend); further deepening physical, mental and emotional neuronal patterning and responses at the same time and thus, to some degree, is a "learned response."

Millions upon millions of neuronal patterns have been established in the brain over years of living and experiencing life, also setting up our patterns of personal likes and dislikes as well. *All* of these millions of patterns, to one degree or another, are competing for the resources of the body.

> When the healing mode is triggered in the body, which definitely happens when someone receives a Bowen session, neuronal patterns of the parasympathetic nervous system designated *specifically* for healing the body are activated at a very inner core level.

Hearing a song that we have not heard for many years, for example, immediately triggers a recall of either the first time or last time you heard the song, or of a time you were listening to the song (or it was in the background) and something either good or bad occurred. In that moment, you "experience" or "relive" the event as though it just happened – in your mind. However, physiological, emotional, mental, and energetic "charges" occur, causing changes to happen in the body. Some of these quickly diminish, of course, returning the body back to where it was, while others can linger for a *long* time, depending on how the initial event was taken in by the mind *and* the body. It is as though an automatic recurring dialogue of sorts has just, *once again*, re-triggered the memory of the event causing parts of the body to be targeted *again* with reactions or responses that are similar to those that initially took place.

For some people, just seeing a needle or someone receiving a shot on television, for example, puts them into a state of shock and they nearly pass out, *and it didn't even happen to them*. At other times, something seemingly insignificant, such as a certain aroma, sound (music, voice, tone, <u>word</u> etc.), taste, action by another, touch, certain movement on our part or that of another, a certain sensation (as in feeling damp, cold, a breeze, rain on your face, etc.) or a perceived or actual insinuation, etc., can often trigger an unprovoked physical, mental, or emotional reactionary response that has become a significant part of our neuronal patterning that we aren't even aware of. Sometimes, when these deep reactionary responses happen, the individual is actually startled and asks "Now where did <u>that</u> come from?"

On the opposite side of the spectrum, look at what takes place with the healing mode of the body. When the healing mode is triggered in the body, which definitely happens when someone receives a Bowen session, neuronal patterns of the parasympathetic nervous system designated *specifically* for healing the body are activated at a very inner core level. Positive energizing and healing patterns and cycles are re-activated and brought back to life, addressing the body from the inside out. The resources and energies which were being drawn to other areas of the body by former events or "patterns" that are no longer needed begin to be quickly re-directed to where they are most needed, for relaxation and healing.

The restoration of these neuronal patterns *combined* with the freeing of energy and resources very frequently initiates a miraculous chain of events in the body and mind where immediate revitalization and restoration of the body occurs. When this happens, tension is rapidly released and pain is very commonly eliminated.

Through *these* freshly restored healing neuronal patterns, a whole new set of responses emerge which radiate excitedly throughout the entire body, saturating it with resources that have been needed for a very long time, in some cases. These restored patterns also begin to restore synchronization, synergy, balance and energy throughout the body, thus naturally producing profound calming effects on the entire body and mind *as a whole*, while accelerating the repair and healing rate of the body at the same time.

These restored healing and relaxation patterns also set up a positive chain of events in the body which directly influences the overall function of the body, re-opening and re-establishing other blueprinted neuronal patterns beneficial for the entire body. They also automatically set up or re-create healing cycles that recur over and over again, substantially assisting the long-term healing of the body over time.

Re-opening of restricted neuropathways and restoring communication between body and brain, releases once-guarded areas of the body, finalizing many repairs. The final completion of these repairs often causes the pain, discomfort, tension, spasm, stress, and many conditions and disorders or long held patterns or cycles to greatly lessen, or simply disappear. The diminishing or complete elimination of these patterns or cycles regularly produces thorough and profoundly positive physical, mental, and emotional changes simultaneously throughout the body. When this level of transformational healing happens in the body, many of the cyclical pains and illnesses disappear as well, in nearly every case. Once again, a "learned response" or shall we say a "re-learned healing response" occurs, which is actually a form of conditioned reflex within the body.

A conditioned reflex is a reflex developed through the millions of connective communication networks within the body. They utilize the direct sending and receiving connections which are open and *working*, using the path of least resistance within the physical, electrical, hydraulic, chemical, and energetic parameters of the body. The conditioned reflex can often be triggered in the body though our senses of sight, smell, touch/feel, taste, sound, *and* sense (intuition). Our senses actually are specific kinds of <u>sensors</u> that signal information from the body to the brain. These senses work together with the brain to inform it of what is happening <u>at all times</u>, even when we are sleeping.

The brain uses the stimuli (input or signals) from these senses. Both the body and brain send signals back and forth, to and from each other, multiple times a second. New signals received by the brain set up an initial series of neuronal patterns to cause the body to react or respond, often starting on a very small scale. These neuronal patterns will develop and lock in as a "normal" pattern over time by use, in other words by "training the brain."

A specific series of stimuli of certain kinds become, in essence, a specific "trigger" for the brain to activate an entire series of other specific triggers in the brain, to then activate the body to reflexively react or respond. These will eventually set up conditioned or "known" reflexive patterns or cycles, that the brain and body will automatically respond to and live by. This reflex will then *automatically occur* when a specific stimulus <u>from the senses</u> triggers it. In other words, a specific stimulus received in the brain will automatically trigger a specific stimulus to the body from the brain, causing the body to immediately and automatically take action.

Sometimes though, because of the tremendous impact of an event and/or the high magnitude of a strong stimulus from one or multiple senses simultaneously, this pattern can be imprinted in the brain in a <u>very</u> short period and in some cases immediately – as in touching something very hot. In this case, the brain will *immediately* remember *and* trigger the programmed response, causing the body to automatically and involuntarily "reflex" the next time something touched is hot, or just perceived or anticipated to be hot. During this reflex, the reactionary response can be so strong that it can actually induce high level and extreme physiological changes in the body.

There are multiple cases where people who were under hypnosis were told that they were going to be touched by something "red hot". However, they were only touched by a simple pen or pencil. The perception that they were going to be burned was so strong in the brain that physiologically the body immediately "created" an actual burn mark and/or blister on the point were the body was touched by the room-temperature pen or pencil.

How many times have you told yourself that a particular incident would produce a specific outcome and you either became totally elated or sick in anticipation of the possible outcome, and for some reason or another the outcome you perceived and anticipated <u>never</u> happened? You got all excited, or in some cases sick, over the possibility of "what if"-- over nothing.

You have conditioned yourself to be elated or sick *just in anticipation* of the possibility that some event may happen, not that it even ever will – also a learned response or conditioning.

> **Conditioning**: psychological term for any of several types of learning which leads to specific responses to particular stimuli – (and, I add, whether actual, perceived, or anticipated)

The level *and* the strength of *energy* within the mind (individually) and within the body (individually) directly affect one another. The stronger of the two *always* wins. The entire body needs a balance within these two differing energies, so one doesn't overpower the other. An imbalance either way causes a domino effect which radiates throughout the entire body, directly affecting systems and organs down to cellular levels, thereby disturbing chemical and electro-chemical balances as well. To assist the body in defending itself, it is designed with two separate, connected lines of defense.

TWO LINES OF DEFENSE

In order for the body to defend itself, it must *immediately* decide how much of a threat exists and whether it is life-threatening. When the body senses or perceives an outside threat, it produces more adrenalin, triggering the "fight or flight response or mode." In this mode, the body will *automatically* do one of two things: it will either fight, or it will cause us to run (flight.)

For internal protection from intrusion, the body automatically produces and injects higher amounts of a steroid hormone called "cortisol," which is produced by the adrenal glands. An increase of cortisol within the body sets off a huge chain of events which causes the body to launch the internal protection mechanisms.

Cortisol's important function in the body includes regulation of blood pressure, cardiovascular function, and the regulation of the body's use of fats, carbohydrates and proteins. Cortisol secretion into the body increases in direct response to *any* stress existing in the body. Whether the stress is physical (temperature extremes, illness, trauma, or surgery, etc.) or psychological pressure (finances, relationships, career or employment, etc.).

When cortisol is secreted into the body, it causes a breakdown of muscle protein, releasing amino acids into the bloodstream. These amino acids are utilized by the liver in order to properly synthesize glucose for energy and muscular use. Cortisol also releases energy that is stored in fat cells for use by the muscles. All this occurs to assist the body to more adequately deal with stress, while ensuring that the brain receives energy sources that are adequate for its needs. Almost immediately, either during or right after a stressful event, cortisol levels elevate in the body. When the adrenals are chronically over-exerted, the naturally-occurring chemical signatures which help the body to produce and release cortisol are greatly reduced and the body automatically goes to other parts of the body (such as ovaries and testes) to release the chemical signatures so cortisol production can continue, even though this may cause over-taxinging of the body's resources.

EXTERNAL PROTECTION

Using the fight or flight response, the body does what is necessary to protect itself from outside physical, mental or emotional attack. The body will automatically launch into this mode *even if it is only perceiving* something or someone is attacking.

The attack or perceived attack spikes the production and release of adrenalin as the body is put in a state of high alert. These spikes immediately cause the body to take drastic, even very radical, life-saving action. The heart pumps harder and faster causing increased blood flow, breathing becomes more rapid and deep, the pupils dilate, body heat increases causing increased sweating, the brain functions at a much quicker rate, reaction times significantly decrease, and the ability to intensely focus and higher levels of awareness appear.

If chased or attacked by a wild animal, for example, the body will fight for its life and inject every bit of cortisol it can produce into the adrenals to keep the body fully on guard, giving us inhuman strength, ability and endurance. In these cases the body sucks the body almost dry of cortisol!

Cortisol is an important hormone which is needed and used by *every single cell in the body*, and is essential for the optimal health of cells. Cortisol also is an anti-inflammatory, a stress hormone, helps regulate blood pressure, promotes vascular tone, insulin release for blood sugar metabolism, and also supports the immune function as well. Cortisol helps the body to release sugar into the bloodstream that can be readily used for immediate energy for use when the body is in the fight or flight mode.

Small releases of cortisol have some positive effects, such as raising awareness levels, increasing immunity, and increasing pain tolerance, while also assisting the body to maintain homeostasis. Higher and prolonged levels of cortisol have negative effects, such as suppressed thyroid function, blood sugar imbalances (hyper or hypoglycemia,) impaired cognitive performance, decreased bone density, decrease in muscle tissue, higher blood pressure, and lowered immunity. Chronic unrelenting stress can have a very dangerous effect on the body, making you much more susceptible to colds, flu, fatigue or exhaustion, illness, and infection.

Normally, short periods of the body being in a state of high alert or defense occur infrequently and can easily be supported by the body. People who constantly surround themselves by highly stressful situations, however, actually cause the body to hold itself in a state of high alert or defense. Constantly doing so, by not reducing or eliminating the stressors altogether, creates a new neuronal pattern as the brain begins to accept the existence of these high alert and high stress levels as a normal state that is now necessary to keep the body stabilized and functioning properly.

This new "normal" state, which includes excessive amounts of cortisol in the body, begins to produce disproportionate tension and wear-and-tear on the body, leading to a dis-eased (ill-at-ease) state of improper body system and organ functioning. Over a period of time this state leads to the adrenal depletion and therefore a great reduction of cortisol production, and cortisol reserves quickly diminish. Adrenal exhaustion commonly creates a number of very common conditions, disorders and syndromes, beginning, of course, with exhaustion and chronic fatigue.

When a person is experiencing adrenal exhaustion, the usual "pick-me-up" is some form of artificial stimulant such as coffee, espresso, chocolate, sugar, easy-to-get over-the-counter medications which contain a heavy dose of caffeine, or any number of stimulants. These artificial stimulants produce a false signal to the brain that there is plenty of reserve cortisol, although the reserves are gone. This exhausts the adrenal glands of nearly all cortisol production. Constant consumption of stimulants also eventually leads to the depletion of resources in the body, which can lead to reduced and improper functioning of life-sustaining systems and organs, leading to their eventual failure. In these cases, the adrenal glands become exhausted or worn-out, seriously needing a break.

Most people are generally unaware what state their body is actually in or how it got there, and how this state directly affects the entire health and vitality of the body. Chronic stress seems to be a *very* common denominator in illness and dis-ease related health issues.

In order to keep cortisol levels healthy and under control, the activation of the body's relaxation response is critical, especially after the fight or flight mode was triggered in the body. Finding ways which work for you to help manage your level of stress is one way to lend a hand to your body; however, utilizing ways which actually help your body to *eliminate* or quickly and naturally rid your body of stress is much better.

INTERNAL PROTECTION

Internally, the immune system generally remains balanced and occasionally has to protect the body from internal attacks. The immune system uses whatever resources it has at its disposal, in order to quickly and effectively counter-attack any unnatural source which was introduced into the body that could potentially be harmful. When unnatural sources are brought into the body by swallowing, inhaling, injection or injury, the internal protection system in the body immediately attacks the source in an attempt to overcome and then purge it from the body.

Occasionally the body will naturally flush or detoxify itself to cleanse and purify it from accumulated unwanted wastes. The common cold, flu, low-grade fevers, and occasional loose stools or even diarrhea are some of the ways the body makes this happen.

Usually, this natural detoxifying process occurs twice a year for many of us, and once in the spring, and once in the fall is the usual course for most people. This indicates that the body is naturally purging built-up toxins. This purging occurs especially in those who eat excessive amounts of foods and beverages which contain preservatives and excessive sugars, which builds up potent toxins in the body. Those who eat very healthy diets and exercise regularly, very rarely, if ever, contract a cold or flu. This is due primarily to the fact that their body is very strong and their systems are very resilient; therefore, their body continually rids itself of toxins, so build-up is less likely.

The immune system, though strong in most people, only has the ability to resist attack on a constant scale for a limited time. Overloading the immune system long-term often causes it to become sluggish and weakened. In this condition, the body becomes easily tired and fatigued and its resistance-fighting ability decreases considerably. This leads to increased stress on other organs and systems as they take up the slack in order to protect the body as a whole, which eventually lead to more severe states of fatigue and exhaustion if something isn't done to reverse it.

Initially, a sluggish, weakened or impaired immune system often shows up as a person being tired all the time or suffering from insomnia, for example. More serious immune system impairments begin to show up in more chronic forms and conditions, commonly progressing categorically into more serious disorders such as chronic fatigue, Epstein-Barr, Fibromyalgia, and then into Multiple Sclerosis for example.

The body *always* gives signs of what is happening deep inside. The body will alert you in an attempt to get you to rest, exercise, *and* take care of yourself for your own survival. The solution for many ailments is simple: break detrimental, injurious or dangerous patterns, receive proper nutrition and hydration, adequate and proper exercise, *rest and relaxation*, while also giving the body the correct information it needs to heal.

One of the keys to restoring and maintaining optimal health is to become aware of the signs the body is displaying and what it is telling you.

SIGNS and SYMPTOMS: Part of the early warning system

The body doesn't suddenly give out just because we turn a certain age. The body does, however, often give numerous small signs that something is not quite right along the way, long before problems arise. We call these signs symptoms. Ignoring or masking the symptoms generally leads to other, more serious problems. If it is not balanced, the body over time will decipher the imbalance as normal state (a new neuronal pattern), and will then attempt to keep the body in this abnormal state of ill health.

As already mentioned, when imbalanced, the body begins the process of slowing or shutting down a system or organ. It is at this point that the systems and organs in the body no longer work together in a normal synchronistic manner. Each individual system or organ begins to slowly "do its own thing" to keep the body alive, though not necessarily well.

Each organ eventually struggles to play its part in the body's survival. This struggling radically increases the demands on the already depleted supply of energy and resources of the body, thereby increasing the depth of ill health. If something isn't done to put a stop to and begin the reversal of the worsening condition, the individual becomes quite sick, and irreparable damage can result.

> Each symptom or dis-ease has an initial physical, mental, or emotional cause.

Each symptom or dis-ease has an initial physical, mental, or emotional cause. Research shows that nearly 90% of all disease has an emotional factor. When combined with physical or mental factors, health problems worsen at a highly accelerated rate.

The body has unique warning systems. All too often, people have not received adequate training to understand what is taking place in their bodies. In all too many cases, shown in various documentaries, physicians often do not have or take the time to properly educate the patient. Most physicians will admit that they have been taught to treat symptoms and not the core issue, primarily beginning a course of treatment using some form of medication. Medication can be very useful at times; however, using at as the only course for treatment may not be wise.

Symptoms are acute outward signs of what is taking place *within* the body. They are the alarm system of the body which indicates that the physical, mental, and emotional demands placed upon the body have exceeded safe levels. They are *supposed* to annoy you to get your attention.

When symptoms occur, you can ignore the signs and just "learn to just live with it." Because most individuals do not understand their body or the signs it gives that something is not right, they make the choice to just let it be. Unfortunately, ignoring the signs does not lessen or eliminate the consequences associated with them. This choice is definitely not a healthy one, nor is it the best one. Unwise choices pertaining to your health and well-being will most likely lead to more severe problems further down the road.

A second choice would be to "make the symptoms go away," at least for now. This temporary choice of suppressing the symptoms includes using pain-reducing medication, anti-inflammatory medication, muscle relaxants, heartburn and digestive liquids or tablets, and similar over-the-counter medications, or steroids in its many forms. This choice has a tendency to deeply suppress, mask or even temporarily eliminate the natural warning signs given by the body, as well as push the things the body wants to rid itself of, back in again.

This would be similar to placing a piece of dark colored tape over the *check engine* light on the dashboard of your car, or unplugging the warning light altogether. Ignoring or unplugging the warning light removes the annoyance, but the possibility of extensive or serious engine damage still exists. The problem is <u>not</u> the warning light. The problem is far beyond normal maintenance and needs to be found and repaired quickly.

Understand that a *symptom* is a *warning light*. The symptom is not the problem, *nor has it ever been*; therefore, the real problem must be addressed, not the symptom. The longer you ignore a symptom, the more serious the problem can become.

When treating symptoms, I believe that Andrew Weil, Harvard Medical School graduate and world-renowned alternative medical physician said it best: "Treating the symptom is not only futile in most cases, it may do greater harm than good in the end." A symptom signals that something is out of balance and if it gets worse, it may be difficult to discover what the core problem was to begin with.

Treating symptoms and not the cause can be compared to trying to find a lost person at sea. The search, though relentless and intense, often does not produce the desired results because there are too many variables and too vast a territory that has to be searched.

A third choice is to listen to the body and its needs, because the body has its own unique tell-tale system. It is important to consult a qualified healthcare professional who really understands what is happening on much deeper levels and knows what needs to be done.

For most people though, a completely new choice would be just reducing the amount of stress on the body and mind. This alone commonly helps immensely in quickly restoring health to higher levels. In addition, avoiding unhealthy foods, places, events, situations, and in some cases, people, which trigger symptoms or illnesses, can easily be the beginning of a cure in and of itself. For others, losing weight, exercising, refraining from smoking, drinking, or using drugs often leads to greater health.

> Given the correct information, the body can *greatly* reduce the time it normally takes to heal itself, and sometimes with instantaneous results.

The best choice, however, is to revive and restore the body's own healing system, to help the body do its natural work of healing and restoration of optimal health just as it was designed to do. Treatment that peels away the layers which hide the core issue, and addresses the cause, usually proves to be the best solution.

Using known medical models as a gauge, physicians know that it will "normally" take a minimum of one month of proper treatment for every year the patient has had the problem, in order to remedy the problem. For example, if someone has had a disorder for five years, it will normally take a minimum of five months of proper treatment, including proper nutrition, rest and exercise, to bring the individual back to good health.

However, given the correct information, the body can *greatly* reduce the time it normally takes to heal itself, and sometimes with instantaneous results.

THE INTERCONNECTED BODY

Because of the complexities and intricacies of the human body, it can be affected in a seemingly infinite number of ways. Every part or portion of the body is interconnected either directly or indirectly. This means that a change in health in one area of the body directly affects or impacts *all* other areas to some degree.

Systems and organs can be thrown off balance by changes in physical, mental, or emotional states which cause chemical alterations or imbalances. These chemical alterations or imbalances directly influence the mechanical and electrical aspects of the body as well, causing some area of the body to destabilize in some way.

Each part or portion of the body is either directly or indirectly connected by:

» Structural contact – as in the skeletal structure of the body

» Circuitous connection – through the central and autonomic nervous systems

» Hydraulic connection – through fluids moving throughout the body via the circulatory, digestive, or lymphatic systems

» Mechanical connection – through muscular and connective tissue attachments

» Physical connection – through the fascia tissue that surrounds every muscle, organ and nerve in the body

» Electrical connection – through electrical impulse or stimulation through the central, autonomic nervous, and circulatory systems or piezoelectric generation

» Mental connection – through thinking, reasoning, and analyzing

» Emotional connection – through feeling and sensing

» Chemical connection – through ever changing chemical processes that constantly occur throughout the body

» Fluid connection – through the gigantic assortment of fluids that exist in the body

» Sensory connection –
    Auditory – through sound
    Visual – through sight
    Tactile – through feel and touch
    Taste –through contact with the tongue
    Olfactory – through smell

» Experiential connection – remembrance of past experiences and the body and mind's reaction or response to them

» Energetic connection – Chi, Ki, Prana, or Life Force energy

Each one of these connections requires a closed loop to generate and provide instantaneous stimuli through the autonomic and central nervous systems, to the brain, and back to the body. The brain constantly receives information and gives *instant* feedback. These responses can either be voluntary or involuntary or some combination of both.

If the imbalance is not properly attended to, the cycle of imbalance becomes magnified as other factors come into play. Take the example of a very minor injury - stubbing your toe. Visualize it. To begin with, your foot rapidly recoils in the opposite direction of the blow. The opposite leg takes on all the weight of the body. The rest of the body compensates attempting to keep you from falling. When any structure receives damage, the body will torque around the source of pain. In the case of physical trauma, the muscles contract or spasm to protect the body as it automatically alters its alignment in an attempt to attempt to keep the head erect and the eyes level and horizontal to the ground.

In this case of stubbing your toe, a signal travels from the toe to the brain and back again - all the while the brain sends signals to release endorphins to dampen or kill the pain. Your breathing increases, you may let out a yell, and you hop around on one foot. Your heart pounds wildly to get the endorphins to the foot. At the same time, the brain rapidly assesses and re-assesses the situation repeatedly. *It's all connected*!

This may be an extreme example, but things that happen in or to the body which require a rapid response occur throughout each and every day. Remember the time the driver next to you cut you off, missed hitting your car by inches and nearly caused an accident? One mere miss, right? Your car wasn't even hit. Well, how many hours did it take your body and mind to calm down from just one little incident?

Once the body is put into the fight or flight mode, it takes significantly longer for the body to recover. Sometimes it may take days or weeks, and in rare instances, many years to recover from a close call of a very traumatic incident, such as being in a bank when it is being robbed at gunpoint.

Incidents that cause the body to go into the fight or flight mode happen, it is a part of life. We call this re-occurring cycle and the effects it has on the body *stress*, and too much stress can cause momentarily loss of our normal behavior. Regular maintenance on the body and mind to rid ourselves of unnecessary stress that we are holding onto is essential.

The body and mind together, just like an automobile, constitute a finely tuned mechanism needing regular maintenance to keep it running at optimal performance.

Excessive stress and outflow of resources take their toll on the body. Those who expose themselves to higher levels of stress must receive maintenance more often than normal in order to simply maintain good health. Receiving less maintenance than what the body requires eventually produces greater wear and tear on the body and may cause conditions which exceed regular maintenance capabilities of the body, causing repairs to become necessary. As far as the body is concerned, repairs are a much higher priority than maintenance and require more attention.

Physio-structural repairs become necessary when the body is physically injured, weakened, or damaged, i.e. when a bone is broken. The more serious the emergency, the more immediate attention, reserves, and energy it will receive. The healing of a bone fracture, for example, begins within $1/10^{th}$ of a second after the fracture occurs. The body doesn't wait until you are brought to an emergency room to start the repair processes.

Any emergency response, once it is triggered in the body, will often have long-term repercussions if they are not taken care of. These repercussions can continue in the body to one degree or another throughout a person's lifetime and be very influential throughout their entire life. This is because it becomes a part of the cellular memory unless the body and brain receives a very rare and specific kind of signal which will cause the body to generate or create a counteractive/corrective course that causes the body and mind to restore itself.

As far as injury and trauma are concerned, both are multi-dimensional. There are physical, mental, and emotional aspects that are directly linked to every injury or trauma we have ever suffered. One aspect of an injury rarely, if ever, happens without impacting the others. "Disappearing" the entire collection of all aspects which are detrimental to one's health, I sincerely believe, is possible. I have seen it happen.

Alternative healthcare choices offer a good source of outside help, to enable the body to recover to some degree, especially when the condition is minor or moderate. Alternative healthcare, in many cases, takes a gentler approach to healing the body and can often assist the body back to some degree of good health.

In severe and immediate life-threatening situations, invasive measures may be necessary to "put the body back together again." The help of a qualified doctor and/or medical or hospital staff is <u>vital</u> since the body can't do this on its own. In these instances, modern medical experts play a vital role in resetting the stage to allow the body to do its own healing.

SYSTEM AND BODY REGULATION

When one or more of the systems or organs become overburdened, the others join in to compensate in an attempt to keep the body functioning and in good health. This works for a while, to give the overworked system time to regain its optimal functional capacity.

Overburdening can originally be caused by an accumulation of bumps, bruises, sprains, strain, minimal stress, and small traumas. Severe overburdening is often caused by continual and prolonged stress, improper nutrition or physical, mental, or emotional trauma, surgery, or and accident and can take a larger and more lasting toll on the body.

> **System and organ balance go hand-in-hand. Each system, each organ plays a vital role in balancing and regulating the other.**

71

If the systems and organs cannot return the body to a state of balance, they eventually lead to each struggling for survival as individual units. The brain takes on the tremendous task of attempting to keep everything functioning in a proper and efficient manner. The brain causes massive rerouting of resources to the systems or organs which can most effectively assist to keep it in its present state of health. This rerouting helps to temporarily stabilize the declining health of the body. .

Once this cycle has begun, it becomes crucial that the body return to a normal state *as soon as possible* through adequate and proper care. Good and balanced nutrition, rest, exercise, and most types of physiotherapy alone do not fully reset the body to heal at core levels. They may *temporarily* help to re-stabilize the body back to a specific level of health, but since both the body *and* brain have not been reset, the body will not *fully* recover. Core issues must be addressed to assure permanent recovery.

Contrary to common belief, *it is, and has always been* the responsibility of the individual to listen to his or her own body, and for that individual to find ways lessen the causes of overload on the systems and organs of the body. I'm sure you have heard, "People are what they eat, drink, and do." If you choose not to eat properly, or drink too much alcohol, or choose to remain in a state of stress or exhaustion for extended periods of time, you significantly diminish your chances of staying in good health.

> *...it is, and has always been, the responsibility of the individual to listen to their own body **and** for them to find ways to lessen the causes of overload on the systems and organs of the body.*

PAIN AND PAIN CYCLES

Neck and back strains and pains are commonplace in humans, worldwide. The frequency of such injuries is something that is new in this modern age, due to modern technology such as computers and automobiles. In classic cases of back and neck strain or injuries, muscle spasm and inflammation naturally occur. Together, spasms and inflammation protect the strained or injured areas. In other words, the body is doing its job.

Often the injured person takes pain medication and just keeps working. This deprives the body of proper rest and healing time. The medication triggers the body's tolerance to pain. The person continues on as though nothing has happened, resulting in a pain/spasm cycle.

> Muscles go into spasm to help protect the area that has been injured and to tell the person that healing the area is a must.

When someone's back or neck "goes out" they are generally laid up for a time. A healthcare professional may mask the pain again with medication or manipulation. This merely interrupts the pain/spasm cycle temporarily, but the pain and spasms *will* return if not properly addressed and erased.

Without sufficient time to rest and recuperate the back or neck muscles remain in spasm, protecting this area. The pain tolerance in the body is just increased through more medication. One day out of the blue the pain returns, with a vengeance in many cases, and is so excruciating that the individual is not even able to walk, sit, or move.

In more extreme incidences, pain can block the ability to breathe. Doctors generally diagnose these instances as ruptured or herniated discs in the neck or back and their interpretation is that it requires surgery.

In most cases when some of the muscles of the neck and back become spasmodic, other muscles surrounding the area also go into spasm attempting to realign the body.

Continual spasm of muscles leads to other muscles getting involved to balance out the area, which usually or eventually leads to the compression of spinal discs. The compression causes more muscles to spasm, in order to protect the area and in many cases, either herniation or rupture of these discs do occur. This compression or herniation of the disc(s) cannot be effectively reduced or eliminated by muscle relaxing medication or manual vertebral manipulation alone. Temporarily relaxing a muscle through medication *will also not* resolve this deep pain/spasm cycle which is happening on much deeper levels in the body.

Just manually adjusting vertebrae temporarily relieves the pressure and lessens the seriousness of the pain, interrupting the pain/spasm cycle; however, it doesn't necessarily eliminate the cycle. To alleviate the pain, it is necessary to get the proper help to assist the body to erase the pain/spasm cycle.

Besides getting the proper help, rest and relaxation will greatly help in moderate to serious cases. Resting means: learning the lost art of doing *nothing* for a while in order to give the body the time it needs to recuperate. Sometimes the only rest people get is in the hospital during a serious illness or injury. Even there they don't get the proper rest because people visit, nurses wake them up to administer medication, injections and takes vital signs, and hospital personnel keep coming in and out of the room.

Although it is commonly only a temporary condition, nerve pain can cause major discomfort, pain or even disability if it is severe enough. Severe nerve pain commonly radiates throughout the entire body causing to body to stop--instantly! The body that is experiencing severe nerve pain often doesn't heed other signals which need attention, too.

To understand what happens in the body regarding nerve pain, visualize this: picture what happens when you crimp a running water hose. The hose swells as the pressure increases. Minute amounts of water forcefully squirt through any opening that exists, causing extreme turbulence as it shoots past the blockage.

> ...stress is an unnatural state of the mind and body that is contracted from outside sources. Anxiety, an advanced state of stress, decreases the ability to focus.

To a large degree, this is what happens in the case of nerve pain or energy blocks in the body. Frequently, these immediately provoke muscular spasms and inflammation to protect the affected area. High levels of stress and tension alone can cause this to happen too. Left to itself, the inhibited region causes more tension and even more spasm and inflammation as the body protects itself. If nothing is done to release and get rid of the cycle, it just gets worse.

Chronic pain often occurs when the nerves have been struck, crushed, damaged or severed, causing inflammation to occur. Common causes for chronic pain are usually physical ones: trauma, burns, lacerations, surgery, high concentrations of metals, nerve damaging or destroying chemicals, excessive alcohol consumption, and in some cases certain medications.

This kind of nerve pain regularly resists conventional heavy duty painkillers, and anti-inflammatory medications. Research reveals that chronic pain and suffering can actually cause a rewiring of the brain. In this rewired state, the body and brain's sensitivities to heat, cold, light, touch, smell, taste, and sound now become so heightened that some of the input may be intolerable. Medication given at this stage becomes almost useless.

STRESS

The American Institute of Stress has announced that workplace stress costs $300 billion per year in healthcare costs alone, not including lost productivity.

Stress is an unnatural state of the mind and body caused by outside sources. Contemporary lives are so full of pressure that constant worry, anxiety, nervous tension, apprehension, and stress become a lifestyle. People, especially in the United States, do not know how to relax. They take a vacation to relax but come back exhausted. The focus of most vacations is not on relaxing but on "doing as many things as possible, while we have time off."

Others use their vacation to "catch up on a few things" and exhaust themselves in the attempt. In both cases, the body and mind are never given a chance to rest. All bodies need rest. Many people sleep, *but they do not rest*. Their minds run incessantly while they sleep and their bodies remain in the "fight or flight" mode.

When they are drained physically and mentally, many people turn to coffee, chocolate, caffeine and similar substances to give them the boost they need to "keep up the pace."

These substances trick the body into producing more cortisol, thereby increasing energy for a short period before the body fatigues again. When the body slows down, they take more of the same substances overriding the body's danger signals.

Overriding these signals weakens the body, making it unable to function effectively. At the same time the body attempts to rebalance itself. In turn, this causes more weakening of the body because of the lack of energy. The cycle continues over and over again without ever regaining full strength.

When the systems and organs are affected this way, poor health quickly follows. When unbalanced or overworked, the body gives us very distinct signs alerting us that something is not right.

> *Stress, anxiety, and tension are the greatest indicators that the body <u>is</u> out of balance.*

Stress, anxiety and tension are the greatest indicators that the body is out of balance. Other indicators may include unexpected and uncontrolled bouts of panic, anxiety, depression, fear, anger, rage, a state of unwillingness to make necessary changes in your life, job or relationship, physical and mental fatigue, severe muscle spasms, decreased sense of self-worth or self-esteem, for example. In other words, the body thrusts a person into an out-of-control physical, mental, or emotional roller-coaster ride in order to get some attention.

Panic attacks unmistakably transmit strong signs that the body needs rebalancing. The American Medical Association (AMA) states, "Stress leads to an 85% increase in heart problems" and "Stress reduces the body's ability to heal."

The National Institute for Mental Health (NIMH) states, "Stress leads to anxiety, depression, and suicide." Removing stress and tension alone reduces many systemic imbalances, muscular, structural discrepancies and chemical imbalances, while also rejuvenating and renewing the body's energetic fields.

ILLNESS AND DISEASE

Poor health is often due in part to an imbalance in structural, chemical, mental, or energetic levels. All four pieces are closely interrelated and interactive; therefore an imbalance or substandard health condition in one area will affect and produce a substantial unbalancing effect on the others.

An imbalance in one area causes the entire body to overexert to try to bring itself back into a state of perfect balance.

General illness can often be overcome with little or no outside medical intervention if the body is properly assisted to return to a state of balance. Moderate illness may require medical intervention depending upon the illness, but often the body and mind can be rebalanced with proper assistance. Invasive measures may not be necessary with many illnesses. So the question arises, "Why take invasive measures if invasive measures aren't necessary?"

Many hundreds of thousands of people throughout the past century have experienced a reversal in the state of their health by simply making much needed changes which include, rest, proper nutrition, some moderate exercise and proper intervention if and when necessary. Many people today do not feel they have the time or resources necessary to properly rest and relax, as their body really needs.

A severe illness or an emergency may necessitate invasive and/or aggressive action. Even Chinese herbalists and medical doctors concede that when the body has been pressed past the point of diminished resources, Western medical intervention combined with other approaches may be the only answer.

Physical signs and symptoms such as paleness, acute and chronic fatigue and pain, irritability, lack of mental clarity, headaches, insomnia, fibromyalgia, and digestive disorders are just a mere tip of the iceberg as to what is truly happening inside the body.

Illness normally does not appear overnight. The health of the body slowly and gradually declines as our bodies go through a variety of steps that lead to dysfunction, because many people choose to ignore the body's signs and signals.

When signs and signals occur, it is best to receive effective help as soon as possible. Alternative healthcare is a good source of outside help, especially when the signs or conditions are minor or moderate. Alternative healthcare, in many cases, takes a gentler approach to healing the body and can often assist the body back to some degree of good health. There is no reason to take invasive measures unless invasive measures are necessary.

In severe or immediate life-threatening situations, invasive measures may be necessary to "put the body back together again" or to remove or repair serious conditions from the body. In cases such as these, the help of a doctor and/or highly trained medical staff is _vital_ since the body can't do this on its own. In these instances, modern medical experts play a vital role in resetting the stage to allow the body to do its own healing.

STIMULATING THE PHYSICAL LEVEL OF HEALING

Manual manipulation and other physio- or therapeutic techniques are designed to enhance body functioning by working from the outside inward to help improve the mechanical and overall functioning of the body. Many of these work to some degree, having limited roles or scopes of practice. Many do not provide the essential elements that the body needs to fully revive the healing mechanisms in the body.

In the course of returning the body back to optimal functioning from acute or even long-term or severe conditions or dis-eases, various healing changes and healing stages are common.

HEALING CHANGES

The most common and easily recognizable changes which take place as the body begins to heal are the repair and healing of external wounds, the increase in fluidity of motion or flexibility, and the increase of range of motion or ease in which a person moves. Other common healing changes are the reduction or elimination of inflammation, pain and suffering, as well as the acceleration of healing or reduction in the time it normally takes to heal a certain injury or condition. As a person begins to heal and feel good again, other significant, positive, and welcomed changes are both noticeable and common, such as: a calmer character, increased ability to focus, and balanced behavioral patterns, to name a few.

HEALING STAGES

As has been discussed previously, the body is not just a physical unit. It is connected physically, mechanically, electrically, chemically, mentally, emotionally, energetically, and spiritually on many different levels

Every neurological function in the body also affects a person's physiology, physical, chemical, mechanical, mental, emotional, energetic, or spiritual aspects to some degree or another. Imbalances caused by too much or too little of something are all too common in many healthcare approaches used today.

Part of the problem is that we live in a "microwave and internet world" where we are used to everything being done in an instant; therefore, we expect the body to respond and heal in the same way. In most instances, it may take some time.

The body commonly needs to go through various healing stages as it supports itself to return to health, depending on the severity of the injury or trauma. The releasing or purging of old patterns or cycles in the body may show up in ways that are quite different than those which may be expected. As the body begins to release long-held patterns of stress, spasm, tension, emotion, mental distress or disharmony, it may need to unwind or untorque (unloosen) itself.

In cases where chemical or alcohol addiction or toxicity is prevalent, the body must purge itself as well. If, and when, the body is ready and these changes begin, the body often displays crystal-clear signs that a healing cycle was induced.

When a healing cycle is induced, the body will do whatever is necessary to make the changes that are required. These changes may possibly consist of temporary short periods of being uncomfortable, intensification of pain, surges of emotion, certain physical signs that changes or releases are happening, or the individual simply closing down. These observations are often just the tip of the iceberg, and may not portray the entire picture.

Yet the individual may not know where to go or who to turn to for proper assistance for each level or stage. Each stage takes time to allow the body and mind to go through the required courses which affect some degree of healing. These various stages have no time limit. Many Western and alternative approaches often assist the body or mind to move through some stages of healing, but often fall short because they do not address the body/mind as a whole. Colds, flu, fever, or diarrhea often take a toll on your entire body and mind. Remember how miserable some of these illnesses made you feel? They were temporary, however and minor compared to the effect severe physical, mental, or emotional traumas have on the body.

Severe traumas have a resounding reflection in every area of your life. I have found that often the conscious mind does not want to remember the trauma and the immense pain it caused, but the sub-conscious mind and the body remember as though they just happened. Physical, emotional, and mental traumas often cause abnormal heightened tension and spasms in the muscles and organs. These spasms almost immediately affect the Central Nervous System (CNS), and Autonomic Nervous System (ANS), which in turn affect the functioning of every system and organ in the body.

The systems are commonly affected before the organs begin giving signs that something is "out of whack." These signs, if unheeded, often express themselves in areas removed from the actual problem. It takes a highly qualified practitioner to truly understand what is wrong. Experienced healthcare practitioners often understand that the body can express or indicate what is taking place before they treat the patient. This assists the practitioner to more effectively pinpoint the cause.

The physical, mental, and emotional affects of traumas or injury can often be cleared. Occasionally, the body may need to go through what is called a *healing crisis*. A healing crisis can occur at the time of intense emotional release. It can also happen during times of illness when the body tries to get rid of life depleting toxins. You can also induce a healing crisis by deep relaxation and reflection on the true nature of the trauma.

If you have experienced a cold, flu, fever, or diarrhea, then you *have* experienced a healing crisis. The body's responses to these are a positive sign that the body is battling the problem by detoxifying and cleansing itself. The detoxification process is actually a natural one which often occurs twice a year. What two times? Let's say that the bi-annual cold and flu season may just have something to do with it. The common cold is just the body's natural way of detoxifying the body. This is the body's way of "cleaning house," while getting you to slow down and stop so the body can detoxify itself and rest for a short time. A fever, on the other hand, is the body's way of burning away and consuming harmful bacteria.

The body also detoxifies to rid itself of the harmful effects caused by unnatural preservatives, flavor enhancers, fillers, sugars, sugar substitutes, hormones used to enhance the growth of animals.

Food poisoning, for example, causes the body to literally eject the poisons through projectile vomiting and explosive diarrhea. There is nothing the sufferer can really do about it. You can use medications to suppress the symptoms, but the fact is that the body wants the poisons out, and *it wants them out now!* **The body wants to eliminate anything that is not for its own good.**

Toxins in the body or a toxic body can be the result of more than just physical interaction or reaction with products that are ingested or consumed. Toxins can also be a result of accumulated emotions and mental stress which causes chemical changes in the body that, in the long run, can be very detrimental to one's health.

On the other hand, healing is a natural, unconditioned reflexive response that is instinctively interwoven in the inner workings in the body. In other words, the body is pre-programmed to naturally heal when the program is triggered or turned on.

For most people, and I add, particularly those who are stressed or tense most of the time, triggering the healing response may take a few times, and in some cases, a bit longer. This is primarily due to the unfamiliarity of the body to being in a relaxation state, and the body must *first* be brought to full relaxation in order to initiate the healing response or mode. The relaxation response is just simply the body's way of getting itself and the brain to "let go for a while".

Just as something being learned by the body and brain may take several times and the *minimal* course of 21 consecutive days for the body and brain to "get it", a true course of treatment that incites the body to heal will naturally take a minimum-course of a 21-day-period to take full effect. This DOES NOT mean 21 consecutive days of treatment, nor does it mean receiving just any kind of treatment either. It does take the right approach that works WITH the body and brain the way they are DESIGNED to work.

This consecutive 21-day-pattern often holds true for getting the body to get to and then *remain in its* natural healing state, in other words, to hold the healing patterns once they are instilled in the brain and body. In most cases, where pain or spasm cycles have been there for some time, the body will just naturally take a minimum of 21 consecutive days to just begin to erase the old patterning in the brain and the body. Could it happen sooner than 21 days,? Absolutely! I've seen it happen thousands of times. When the body is set up to allow itself to heal it may do so at any time IT is ready to.

However in most cases, the way the body is designed to work, it is necessary to give it time to be with the correct information, to begin to allow it to peel off the layers in its own due course. This way the body will heal what it knows is most important first. It will peel the layers back strategically and begin to heal on much deeper emotional and mental levels as well.

When the body is properly stimulated to heal, it will generally continue to heal for 3-5 days afterwards, *as though it received a treatment everyday.* This will depend, of course, on the individual, their healing cycle, and the seriousness or extent of that which needs to be healed. In this way, the body uses less energy as a whole to heal, and the body happily begins to cooperate and work together as a whole, just as it was designed to do, returning the body back to normal, vibrant health a little at a time.

Usually around the sixth day, the body will peak and will begin to return to old patterns. This is just a tendency the body and brain have to return to what they are familiar with. It is imperative when the body starts to "go backwards," so to speak, that re-stimulation or re-activation of the healing system occurs. This is necessary for four reasons: (1)to refresh *and* deepen the healing neuronal patterns in the brain (2) to cause the body to begin healing on deeper levels while (3) at the same time naturally bringing your body back to optimal health, and (4) to cause the brain to eliminate the old pain, spasm, or illness cycles so as to make them disappear. Because the brain created them to protect the body, it can also make them vanish to help heal the body as well.

By understanding this one key point on how the body is designed to work, you can readily know if a certain course of treatment is actually working for you or not. Not all treatments work for everyone or in every case. Finding one that works for you *and* your body is such a huge factor in both restoring *and* maintaining your optimal health.

Proper healing signals given to the body are clear, direct, and in many cases, strong messages which are sent to the brain often which set off latent, primal, "blueprinted" healing configurations and cycles already existing in the body. Proper healing signals profoundly affect both the brain and body simultaneously. They are primarily governed by the potency or concentration of the signal given *and* its effectiveness in triggering and turning on healing responses for a particular physical area of the body, while simultaneously effectively triggering and turning on healing responses for other physical, emotional, and mental levels as well. This can effectively erase pain, spasm, and illness in nearly every case.

These proper healing signals are not governed by the physical strength, forcefulness, or know-how of the person doing "something," or just any application of "any 'ol kind of therapy" or approach that attempts to force an outcome, or some machine that is supposed to do such and such.

True, the application of different kinds of therapies, approaches or mechanical, electrical, or other stimuli can offer some assistance and have some affect; however, the spectrum of the range of their effectiveness is usually found over time to be *extremely* narrow. In most cases, this will just lead the body to merely temporary interruption of pain or spasm cycles, and not the erasure of them. In most cases, the pain or spasm will subside for a time--whether a day, a week, a month or a year--then it will return to some degree or another.

When the brain and body *are* given the proper healing signals, the body can be restored back to optimal health in a relatively short period of time, usually within five weeks, in nearly every case. During any healing process, the body only partially will heal at any given time, due to its limited resources.

The level *and* the strength of the energy both within the mind and within the body directly affect one another, and are considerations which need to be taken into account when a healer "tries" to calculate how long it may take for a person to return to optimal health. I say "try" because there is no way to calculate how long it will take for a person to be restored to optimal health. There are parameters which can be considered "normal." However, I have seen severe cases restored in two weeks with proper care, and I have seen what *appeared* to be simpler, much less complex cases, take 6-8 weeks to resolve, perhaps because.

Healing as a whole is not something which can be controlled or forced from outside sources no matter how much knowledge or experience the healthcare practitioner has, as they can only assist in setting the stage for any healing to take place. Herbs and medication have their place in returning the body to normal parameters.

Forcing the body to heal quicker than it is able; using *any* approach, often causes the body to spend energy defending itself first. This energy could be better used in other areas for repair and healing. The body is so intricate. It already knows what it needs to heal itself. It always takes into consideration its present level of health, overall condition, strength and ability, and available energy resources. If it is able, the body will always heal when given the correct information.

For full multi-dimensional healing to take place, the body needs to be treated gently, as a whole, and in layers in many cases; simultaneously addressing all systems, organs, levels and areas, in order to give the body exactly what it needs at levels *it* can currently handle. And that's what Bowen does.

Chapter 5

Bowen?
Never heard of it.

Well, neither has 99.9999 % of the world

Bowen: A very advanced, gentle and revolutionary healing system for the body and mind that bridges the gap between Western and alternative medicines. It is a brilliantly simple approach which produces consistent, reproducible, and highly-satisfying results that commonly eliminates tension, pain, and repeatedly resolves troublesome health issues while realigning the body and mind, and restoring optimal health.

It unmistakably and naturally promotes rapid physiological, mental, emotional, and energetic modifications in the body which are necessary for optimal health. It causes fine-tuning to occur throughout the entire body, prompting it to reestablish wholistic (whole body) balance in every system and organ down to the cellular level. It removes unneeded re-occurring cycles and patterns in the body. It produces maximum predictable results with minimum intervention.

It unlocks and releases a core primal survival receptor, re-educating the body and mind to function at its most efficient and vibrant "at case" state. Bowen is a gentle and non-invasive alternative approach to optimal health that can be used on anyone, from infants to the elderly.

Many physicians and healthcare professionals around the world are becoming convinced in the profound effectiveness of Bowen in addressing difficult pain and difficult health-related issues.

Bowen uses a "least threatening" and minimalist approach to addressing the body. Bowen slightly "challenges" a muscle, tendon, or connective tissue, while it minimally disturbs the fascia tissue that surrounds muscle, connective tissue, and organs. The fascia tissue is the opaque membrane-like fibrous connective tissue which supports and surrounds soft organs and sheaths various structures in the body, such as muscles. It interconnects all the muscles and organs, forming a kind of mesh or web around these structures. The fascia tissue throughout the entire body connects near the knee. This connecting point is a *very* key point in the body, which I will discuss more in depth later. The fascia tissue can easily become dehydrated through not drinking enough water.

Bowen does not forcefully separate the fascia tissue, as in many other therapies. Bowen is not diagnostic, nor does it include any form of spinal manipulation, clinical nutrition, or dietary management. With Bowen, the body establishes the solution(s) necessary to re-balance and heal itself. Through Bowen, the body once again begins to communicate with itself and makes changes on subtle, life-transforming levels.

Bowen is a highly specialized, hands-on technique which uses gentle movements over muscle and connective tissue to increase the vitality and strength of internal organs while also activating the systems as well. It also stimulates the innermost healing abilities of the body, down to the cellular level. Using standard movements in specific locations, "Bowen Moves" activate and create a relaxation response in a particular area for a short period of time before releasing.

The Bowen Activation Moves, or "Moves," performed by a skilled Practitioner give the body instructions which allow it to "let go" on multiple levels simultaneously. This reduces muscle spasm, improves the blood and oxygen supply to the body and also increases lymphatic drainage.

Bowen mechanically separates closely connected and adhered fibers without a trace of pain, while stimulating both muscle and connective tissue. Moves performed on the body produce positive affects by closing the communication lines, or energy flow, called Ki or Chi. These Moves cause direct beneficial healing and balancing effects by stimulating physical, mental, and emotional healing.

The primary focus of Bowen is to trigger "a response" in the body rather than to physically attempt to change or alter the body in any way. Bowen generally does not seek to "fix" specific health problems; it merely resets the body's systems to allow it to accelerate its own cure. Short-term benefits include a deep sense of relaxation. Longer-term effects often include better overall well-being or improvements in dis-eased states.

Bowen has the ability to improve connections between the Central and Autonomic Nervous Systems and brain, along with the different body systems by "waking them up". Bowen actually transmits natural waves of different kinds throughout the body addressing: physical, mental, emotional, fluid, neuropathic, and energetic levels simultaneously. By stimulating the body to create specific harmonic frequencies, Bowen opens communication channels while also balancing the autonomic nervous system (ANS). A balanced ANS may indeed hold the key to improve the quality of life, mobility and over all wellness.

Bowen also strengthens the immune system, while at the same time reducing and eliminating pain. Many individuals report that they have reduced or eliminated their need for medication after just a few Bowen sessions.

Bowen does not attempt to treat anything in the body. It merely addresses the entire body, and addressing a particular problem with Bowen produces changes throughout the body. If you compare addressing a sprained ankle, which affects your entire body, with fixing a flat, which affects the proper functioning of your vehicle as a whole, you can see similarities.

Generally speaking, the longer a problem has existed the more sessions it may require to achieve the desired results, but not in every case. Bowen can work alongside your present medical or physical treatments to enhance the healing process,, when combined properly. Exclusively receiving Bowen though, will greatly enhance the results in nearly every case. The intention is always to find and address the cause of 'dis-ease' or to work through why the body is ill-at-ease.

Bowen sessions may last from 30 to 90 minutes, and are customized for the individual to address what the body presents "that day". Initially, it is generally recommend that a person receive three to five sessions spaced 5-10 days apart.

Bowen consists of a series of very precise Moves at specific points on the muscle and connective tissue throughout the whole body, producing benefits which extend from the physical right through to the emotional, cognitive and spiritual levels. Bowen – also referred to as Bowtech℠ and more recently Bowenwork™ is a revolutionary approach which complements rather than interferes. Bowen is an all-natural hands-on therapeutic approach to healing the body that addresses every system and organ in the body down to the cellular level. It primarily consists of light-touch "Moves" that are performed throughout the body

A specific set or combination of Moves which are put together to address a particular area, condition, or kind of pain are called a "procedure." The very basic aspects of the Move consist of moving the skin, applying light pressure, and then rolling over the muscle, tendon, or connective tissue in a gentle and non-invasive way. The Moves are, of course, much more complex in nature than can be described here. These Moves also moderately stimulate specific nerves that underlie the area, causing a soothing rippling effect to radiate throughout the nervous system extending to other areas of the body.

Each Move has its own finger, thumb, and hand placement and positioning. Each Move also may use a single finger or thumb, or any combination of fingers and thumbs, to execute the Move. The Move also has its own direction of travel, whether toward the center of the body (medial), toward the outside of the body (lateral), forward toward the front of the body (anterior), toward the back of the body (posterior), toward the top of the body (superior), toward the bottom of the body (inferior), or in combination with an angular (oblique) direction of travel.

The acceptable pressure used in a correctly performed Bowen Move falls somewhere between a tickle and on the edge of being uncomfortable. The pressure is not light enough to tickle the body, nor is it deep or firm enough to cause any harm. Going near or to the point of discomfort and not through it is a part of the objective when performing Bowen correctly.

When addressing the body in this unique way, the brain immediately performs a quick self-assessment to determine the extent of the incident. It also does its best to determine the cause and the effect it has on a particular area. It will also determine how it will influence the entire body long-term. In Bowen, each Move or Procedure is designed to be performed in complete harmony *with* the body.

Commonly when Moves are performed, a "heating up" begins to occur in the body at or near the point where the Moves were performed. The heat generated by the body from the Moves speeds up specific healing processes in the tissues and cells, thereby increasing blood flow and oxygen supply to the region also causing the muscles to begin to relax.

The nature of the Moves causes them to radiate deep into and throughout the entire body; into the arms, hands, legs and feet or to any other system, organ or other part of the body that is in need of a release or relaxation response. Performing a Move on the body is much like an instantaneous heat-seeking missile searching out and finding its target. However, with Bowen it goes from one target to the next, activating each target along the way.

> In Bowen, each Move or Procedure is designed to be performed in complete harmony *with* the body.

The Bowen Relaxation Moves, or "BRM," are specific sets of Moves which are core Moves that generally act as a kind of body pre-treatment that opens initial communications within the body and brain which have been stalled or shut down for some time. The BRM has a way of opening the body and brain in such a way that actually enhances the body's ability eliminate pain, while also preparing other specific areas which need to activate and receive healing from the body as well. Other Moves or procedures performed in these areas after the pre-treatment BRM's are performed allow greater direct access to these areas and on deeper levels.

The precise location of each Move must be taken into account for each individual. Even though performing Bowen Moves may look or even sound simple, it takes extensive in-depth training to correctly execute each Move in order for the body to receive a proper signal. Learning the sequential patterning of Moves used to commonly address individual conditions can be quite challenging, even for seasoned veterans of other forms of therapy or bodywork.

Moves that are performed throughout the body use a specific pattern, consisting of singular or multiple Moves (depending on the procedure performed). Usually, a Bowen session begins in the low back region, performing Moves in conjunction with the natural breathing rhythm of the individual. Moves are sometimes performed after the person is asked to take a deep breath to further enhance relaxation in the body. This greatly assists the body to transfer from a state of tension into deeper levels of relaxation. Specific procedures also require that the person take a deep breath, especially when addressing the respiratory system or kidneys, and in most instances tend to create profound outcomes. Each individual Move is unique in its location and in its execution *for the individuals' body*, because everyone's body is slightly different.

The proper execution of a Move depends upon:

= The physical condition of the person receiving Bowen
= The level of health of the person
= The type of condition or injury that is present
= The area of the body addressed
= The sensitivity of the person due to age, injury and other factors
= The degree of discomfort, pain or injury present
= The length of time the individual has had a particular condition or injury, and the actual extent of the condition or injury
= The amount of tension the muscle, tendon, or connective tissue has
= The range of motion the individual has in the area being addressed
= The amount of available skin slack
= The timing of the Move
= The direction of the Move
= The depth of the Move
= The speed of the Move
= The amount of pressure used
=   etc…

These are just a few of the factors that a properly skilled and experienced Bowen Practitioner takes into consideration to perform just one single Move on the body in order to stimulate a healing response for a particular area and to assist in alleviating a condition, suffering or pain.

It is crucial that the Practitioner *must always* strive to perform the minimum number of Moves or procedures to activate the preferred self-healing response. Performing too many Moves or procedures often produces counterproductive results because the body and brain get overloaded with too much information to process at one time.

The more serious your illness, the less Bowen will be performed during the session, using less pressure. The Practitioner must see, feel or sense changes as they happen in your body when he or she works with you. He or she must also know when the body has had enough for that session.

After the Practitioner performs a Bowen Move, the body begins to eliminate and erase the old unneeded pain/spasm programming. It doesn't just merely interrupt the pain/spasm cycles like most other therapies--it actually begins to help in the reprogramming processes for the entire body and brain so they can heal. Practitioners frequently find that very long held patterns or pain/spasm cycles in the body simply disappear after a just few Bowen sessions.

Each Bowen procedure is commonly named after the specific muscle, region, system, organ or condition that it addresses. Bowen also uses frequent pauses or waiting periods between sets of Moves. The waiting time (two minute minimum) is a **key** and **essential** element in triggering the body's healing ability. The waiting periods give the body and brain time to receive the direct message sent by the Moves. They also give the body time to respond and make necessary physical, structural, chemical, and energetic changes before the Practitioner performs the next set of Moves.

Bowen Practitioners commonly refer to these waiting periods as "Cooking Time" because the body often heats up after a specific Move or procedure is performed, which is a signal from the body that changes are definitely occurring. These short waiting periods are integrated throughout the session and are a very vital, essential and necessary part of Bowen. The Moves performed on the body give the body a very direct signal to start fixing itself. The waiting period gives the body time to assimilate the message and to respond.

During a session, it may not seem like much happens as the Practitioner uses light pressure, but as I explain to people, "You can use a 20 pound sledge hammer to turn the light switches on at home, but it is not necessary" or "Just put your finger in the light socket when someone turns on this little switch!" The person turning on the switch didn't do much, but the electrical current creates a substantial shock. Of course, they get the point.

Similarly, the Practitioner is turning on or activating the body's switches, so to speak. The primary objective of Bowen is to perform the absolute minimum amount of work to activate the healing mechanisms and redirect the body's resources where they are most needed first.

> **Bowen naturally promotes physiological, mental, emotional and energetic adjustments and corrections throughout the entire body, prompting it to re-establish wholistic (whole body) balance. It does this by fully utilizing the body's own nervous system pathways to reflexively jump-start and awaken the preoccupied brain.**

Bowen consistently gives *Maximum Health for the Minimum Price*™. Bowen is highly effective in addressing all levels of pain and functional illness. Functional illness is the state between optimal health and pathological conditions. A pathological condition is obvious. A functional illness, on the other hand is quite obscure.

A person, for example, has pain or a disorder that has been present for some time, yet an MRI, x-rays, lab and blood tests indicate nothing is abnormal. These disorders seem to exist without cause and are exhibited in or on the body resulting in "functional illness."

Functional illness often leads to substandard health. Examples of functional illness can appear as rashes, headaches or migraines, TMJ, hemorrhoids, digestive and eating disorders, ADD/ADHD, fibromyalgia, emotional upset or instability, physical and mental fatigue, kidney and bladder problems, minor circulatory problems as well as other health concerns.

Functional illness complaints also include Irritable Bowel Syndrome (IBS), sciatic pain, infertility (both male and female), joint and muscular pain, back or leg pain, breathing difficulties, lack of energy, or inability to focus.

Any one of these can be debilitating, and yet modern medicine often cannot clarify what is wrong in many of these cases and the person is told to "Just learn to live with it".

Bowen acknowledges these functional illnesses, then opens and restores health by turning on the internal healing intelligence within the body. This internal intelligence is able to balance physical, mental, and emotional levels simultaneously because Bowen opens the body to work at its greatest capacity. Optimal health is the only true state of the body.

Bowen has proven itself over and over again to be extremely effective for functional illness and pain. Bowen can be of tremendous benefit for *many* people. The ailments Bowen can address exceptionally well include:

- Pain
- Numbness
- Neuralgia
- Heaviness of the head
- Stiff joints
- Constipation
- Sluggishness
- Insomnia
- Disorders of the Autonomic Nervous system
- Cold hands and feet
- Pains in the knees experienced during standing or going up or down stairs
- Upset stomach
- So-called middle-age or old-age pains
- Stiff or tight neck and shoulders

These are just a few of the ailments Bowen readily addresses. A more comprehensive list is presented in another chapter.

Bowen also works especially well for those who don't suffer from a definite illness. These persons may feel sluggish, lack appetite, tire easily, need an attitude adjustment, have poor facial color, or need an overall health "tune-up."

Those who have received Bowen sessions find it to be far more effective and much longer lasting than chiropractic, physical therapy, massage, and energywork combined.

Because of the unique way Bowen addresses the body:

- Vertebral misalignments commonly right themselves – yet there is no manipulation of the spine as in chiropractic

- Muscle tension and strains are relieved and normal lymphatic flow is restored – yet muscles are not squeezed as in massage

- Meridians show immediate improvement – yet the work is not based on energy meridians as in many Chinese therapies

- It opens energy flow like acupuncture – yet it uses no needles

- It changes energy flows in the body like acupressure – yet the pressure is very light, subtle, and gentle

- Fascia rehydrates, adhesions release, and scar tissue softens – yet there is no heavy pressure as is Rolfing®, Shiatsu or other deep tissue therapies

- The body commonly becomes limp and very relaxed, as in Trager® therapy or yoga – yet there is no rocking, shaking, or continual body stretching or moving

- The mind commonly goes into a very deep state of rest and relaxation, as in meditation – though no meditative techniques or suggestions are offered (the altered state experienced by most people during Bowen is often quite different and much deeper than meditation or hypnotherapy)

- Internal psychological shifts are common – yet it is not necessary to evoke emotional releases or responses as in mind-body therapies

- Nearly everyone reports a pleasant, relaxed state, and deep sense of well-being, ease, and a sense of peacefulness and calming after just one or two sessions

- Many have lost weight naturally, though this is not a weight loss program

- ADD/ADHD in children and adults commonly lessen to a greater degree or is eliminated altogether

- Stress and tension is commonly <u>eliminated</u> – therefore, stress and tension has no more need to be managed

- Insomnia is gone after a few sessions, in most cases

- Depression commonly diminishes

- Anger regularly dissolves ← *oh yea...... a sigh of relief....*

In nearly every case, Bowen begins where most other treatments or therapies stop or have failed altogether. The bottom line is that Bowen is legendary for reducing and eliminating many pains, discomfort, disorders, and dysfunctions in the body.

The sequential Moves performed on the skin over muscles, tendons, and connective tissue stimulate changes beginning with the autonomic and central nervous systems. Some of the Moves cause sedating effects within the systems and organs in the body, while other Moves cause stimulating affects. Most Moves cause a relaxing effect throughout the entire body and all Moves assist the body to re-balance itself.

The Moves generally produce healing responses in the body which often also effectively reduce or eliminate sympathetic transference or referred pain (a pain or discomfort which occurs from something that is happening in another part or on the opposite side of the body.)

> Commonly, after just the first Bowen treatment, people walk away with nearly 50% of their ailments completely gone within the first week.

Modern advances in medicine have failed many who report that the conditions they suffer from are the same or even worse after years of Western medicine, physical therapy, or chiropractic treatment. They often come to Bowen with a long list of ailments.

When watching a Bowen Practitioner at work, the process seems relatively simple and it's definitely non-invasive. Clearly, at least on the surface, it appears that they are doing very little, if anything at all.

After performing just a few Moves, the Practitioner will leave the room for at least two minutes, occasionally longer after some Moves. They then return and perform a few more light Moves on a different part of the body, then leave again. This course of performing light Moves and leaving continues throughout the entire session.

The question an observer might ask is, "What is this light touching and then leaving the room actually doing that causes or produces such profound and extraordinary results in nearly every case?" Initially, the Move addresses the fascia tissue and then turns on what I call the "circuit breakers" in the body.

TURNING ON THE CIRCUIT BREAKERS

These "circuit breakers" have been turned off due to a variety of factors which include bumps, bruises, sprain, strain, stress, trauma, surgery, accident, and life in general. Many of these have been tripped due to some incident and have been off for quite some time.

When these "circuit breakers" are turned back on, the proper "electro-chemical neuropathic flows" in both the autonomic and central nervous systems begin to reopen using the natural routes that are imprinted in the body and brain since just before birth. After a while, the neuropathic detours that the body had put in place to re-route itself after an injury or trauma, for example, simply become useless and are basically discarded.

The region which was affected by the Move or Moves performed on the body experiences a rippling wave-like effect which is radiated throughout the entire body on both physical and energetic levels. This wave causes other subtler modifications and adjustments to begin taking place in other regions of the body. This ripple effect is relatively similar to throwing a stone into a pond of water. With Bowen, however, this wave continues to ripple throughout the body for 3-5 days or more after a session, causing continual changes to take place.

One Bowen Move performed in one area of the body, though specifically addressing the region adjacent to the Move, very often directly affects something else in another part of the body, be it a muscle, organ, joint, or system, as each and every part of the body is connected directly or indirectly.

The condition doesn't just automatically disappear in every case, even though the Practitioner has performed the "right" Move for what the body needs for a particular pain or injury, per se. The Practitioner only uses the Moves to turn the healing mechanisms on. Once the healing mechanisms are awakened, *the body will always heal what* **it** *knows is most important,* **first**.

The body may not begin to heal the health or pain related issues the individual *thinks* needs to happen first or feels are most pressing or prevalent. The body may have to make countless other corrections, using an exact order yet unknown to researchers and experts, to correctly rebalance and reprogram itself, first.

These corrections may include structural, muscular, neuropathic, energetic, or chemical rebalancing so minute as to be undetectable using the most technologically advanced and sophisticated equipment available today.

To the trained Practitioner, many changes can be observed within a few moments after a Move or procedure is performed. Those who receive Bowen can often feel changes taking place in their body during a session as it begins to naturally untorque, unwind, reprogram, and rebalance itself.

The role of the Practitioner is only one of being a facilitator, which can be likened in many ways to a person working at a computer. The operator enters information into the computer using a keyboard.

The body's information is automatically sent to the brain (the body's computer), where the brain calculates the changes that need to take place throughout the body and then inputs information in the form of changes or responses. If inaccurate information is entered, it often results in an incorrect answer which occurs with some of the standard or known medical treatments.

In Bowen, the person responsible for keying in the information must do their part accurately, and then they *must* allow the body to do *its* part. Waiting for the process to complete its cycle is also another important factor. You cannot speed up the outcome once the healing mechanisms are revived. Each body is very different. Each has their own speed and abilities heal.

With Bowen, the body needs its time to make the necessary changes on a variety of levels and to properly process the information that it has been given. Performing Bowen sessions too close together is like trying to add fuel to a fuel tank that is already full. It is unable to take any more.

In case of the computer or the body, immediate answers can occur. Through this process, the answer is a result of input, processing strength and ability.

> Every Body knows that Bowen is best for the body.
> *The predicament is that everybody doesn't know this yet!*

Based on the results that other Practitioners and I witness on a daily basis, I am thoroughly convinced that there is no other therapeutic system in the world that even comes close to the results Bowen can consistently achieve. It consistently surpasses every other therapy in the world.

I have seen this therapy execute such remarkable changes in the body that people cry tears of overwhelming happiness and joy when their pain or discomfort disappears and their agony is finally gone because they found a solution.

In rare cases where the body is not able to respond as well for some reason or other, Bowen may not be able to produce "miraculous changes" each and every time. Regardless, its ability to significantly reduce or eliminate pain and promote positive changes *in nearly every case* makes it incredibly obvious that Bowen is an extremely effective, results producing approach to healthcare.

Chapter 6

Bowen

What is it again?

Bowen offers a simple course of treatment (remedy) for pain and many ills. <u>Period</u>.

Bowen is *very* straightforward. It produces maximum predictable results using minimum intervention by penetrating into the innermost core of the body and resetting its healing mechanisms from the inside out.

Explaining Bowen to anyone who has not experienced it is somewhat like attempting to explain the meaning of Life. It is not just one thing, nor can it be explained in just one way, depending on the point of view or which level you want to explore. Understanding the countless events that occur in the body after only one Move is performed makes understanding Bowen complex, primarily because it seems like the Practitioner is not really doing anything at all. The many areas and levels that it addresses and reaches in the body exponentially expand with each subsequent Move.

Because of its wholistic nature of addressing the entire body and resetting it to heal, and not any specific condition or dis-ease, Bowen has been instrumental in breaking the cryptic code of health that has eluded health experts for thousands of years.

Bowen is comprised of a series of organized sequences of "Moves." Most Moves can be performed through loose-fitting clothing on a soft comfortable treatment-type table that is similar to a massage table or single size bed. Although Tom Bowen usually had people remove the outer layers of clothing and covered them with a blanket, as was customary in his day for alternative practitioners to do so, it is not necessary to disrobe to receive a proper Bowen session. Just loosening trousers, removing a belt, shoes and socks is all that is necessary, in most cases.

The Moves can be performed in such a way that can either stimulate or sedate systems and/or organs in the body depending on the direction *and* location of the Move or the specific procedure that is performed.

For those who have some knowledge of the body and of physical therapeutic modalities, Bowen can be viewed by them as a very distinctive and original form of physical, neuro-muscular, chemical, and energetic re-patterning that commonly erases unneeded recurring cycles in the body.

To erase the unneeded recurring cycles, Bowen first initiates a chain of events to begin the reversal of the offending causes.

To understand Bowen on another level or from a different view, let's look at Newton's First Law of Motion, "A body in motion will tend to stay in motion, a body at rest will tend to stay at rest"- unless something causes it to do likewise, and Newton's Third Law of Motion, which states, "For every action there is an equal and opposite reaction."

Taking a look at these two "laws of motion" and then adapting them to what occurs in the body in a simplified form, you may begin to see what occurs in the body in a different light.

"A body in motion will tend to stay in motion, a body at rest will tend to stay at rest"- unless something causes it to do likewise. A healthy body will remain healthy, calm, peaceful etc. unless outside factors come into play that are large enough to cause a change. In the body though, it is not just one thing on its own that causes changes to occur.

Bowen first initiates a chain of events to begin the reversal of the offending causes.

In most cases, it is a combination of MANY small and seemingly insignificant things on the physical, mental, emotional and energetic levels that add up together in the body that cause a chain reaction of sorts to occur that begin to cause an imbalance in the body. This is due primarily to the natural great resilient and flexible tendency the body has to ward off outside influences so it can remain healthy.

For example, when a person starts running they do not begin breathing hard as soon as they begin to run. It takes some time for the oxygen levels to become depleted enough to trigger responses in the body that cause much deeper breathing to occur. It is not just the movement of the feet that cause this to occur, neither is it just the movement of the legs, or just the movement of the arms that trigger the deeper breathing. It is a combination of all three in this simple case that triggered a physical reaction in the body.

The same happens in and with the body. It isn't just the digestive system that is temporarily out of balance a bit, but a combination of lack of water, improper nutrition, insufficient rest, not enough exercise, too much work, emotional reactions, and mental strain, for example, together that cause the digestive system to be out of balance. The temporary imbalance in the digestive system sets off temporary imbalances in other systems and organs as well, which brings in "for every action there is an equal and opposite reaction," moving our health in the opposite direction from where it was.

Because of the neuro-chemical factors contained in the nervous system and brain, a reduction or amplification of the signals is sent to the systems, organs or brain occurs, and sets off a chemical reaction in the body, which commonly leads to emotional reactions, which commonly leads to physiological reactions, which lead to other chemical reactions leading to other emotional reactions leading to other physiological reactions... and over and over again affecting the entire body and mind, leading to declining health.

In the body a singular reaction which only affects one thing is not ever likely. A single reaction will always affect other systems and organs to some level. The "equal and opposite reaction" in the case of the body is not singular, but a combination of many small reactions that take place that add up to the "equal and opposite reaction" or reactions in the body. These reactions are causative factors which begin the decline in health, primarily because the "reaction factor" has a tendency to put and/or keep the body in the defense or emergency mode.

Reversing the reaction factor(s) that are occurring in the body as the body begins "rejecting" itself to some degree, typically requires the exact opposite "action" that in turn causes an equal and opposite response in the body.

A *single* gentle, yet, direct and definite coaxing, encouraging, and persuasive signal given to the body causes (stimulates) the neuro-electro-chemical firing of the nervous system using responsive chemicals that lead to the beginning of the direct sedation of only one reactive system or organ. The mere beginning of the sedation of just one system, for example, will set off the beginnings of a positive chain response in the body that once again, sets off a small chemical change in the body, which commonly leads to small emotional changes, which commonly leads to small physiological changes in the body, which leads to other small chemical changes leading to other small emotional changes leading to other physiological small changes... and over and over again that can add up, effecting the entire body and mind leading to increasing health. Just one single Bowen Move, performed alone, can produce very powerful and profound effects on the body, causing it to reset itself and make instant changes.

Practitioners and students alike observe and experience that by just performing the same few Moves on the body, just the amount that the body needs, repeatedly over a couple of sessions, typically produce profound effects even in systems, organs, parts of the body, or areas in life that were not even addressed.

When a signal is given to the body as a Bowen Move is performed, an amplified, clear and distinctive signal is sent *to* the body. This signal goes where it can in the body. The system or organ that receives the signal sends out signals to other interconnected systems and organs that is stronger than normal causing the system or organ to respond, sending out yet another stronger *modified* signal to other interconnected systems or organs as well, until the signal, now modified, returns back to the point or area in the body where it was performed.

This sets off other chains of events that steadily send signals from the point of origin in the body where the Move was performed, back out into the body. The system, organs and the brain, receive the signals, modify them, and send them back, to do the same over and over again, while also re-opening the neuropathways and strengthening neuropathic flows improving and restoring neurological flow and function.

This course characteristically continues until the original signal has gotten to a point where it no longer affects the body or mind anymore, because the strengthened signal becomes the new standard by which the body functions. This typically takes around 3-5 days for most people and the body will make all the changes it is able to in this time. This is one of the reasons why the effects of a Bowen session do not disappear after 24 hours like many other conventional or more recognized treatments.

Once the neuro-electro-chemical pathways are re-opened and the systems and organs are beginning to stabilize and begin some degree of normal balanced functioning again, the *next* Bowen session will have a great tendency to open the neuro-electro-chemical pathways even further. This allows an even stronger signal to be sent out through the entire body causing subtler and deeper level relaxation to happen and other positive changes to occur as well.

Because Bowen can produce very powerful and lasting results in the body and mind, the greater the health problem or the more specific the issue is, the less work a practitioner actually has to do, in order for the desired results to occur. In most instances, a set or series of complimentary Moves performed together is all that is required to complete a proper treatment. A limited number of Moves during a session provides the maximum impact. In this manner, Bowen returns the full responsibility of healing back to the body of the person who received the session. Bowen is merely a gift given to the body. Whether the body wants to receive and use the gift is up to it.

To assist the body to obtain the greatest degree of healing in the shortest amount of time, the Practitioner must be acutely aware of what is happening in the body and what the body is showing or "telling" them. He or she must perform a Move, a set of Moves, or Procedure that the body is "asking for". Performing only the Moves that the body is precisely asking for, no more, and no less, while also performing them firmly enough (to address the body structurally), yet at the same time, gently enough (to address the body energetically), produces the greatest results.

> Bowen is merely a gift given to the body.

Every Move is *always* intended to be performed within the comfort level of the person to allow the person to truly "receive" the Move. However, occasionally, a deeper Move or two may be needed in order to give the body a signal that is stronger than the signal that it used to, or stronger than the signal it is currently sending, to enable the body to address a particular very specific health or pain related issue.

In these rare cases where a deeper Move is used, the Move is intended to be performed firmly, yet also *to* the point of discomfort, and for all intents and purposes, not through the point of discomfort. In this way, the Move(s) will tend *to* the body, deliberately and purposefully coaxing it back into balance. This coaxing stimulates healing responses that repeatedly invigorate, revitalize, and enliven the body to its core, beginning its return back to balance, well-being and total body awareness *and* wellness. Moves that are performed properly are absolutely safe to use on anyone in any condition and will cause no harm whatsoever.

The power that made the body, heals the body - it just needs to be turned on again!

BOWEN RELAXATION MOVES (BRM)

The Bowen Relaxation Moves, or BRM, are the initial set or series of Moves (Procedures), which form Bowen's foundational core. The complete set of the BRM consists of the Lower Back Procedure (LBP), the Upper Back Procedure (UBP), and the Neck Procedure (NP). These primary Moves address the entire body as a whole, multi-dimensionally.

These first Procedures are considered to be the basic essential and foundational Procedures. They are pre-requisites that must be performed first, except when very specific injuries, such as a sprain, have "just occurred." They are used in nearly every case prior to performing *any* other Bowen Move or Procedure which would normally be used to concentrate on an area of the body that has a particular health issue, pain or injury. They serve to open the body to initiate first-stage-opening-healing sequences that focus the body and mind on present-time health-related issues. After the body is opened and the first stages of healing are initiated, the body is now more receptive and the rest of the body can be more easily taken care of using other Procedures. All other Moves and/or Procedures are built upon the nucleus of these fundamental and foundational BRM Moves.

It is very common for a Practitioner to perform just the BRM, causing the body to respond in ways that actually addresses the problem without any further need to use any other Moves or Procedures in that session. This primarily happens because the body is given the signal to "give it up", while at the same time the brain is given the signal to "get off it", meaning to get off or out of its detrimental pattern. It is one of the amazing ways that Bowen works.

> The first two Bowen Moves performed in the low back region act as the "master keys" that fundamentally serve to open and turn on the body's healing powers.

As a whole, the BRM alone sets up a series of deep relaxation responses that the body and mind readily takes to, and gently begins to immerse them into a state of leisurely relaxation.

Using Bowen and the BRM, the body is basically divided into 3 parts. The first is the lower portion of the body, beginning around the top of the hips, where the LBP is performed. The second is the upper portion of the body, encompassing the region just above the bottom of the shoulder blades, including the neck and shoulder region, where the first part of the UBP and NP are performed. The third includes the mid back region between the top of hips and the bottom of the shoulder blades and includes the lower portion of the UBP.

Addressing the lower portion of the body first accomplishes many tasks at the same time. The first two Moves performed in the low back region act as the "master keys" that fundamentally serve to open *and* turn on the body's healing powers. They automatically arouse the Central and Autonomic Nervous Systems, increasing neuropathic and chemical activity throughout the body, especially in the brain, while also increasing oxygen flow and circulation. Having a wealth of heightened of activity available, a powerful release of newly available resources created by the heightened activity energizes the body to new levels initiating and eliciting the blueprinted healing sequences.

Once the initial healing sequences are activated and set in motion, the responses in the body are directly equivalent to the strength of the signal(s) it actually received. This is the initial platform from which healing begins using Bowen.

Performing these first two Moves on someone who has just suffered trauma will begin taking their body out of shock in as little as *10 – 15 seconds!* It doesn't matter what kind of trauma they have suffered, whether it was physical, mental, or emotional. This includes incidents such as accidents and other serious injuries, falls, broken teeth, broken bones, a joint dislocation, or other incidents that induce major emotional or psychological reactions.

Many Bowen Practitioners and other bystanders have witnessed these two Moves in action. They have seen them rapidly work in cases of mental or emotional trauma: the traumatic or sudden and unexpected death of a loved one, an unexpected notice of a lay-off or divorce, for example.

> These two powerful Bowen Moves begin the re-stabilization of both the body *and* mind.

These two powerful Bowen Moves begin the re-stabilization of both the body *and* mind. These "master key" Moves can be likened to the key which opens the main entrance doors of a very large high-rise commercial building. In the building, access to the entire core or inside of the building is only allowed through the front doors located on the lower level, and the doors can only be opened by those who are authorized and have and use the correct keys. Those who enter can open other doors to gain access to other secured or locked areas *only* if they have the correct keys.

In the body's case, opening the entire body to healing begins near the base of spine, by those who have and use the correct keys. Other individual keys (specific Moves) can then be used to gain access virtually every other area.

As an instructor, I commonly teach the first two Bowen Moves to doctors, nurses and emergency personnel who are willing to learn them, as a matter of course, because they truly have life-saving potential. I often receive telephone calls from these people who readily share the details of the extraordinary changes they immediately saw take place in someone who was suffering from some kind of serious physical, mental, or emotional trauma, after these people performed just the first two Bowen Moves on them. They ALWAYS say, "I've never seen anything like it. It was miraculous." There are times when these individuals have shared that they "know for a fact" that a person's life was saved because of the two Master Moves were performed and their vital signs *immediately* began to stabilize.

The LBP (lower back procedure) also begins to open the primary or base energy center or "chakra" in the body. This energy center is located in the area of the sacrum through to the front portion of the pelvic region. Many Middle-Eastern and Asian cultures believe that this is a primary center for balancing the body energetically. The first two Moves performed in this area send a direct signal into this lower region of the body, in essence dividing the body into upper and lower portions via the spinal cord and Central Nervous System. This area is also includes the physical balance point of the body.

When the energy begins to move within this area, and muscle tension releases in the lower back and pelvic regions are very common and almost immediate. The pelvic region is also the main structural balance point for the body upon which all the spinal vertebrae are stacked. Opening and relaxing this area using Bowen begins to un-torque, re-align and rebalance the entire body. This commonly happens in Bowen naturally, *without* the need for any use of force or manipulation.

Most physical therapists and chiropractors agree that when the pelvis is out of alignment, the whole body is out of balance. Adjusting vertebrae and bones alone do little to stabilize the pelvis or any other part of the body when muscular tension or spasm(s) are the main cause of the misalignment.

Releasing and re-balancing the muscles using Moves surrounding the pelvic region alone causes sweeping changes, both structurally and energetically, while initiating a freeing of muscular tension, strain, and spasm. Addressing the lower pelvic area with a specific Bowen Moves characteristically causes a rapid release of most acute and chronic low back pain and discomfort. In most cases the release is instant. In other cases it may take some time for the body to unwind and release itself over a few hours, or in some instances, days.

When performing the LBP (lower back procedure) as a stand-alone procedure (meaning using only that procedure in that session, and no more) it will also commonly address the sacrum, coccyx, hamstring and knee regions, as well as initiating changes in the urinary, bladder, uterus, prostate, reproductive system, descending colon, sigmoid colon, rectum, lymphatic system, ankles, and nearly all the fascia tissue in the body.

In the upper portion of the body, BRM Upper Back Procedure (UBP) most commonly addresses the entire region of the thoracic cavity (rib cage), including the lungs, diaphragm, respiratory, lymphatic, circulatory, and digestive systems, as well as the heart, stomach, liver, gallbladder, pancreas, adrenals, kidneys, and the gastrointestinal tract (small and large intestines), the abdominal aorta, striated muscles, and sweat glands, along with the peripheral and visceral arteries, neck, shoulders, and arms.

Bowen Moves primarily performed in the upper back and chest regions also assist in increasing lung capacity through relaxing tense muscles in and around the chest. Increasing the ability to breathe deeply leads to higher concentrations of oxygen in the blood.

The BRM Neck Procedure (NP) normally begins the release of neck, shoulder, arm and TMJ tension, as well as affecting the eyes, vagus nerve, heart, stomach, liver, gallbladder, pancreas, kidneys, and gastrointestinal tract, bronchi, larynx, peripheral cranial and facial vessels, intra-cranial vessels, and a variety of other glands located in the head region.

Commonly, the NP helps relieve headaches in as little as *15-20 seconds*. When combined with the TMJ Procedure, migraines commonly disappear in as little as 2 minutes!

A very specific set of two Moves applied in the knee region which are used to complete the LBP were considered by Tom Bowen as **the most important** Moves in the Bowen repertoire. They directly address the entire body, by directly addressing nearly all the fascia tissue in the body that converges at the knee.

Decades of research shows that the fascia tissue holds the memory of physical trauma. Bowen addresses the fascia tissue in a very unique manner which affects the structure of the tissue, thereby causing the initial release of stored or blocked energies (memory of trauma) throughout the entire body.

New students, without fail, report that using *only* the BRM achieved phenomenal results in the body of the person they were working with. They also report that these few Moves were much more powerful than they ever realized.

During a regular treatment where the BRM are performed, the LBP is performed first, the UBP is performed second, and the NP third, using the accompanying waiting times, of course.

The Bowen Relaxation Moves (BRM), in and of themselves, are so powerful that nearly 80% of all those receiving sessions from a Bowen Practitioner can be properly restored to optimal health using only these basic foundational Moves.

After just only one or two sessions, many people report that they experience an increase in energy and stamina as their body re-balances, exchanging stress and tension for relief and well-being. Most people who receive Bowen commonly feel a variety of physiological changes happening in their body as the Practitioner performs BRM or other Moves.

Re-balancing the body structurally, energetically, and chemically at the same time causes profound *and* lasting changes. As some of these changes begin, they commonly include a "heating up" of the body, which starts in the sacral region. It can then either radiate to other areas of the body or remain in a specific region to continue re-balancing and healing that area, somewhat like an internal heating pad.

Some people experience small involuntary muscle contractions that occur when a particular neuropathic flow is opened or restored. Others experience mild to strong sensations of waves of energy traveling through the body, as they begin to drift off into a deep state of relaxation. One person described the feeling as if she were "sprouting wings out of my shoulder blades!"

Regularly, changes that occur in the body include the disappearance of muscle and joint aches and pains, nervousness, apprehension, depression, and anxiety. These all naturally begin to diminish rapidly, while many long-held symptoms begin to vanish as well.

As the muscles relax, so do the systems and organs. In the circulatory system, for example, the heart rate slows as the body's need for blood flow slightly decreases. The breathing rate of the respiratory system also slows down and breathing patterns deepen. Occasionally, a very deep involuntary breath occurs and is referred to as a "cleansing breath for the body" as the body begins to release things that are unwanted or no longer needed.

When the cleansing breath takes place, the body often rapidly descends into a deep meditative restful state. When this occurs, grumbling sounds can often be heard from the digestive tract as it begins to release and re-digest long-held stress and trauma.

In this deepened state of relaxation, adhesions tend to loosen, and scar tissue often softens, shrinks and at times even disappears. These benefits occur because the impediments to the natural healing and restoration processes are removed. Energy once again is released and the body begins to more effectively communicate with itself. Once these changes begin, many people report that they somehow feel balanced, wonderful, and yet, different.

During and after Bowen sessions, the feelings of energy being released can be felt internally as a pulse or wave-like sensations which are quite different in rhythm and strength from the individual's own heart rate. This indicates that energetic as well as physical repair and restoration is happening.

The repair processes which occur in the body as it begins to initiate healing can be likened to a computer that has had many programs and files installed and deleted. When this happens, fragmented spaces exist throughout the computer's hard drive. When large numbers of spaces or gaps exist in the computer's programs, the gaps greatly affect the speed at which the computer works and alters the computer's performance as well. Occasionally the system must be defragmented using a specific program specially designed to defragment it in order to restore proper high-speed functioning. The computer must wait until it finishes restoring itself before it can once again operate at optimum capacity.

Bowen works on the body in a similar way as the de-fragmenting and the file/program deletion programs of a computer. In effect, it properly and non-invasively rids the body of old unneeded physical, mental, and emotional pain, tension and injury programs. It also begins to remove the restrictions that have slowed down or impeded the body's healing processes.

As the Practitioner performs the BRM, a portion of the brain begins to filter out excessive noise and outside auditory interference. This allows the body to drop into a yet-deeper level of relaxation, allowing the mental state to stabilize as mind chatter fades, while also re-adjusting the analytical portion of the mind as well. As this happens, the left and right sides of the brain commonly begin to work together, causing relaxation and release to occur on yet even-deeper levels.

As both sides of the brain begin to work together, higher levels of concentration, focus, and clarity become very apparent for most people, often causing a major life-metamorphosis or transformation as past issues, worry, doubt, and fear of the unknown begin to release and are replaced with a kind of inner-sense certainty.

Many people who begin to feel or sense this happening in the body and mind remark that they feel "grounded, centered, and balanced," and that they are experiencing a whole new life of "total body wellness." Many find this single benefit of Bowen sessions priceless.

TRULY AN ORIGINAL APPROACH

Because of its uniqueness as a course of action, using a "Less is More" approach, nothing can in actuality be compared to Bowen. It does not fit into known medical, physical or physio-therapy, chiropractic, massage, acupressure, acupuncture, or Energywork models. What truly makes Bowen stand out from and above all other approaches in helping or healing the body, is that each session has its unique way of compounding or building upon the previous session or sessions.

With Bowen, the body remembers what was previously done and builds upon it. I have witnessed this happening many times over. I have even seen many cases where someone received just one or two sessions and then did not come back for six months or a year and the next session they received *still* built upon the prior sessions(s).

> **What truly makes Bowen stand out from and above all other approaches in helping or healing the body, is that each session has its unique way of compounding and building upon the previous session or sessions.**

When receiving Bowen, it is as though the body and brain welcomes *and* receives a new upgraded healing program each and every session. This is usually markedly evident in those who suffer from severe, chronic or difficult health problems, whose problems significantly decrease during the course of receiving Bowen.

The brain, the regulator of all body functions, uses a variety of electro-chemical signals through the nervous systems to stimulate changes and regulate the body as a whole. Bowen directly uses the Central Nervous System (CNS) and Autonomic Nervous System (ANS), to activate the healing response, thereby to assisting the body to re-calibrate and more properly regulate *all* its functions.

After a Move is performed on the body, increased circulation or blood flow and improved oxygenation to that particular area of the body can often be felt as heat radiating from the area which was addressed. It can also often be seen visibly by patches of redness developing at the point of contact of the Move.

One of the secrets to better health lies in increasing oxygen levels in the body. Decreased oxygen intake accounts for a significant portion of sub-optimum health, including fatigue, inability to concentrate, and the body's inability to repair and properly grow or rejuvenate cells in the body. Decreased oxygen in the body has been found to be a main cause of many degenerative diseases and other well-known diseases and disorders, arthritis being one of them. Bacteria growth is also accelerated with decreased oxygen intake, as bacteria cannot thrive in a properly oxygenated environment.

One of the secrets to better health lies in increasing oxygen levels in the body.

A decrease in oxygen levels also increases aches and pains. This decreased oxygen level lessens the efficiency of the brain, organs, and systems, rapidly leading to declining health.

- Increasing the oxygen content in the body of those suffering from rheumatoid arthritis often leads to many notable changes as the sufferer finds it easier to move.

- Increasing oxygen content in the body of those suffering from depression and pessimism naturally makes them feel happier and more optimistic.

- Increasing oxygen in the body begins to accelerate the removal of sediment in the blood. This sediment not only obstructs the blood's circulation, it also accumulates to form higher concentrations of sediment or sedimentary deposits which end up in the kidneys, gallbladder, eyes, heart, and arterial walls. This means that smaller amounts of toxins are in the blood stream. Smaller amounts of toxins in the blood means that the body will more rapidly receive the nourishment and hydration it needs. Quality nutrients are now more readily available to vigorously restore, regenerate, and rejuvenate not only the cells, but the entire body as well.

- Increasing the oxygen content in the blood increases the enzymatic processes in the liver, greatly enhancing its performance, increasing cell nourishment, cellular regeneration, rejuvenation, and restoration. This single improvement alone increases the overall health of the entire body.

Some people claim that Bowen has helped them "cure" their cancer. Others insist that Bowen has made the difference in the remission of their serious illness or dis-ease. Bowen Practitioners _do not_ make any claims regarding Bowen or its effects on cancer or other serious diseases.

Can Bowen treat cancer and other serious diseases? Definitely not. Can Bowen be used to help increase health for those with cancer or other serious diseases? Definitely YES! Can it be beneficial in helping people with serious diseases? In many cases, definitely YES! Will it help every time? To that I must say, "No." In other words, Bowen can play and has played **its** part to help the body along _its_ path to regaining health.

WHAT BOWEN <u>CAN</u> DO

√ Rid the body of energy robbing pain, tension, anxiety, and stress

√ Provide immediate *and* long lasting relief from acute, chronic, or re-occurring head, muscle, and joint aches, discomfort and pain

√ Clear out symptoms and begin to address root causes

√ Help put the body "at rest," to take the body naturally from protect, fight, flight, or survival mode and begin to put it into its healing mode

√ Assist in healing the body in efforts to prevent surgery – in cases where surgery can be prevented

√ Assist the brain *and* body to receive the message to "heal itself"

√ Turn on the "circuit breakers" in the body that have been turned off

√ Set the body up to begin detoxification processes

ISSUES BOWEN COMMONLY ADDRESSES

Bowen is extremely successful in caring for and addressing many acute (recent) and chronic (long-term) tension, pain and conditions.

People come to Bowen suffering many conditions or ailments and find the solution to their health-related problems. Asthma, allergies, carpal tunnel, TMJ, frozen shoulder, sports injuries, chronic fatigue, fibromyalgia, plantar fasciatis, mild to severe back and neck pain, muscular and joint pain are just a few problems Bowen addresses. Helping people with these very common conditions are an everyday occurrence. After receiving a couple of sessions many of these conditions often begin to seem to melt right before their eyes.

Bowen has been found to be an effective method for addressing an extensive list of wide ranging conditions, disorders, and ailments in the body.

The following list has been compiled based on what Bowen traditionally addresses, i.e. what has worked consistently in the past, and well over ten years of clinical experience and research.

ADD (Attention-Deficit Disorder), ADHD (Attention-Deficit Hyperactivity Disorder), AADD (Adult Attention-Deficit Disorder), AADHD (Adult Attention-Deficit Hyperactivity Disorder), Abdominal pain, Abnormal posture, Acid indigestion, Acid reflux, Acute pain, Addiction, Adrenal Glands, Anal disorders (itching, burning, discomfort or pain), Angina, Allergies, ALS, Ankle pain, Anorexia, Anxiety, Asthma, Arthritis, Arthritic Pain, Athletic performance enhancement, Back cramp, Balance, Bed wetting, Bell's Palsy, Bi-Polar disorder, Bladder disorders, Blood pressure, Breast lumps, tenderness, or pain, Bronchitis, Bunions, Bursitis, Buttock pain, Calf pain, Cardiovascular problems, Carpal Tunnel Syndrome, Cellulitis, Chest pain, Chronic Fatigue, CFS, CFID's, Chronic pain, Cluster headaches, Coccyx pain, Colic in infants, Concussion, Constipation, Cranial pressure or pain, Crohn's Disease, Cysts, Cystitis, Deafness, Depression, Diabetes, Diaphragm pain, Diarrhea, Difficulty conceiving children, Digestive disorders, Disc problems (herniated, slipped), Distention (abdominal), Diverticulitis, Diverticulosis, Dizziness, Dyslexia, Ear aches, Ear infections, Ear problems, Edema, Elbow problems, Emphysema, Engorged breast, Epilepsy, Epstein Barr, Erectile Dysfunction (ED), Eye problems, Eyesight, Exhaustion, Fatigue, Fibromyalgia, Flu, Fluid retention, Foot Problems, Frozen shoulder, Gall Bladder pain, Generalized Anxiety Disorder (GAD), General Cardiac and Circulatory problems, General body aches, General well-being, Glandular fever, Gluteal muscle asymmetry, Golfer's Elbow, Gout, Groin strain, Groin pain, Gynecological issues, Hammer toes, Hamstring pull or tension, Hay fever, Headaches, Head pain, Heartburn, Heavy periods, Heel Pain, Hemorrhoids, Hepatitis, Hernia, Herniated discs, Hiccups/Hiccoughs, Hiatal hernia, High shoulder, Hip problems, Hip pain and disorders, Hormonal disorders and imbalance, Ileo-cecal valve, Incontinence (adult), Infant colic, Infertility – male & female, Inflammation, Inflexibility, Influenza, Inguinal ligament discomfort or pain, Insomnia, Irregular milk supply, Irritable Bowel Syndrome (IBS), Jaw problems, pain or misalignment, Joint discomfort, Joint pain, Juvenile diabetes, Kidney disorders, Knee problems, Knee pain, Learning disabilities, Leg cramps, Leg(s) turned in or out, Liver problems, Lyme's Disease, Lymphedema, Lymphatic drainage, Mastitis, Meniere's Disease, Menopause, Menstrual and Female problems, Menstrual irregularities Menstrual cycle regulation, Mental fatigue, Migraines, Muscular Dystrophy (MD), Multiple Sclerosis (MS), Neck restriction, stiffness and pain, Neuromas, Neuropathy, Nervousness, Nervous exhaustion, Numbness (extremity – arms, elbows, wrists, hands, legs, knees, ankle, feet) Osgood Schlatters's Disease, Osteo-Arthritis, Overwhelmed sensation, Parkinson's Disease, Pectoral region discomfort of problems, Pelvic and pelvis related problems (pelvic torque or tilt, leg length difference, hip imbalance), Piriformis pain, Pitcher's shoulder, Plantar Fasciatis, Poor peripheral vascular supply, Post-Concussion Syndrome (PCS), Post-Partum, Post-Traumatic Stress Syndrome (PTSS), Postural problems, Pre-Menstrual Syndrome (PMS), Pre-Menstrual Dysforic Disorder (PMDD), pregnancy discomfort, Psoas muscle spasm, Pregnancy issues, Prostate, Quarterback shoulder/elbow/wrist, Range of motion limitations, Repetitive stress injury (RSI), Repetitive Strain Injury (RSI), Respiratory problems of many kinds, Restless Leg Syndrome (RLS), Rib tenderness or pain, Sacral or sacro-iliac pain, Scar tissue discomfort or pain, Sciatic nerve pain (Sciatica), Scoliosis, Shin splints, Shoulder problems, Shoulders 'frozen' with restricted arm movement, Shoulder blade region problems or pain, Sinusitis, Sinus disorders, Sinus pain and pressure, Skeletal and muscular problems, Sleep Apnea, Sluggishness, Snoring,

Sprains, Sports injuries (ankle, back, groin, hamstring, knee, neck, and shoulder strains, pulls and cramps, sprains, tennis elbow, wrists, etc.), Sprung ribs, Standing difficulties, Sternal pain, Stiff neck, Stress and tension, Stroke (enhanced rehabilitation), Stuck energy, Swelling, Tailbone pain, Tendonitis, Tennis Elbow, Testicular pain, Thigh pain, Thoracic Outlet Syndrome (TOS), Tinnitus (ringing in the ears) Toxemia, TMJ, Trauma (physical, mental, emotional), Tremors, Trigeminal Neuralgia, Urinary tract disorders, Uterine problems, Tipped Uterus, Vertigo, Vomiting, Walking difficulties, Work-related injuries, and Whiplash

Bowen addresses the whole body and the body as a whole!

The list of conditions that Bowen addresses is lengthy and seems almost endless. Using Bowen alone, complex and chronic conditions very often show huge improvements and in many cases, just disappear. In more complex cases, the number of Bowen sessions which may be needed to achieve the desired results may require more than the usual 3-5 sessions.

Will Bowen work in every case or for every condition? To this I must say no. Rarely, Bowen may work for one individual, but not another with the same complex issue. The reason why this happens is currently unknown - it is just another one of the mysteries of the universe, yet to be discovered. I believe that future research will assist in discovering some of the reasons. The easiest way to find out if Bowen can help with a particular problem is to receive an initial set of 3-5 Bowen sessions from a competent and experienced practitioner. Invariably, Bowen will wake up something inside your body to help it with its healing processes. At the very least, it will result in a wonderful, deep feeling of relaxation.

> ...many people commonly experience stress elimination. There is a **huge** difference between stress management and stress elimination.

Bowen begins by first addressing the whole body and the conditions that are simple to remedy through re-balancing and re-stabilization. Next, the body will then address more specific and deeper conditions as compensatory pain, lesser conditions, and symptoms begin to peel off like the layers of an onion, until the root or core is uncovered and then addressed. Addressing core conditions may include as little as one or two Moves in exact locations, a singular set of Moves, or a series of Moves, using only what is necessary to gain the desired result.

> Giving the body more Bowen than it can handle for the day does not prove anything to anyone and is actually counterproductive.

> **Typically, many people receive Bowen once a week for only 3-5 times before they are restored back to optimal health**

The body will always heal what *it* knows is most important first. A Bowen Practitioner may, however, give sequential treatments to address specific condition or multiple conditions simultaneously depending on the person's overall health and condition of their body. The session given will *always* be based on what the body is displaying and what it can handle that day.

Bowen regularly un-torques the body, and relieves the muscles of spasm, allowing the body to properly align itself on its own. Results of this therapy are lasting and very profound in most cases. Often a treatment restores balance. It also often creates increased range and ease of motion,

For some migraine sufferers the pressure and pain disappears within minutes. Many corporate workers suffer from high levels of stress. Stress management does some good for the body and mind. However, managing stress does little to assist the body and mind to truly let go of the tension, apprehension, anxiety, and depression.

I have found that many recipients of Bowen commonly experience stress elimination. There is a **huge** difference between stress management and stress elimination.

Many sufferers with debilitating back and neck pain, or herniated or bulging discs in the neck or back have canceled scheduled surgery after just a few Bowen treatments. So have others with carpal tunnel symptoms. Health care professionals who have personally experienced Bowen frequently refer *their* clients for a session or sessions.

Chapter 7

Energy and Frequency

Everything exists as a bundle of energy with its own specific frequency. Frequency is the measurable rate of electrical energy flow. Dr. Robert O. Becker, M.D., in his book *The Body Electric*, establishes evidence that the human body has a measurable electrical frequency. Dr. Becker also explains that the level of health in a person's body can be measured by the frequency of their body.

Dr. Becker believes that electricity or current within the human body is a vital key to the life process. His discoveries point directly to the regeneration of damaged tissues and organs through increasing and holding the increased frequency of the body within specific levels.

There are two kinds of frequencies:

1. Incoherent and chaotic - frequencies that fracture human electrical fields
2. Coherent harmonic – frequencies that harmonize with and complement the human electrical field

Electrical Alternating Current (AC) and especially microwave frequencies are incoherent and have a negative effect on the health and healing of the body.

The use of infrared or ultrasound manipulates the natural frequency of the body. The consumption of food, products, and liquids also readily alter this frequency.

Live plants, living foods, freshly picked herbs, and fresh organically grown fruits and vegetables grown in untainted soil contain coherent harmonic frequencies and often increase the body's frequency. These also have a high nutritional value that adds to the health and healing of the body.

> **The body is a complexly bundled mass of energy that can easily be altered, either for enhanced health and healing or toward disease and self-destruction.**

The frequency in a normal, healthy body is between 62 and 68 Hertz (Hz). Higher frequencies build the immune system and the body and promote optimal health and healing, whereas lower frequencies rob the body of energy and health.

During the day, the frequency of the brain operates at 10 Hz higher than that of the body. At night, the frequency of the body is 10 Hz higher than that of the brain. This is the body attempting to heal. When frequency drops, the immune system becomes compromised.

The common flu occurs at 58 Hz, Candida (yeast overgrowth) at 55 Hz, disease begins at 52 Hz, and cancer 42 Hz. Even dead, our bodies have a frequency of 25 Hz.

According to Dr. Royal Rife, every disease has its own frequency. His research indicates that certain frequencies can actually prevent the development of disease and that higher frequencies actually destroy diseases that have a lower frequency. Harmful bacteria, fungus, and viruses cannot survive in a higher frequency environment.

Food, water, beverages, chemicals and pollutants have a direct impact that can either build *or* compromise the body's frequency, depending on the actual frequency that these have. Processed (canned) foods have a zero frequency and actually *rob* health *from* the body.

Research shows that subjects given a cup of coffee to hold, quickly reduced their frequency from 66 Hz to 58 Hz, in as little as three seconds. After removing the cup from their hand, the frequency returns to its normal 66 Hz after an average of two hours.

Other subjects given one cup of coffee to drink had their body frequency change from 66 Hz to 52 Hz in as little as three seconds. They were not allowed to drink coffee until the conclusion of the research. These subjects who drank the cup of coffee took an average 72 hours (3 days) to return to a normal frequency of 66 Hz. It took 3 days after drinking just one cup of coffee for the body to rebalance and regain its normal frequency.

It is estimated that people drink 2.5 billion cups of coffee every day. The caffeine in coffee is not classed as an addictive drug, however, many depend on it for a daily stimulant "fix" and are addicted to it. Caffeine is widely known to significantly increase blood pressure, increase the occurrence and severity of headaches and migraines. It also is known to cause bouts of restlessness, nausea, anxiety, muscular tension, and sleeplessness along with other effects which alter brain functioning.

The ill effects generated through drinking coffee and caffeinated drinks alone are very significant. Another note: it takes 1 gallon of water to counter the negative and harmful effects on the body that is produced by just drinking a 12-ounce glass of coffee.

The body is a complex bundled mass of energy that can *easily* be altered either toward enhanced health and healing or toward disease and self-destruction. This energy has both a positively charged side and a negatively charged one. Each side of the body contains its own energy field – either positive or negative. One field cannot exist without the other, though one side may be stronger than the other in an unbalanced or improper functioning body.

ENERGY, FREQUENCY AND BOWEN

Because Bowen addresses the body on energetic levels by stimulating energetic activity and increasing blood circulation in the body, it is widely known to be paramount in quickly reviving and restoring health. For example, a person who just raises their head to look up, thereby straightening their spine, significantly increases circulation throughout their entire body. This single physiological change begins a large scale chain reaction to occur throughout the entire body. The chain reactions which take place in the body also cause changes in emotional and mental states as well.

Children who seem inconsolable, whose posture slumps with their head down, will immediately look up when someone snaps their fingers above their head. Lifting their head causes increased blood flow to the brain when they straighten up. The diaphragm and chest cavity opens and breathing becomes much easier. This brings more oxygen to the body and brain.

This slight change in lung capacity and increased oxygen releases muscle tension and causes neuro-chemical changes to occur. These neuro-chemical changes, which occur throughout the entire body, play a huge role in immediately changing the child's disposition while beginning to restore balance in the body and the brain, and make the child easier to work and reason with. All this is due to increased circulation, which consequently increases the body's frequency as a whole putting the body back on the path to re-establish its normal frequency. Systematically this contributes to greatly improved health.

Stimulating circulation and body activity also stimulates neuropathic flows to the ends of the nerve pathways. Increased signal strength helps transmission across synaptic gaps (or gaps between nerve endings – especially in the brain). Increased firing of the synapses produces a cleaner and much better connection. This increase in firing strength causes thousands of minute recalibrations throughout the entire body on the neuropathic level. It also eventually leads to other changes in the organ functions which ultimately affect chemical balance.

Increasing the health of a just few cells may seem insignificant; however, these minor changes stimulate similar changes in other cells in that region. These changes trigger signals to other regions of the body to do the same, increasing the health of yet other cells, while simultaneously increasing overall health.

The first Bowen Move performed in the lower back region opens up the negative energy field of the body and allows it to flow. The second Move opens the positive energy field. These first two Moves, as we've already seen, are the "master keys" which begin to re-ignite the positive and negative energy flows. At the same time, these two Moves divide the body's energy into two portions, the lower portion, which is below the hips, and the upper portion, above the hips.

These first two Moves also act as a kind of temporary energy blockers, called "stoppers," that last approximately 10-15 minutes. These Moves have a way of blocking the body's energy from flowing past the mid-point of the body. By "putting in the stoppers," the energy becomes temporarily contained between the waist and the bottom of the feet--and the waist and the top of the head. The distance between the "stopper" point at the waist and the bottom of the feet is then a much shorter distance than that between the bottom of the feet and the top of the head. Within this confined area, Bowen Moves are performed in a specific sequence. Bowen Moves then performed in this "contained area" effectively shortens the distance that energy has to travel, therefore decreasing wave length. This shortened wavelength increases the frequency. The same occurs when Bowen addresses the upper portion of the body. During the course of a Bowen treatment, the upper portion of the body is divided in two by the use of a double set of "stoppers". This double set (located next to the spine intersecting a point located near the bottom of the shoulder blades) divides the body's upper and mid portions.

From this mid-body starting point downward, the practitioner performs a series of Moves. These Moves stimulate both the Central and Autonomic Nervous Systems and at the same time re-establishes vital communication links within the body. These links increase communication, beginning in the lower portion of the body. They focus the magnified energy to the area in and around the sacrum and coccyx. This magnified energy opens the primary energy center of the body that surrounds the sacral region.

This energy center is called the primary or base energy center, or base "chakra." It controls the body's primal survival functions. When energy is blocked in this energy center, the body will automatically go into survival mode and will remain in that state until it is opened. Blockages or confinement of energy to this area often lowers body frequency.

Bowen Moves naturally penetrate the blockage, increasing and magnifying the available energy in this area and often quickly release the blockage. Magnifying and releasing energy in this area is often felt as heat or a tingling sensation that begins in the sacral or lower back region. After some time, usually 10 –15 minutes, many people feel energy radiate throughout their body. This is one explanation of how one or two Bowen Moves can affect the entire body and create subtle changes.

Injury to the sacrum and tailbone (coccyx), no matter how insignificant, often leads to a myriad of health difficulties many years later. When the region surrounding the coccyx is subjected to severe physical stress, fracture, trauma or injury (both major and minor) it can create tremendous long-lasting consequences.

These consequences include infertility, female problems, adult incontinence, bedwetting, colon disorders, severe sinus problems, recurring ear infection, Irritable Bowel Syndrome (IBS), stomach and gastrointestinal digestive tract disorders, migraines, Attention Deficit Disorders (ADD) or Attention Deficit Hyper Disorder (ADHD).

Circumstances that create these consequences in the coccyx area include giving birth, being spanked, being in an auto or motorcycle accident, vaccinations in the buttock, a fall or jump from considerable heights, having a chair pulled out from under you, a fall down a flight of stairs, a bicycle crash and many others.

In many coccyx region injuries, the muscles surrounding the coccyx go into spasm, causing coccyx misalignment where it is torqued to the left or right, or tucked under, like a dog with its tail between its legs, This severely blocks or alters the energy flow, scrambling it throughout the body.

Energy flows through the body from the top of the head and is removed from the body through the coccyx, cleansing the body's energy, and as it flows it removes any stuck, negative, or non-beneficial energy. The neuro-pathways (nerves) and energy meridians in the body serve as conduits for the energy to flow. Tapping into and releasing these neurological release points naturally increases and restores the strength of a person's energy. The coccyx grounds excessive, interfering, or outside energies. The coccyx also acts as the main energy circuit breaker and when it is not working properly, or turned off so to speak, it greatly affects the body.

When the energy is blocked, it is re-run back into the body on an altered course. This excess ungrounded energy has to be removed somehow.

Individuals who are not properly grounded frequently do things to excess. This includes talking too much, moving incessantly, mood swings, chemical imbalances, inability to focus, lack of mental clarity or brain-fog, ADD, ADHD, tendencies to disrupt meetings, school classes, or family time, and a myriad of other similar behavior

A Bowen Practitioner never attempts to physically move the coccyx. A practitioner merely addresses the muscle spasm or tension adjacent to the coccyx by performing a very light Move over the skin and tissue above the coccyx. The practitioner may also activate muscles adjacent to the coccyx by performing a Move next to the coccyx. This coccyx Move commonly restores the proper energetic and neuropathic flows, quickly and gently re-stabilizing the body and mind.

Children and adults with the above disorders often show significant improvement after Bowen sessions that include a coccyx procedure. Infertility in men *and* women is commonly reversed using a specific protocol that includes addressing the coccyx and coccyx regions. Also people with chemical and hormonal imbalance often recover through the use of this same procedure.

HARMONICS AND VIBRATION

Sound and vibration are forms of energy. The relationship of harmonics, resonance, music, and sound to health has been known for thousands of years. Many cultures teach this and also stress the effect harmonics has on the healing of the body, mind, and spirit.

Pythagoras set up an entire school to instruct healers about harmonic healing. Pythagoras was so skilled in knowing the effects of specific frequencies, that it is said that during a match where one man was going to kill another, Pythagoras played a single note at the height of the attempt. Upon hearing this note, the man immediately began to sob deeply and walked away.

Studies of sound and resonance indicate that specific frequencies affect particular parts of the body. Some frequencies stimulate healing, others cause the destruction of cells.

Tendons attach muscle to bone and ligaments attach a bone to another bone, resembling a stringed instrument. Applying the proper pressure on a string instrument (strumming) in the correct location causes the string to vibrate at a particular frequency. If we change the location and strum again we hear a different tone. Skilled musicians who know the exact location of the holding points are sensitive to even a small deviation.

Precise finger placement by a skilled musician on a stringed instrument is crucial in playing the correct note. Likewise, skilled Bowen practitioners must first find the exact location before performing a Move. This Move requires the correct pressure, tempo, and fluidity to create the desired effect.

The body, like a stringed musical instrument occasionally requires fine-tuning to assure superior sound performance.

Visualize several cellos in the corners of a room. Intentionally plucking one string on one instrument causes a vibration to radiate throughout the entire room. Although the other cellos in the room are not connected or near each other, they resonate the exact same note at a much softer level. Taken together they increase the sound (energy) in the room slightly. If you adjust the precise frequency of the room acoustics and played that specific note on one of the cellos, the entire room would come alive with sound.

Bowen has the same effect on the entire body when we find the correct "note" for a particular body. It has a tendency to make sweeping changes throughout the entire body.

Each muscle, tendon, ligament, nerve, system, gland, and organ in the body also has its own frequencies that are matched or "attuned". A Bowen Move performed on or over a specific muscle, tendon, ligament, or nerve projects its own frequency much like the string on the cello. The resonation then radiates between the stoppers and activates the portions of systems, organs, or other tissue that resonate at the same frequency.

Activation magnifies the strength of the signal. After awhile, the signal becomes strong enough to exceed the containment of the "stoppers" and radiates throughout the entire body activating other bodily components with this frequency.

Walking up to a cello in the corner of a room, and placing your ear on it may startle you as you hear the many sounds that continually resonate through it. Even though no one is playing it, the cello still gathers sounds, in a wide rang of frequencies from outside sources.

This solitary cello quietly sitting in a corner automatically picks up sounds of cars driving by, a ticking clock, and television sounds from another room. If you take a finger and moderately strum a string you will hear a variety of resonance levels within the frequency of the note played. At some point, the resonance will be at its perfect pitch. The level of the note will be comparatively louder at that exact moment. It lasts for a while, and then diminishes. The time the sound takes to die out is determined by the condition of the instrument and the strength of the note played.

Like a single stringed instrument played by a single musician, one highly skilled Bowen practitioner can cause an entire orchestra to play within the body as he or she performs various Moves. Performing a series of Bowen Procedures throughout the body can be likened to an orchestra playing, each instrument with its own distinctly unique sound--at different volumes at different times.

Working together the instruments in an orchestra play their parts to create a complete composition. An orchestra warming up, on the other hand, where all instruments play at the same time prior to a concert, sounds like complete chaos. This chaos is one of the things that can happen in the body if too much Bowen is performed during one treatment. Over-treatment has a tendency to erase some of the work already performed. .

There is a major difference between playing a single note well on an instrument and playing the whole instrument range well. Likewise, there is a huge difference between playing an entire instrument well and being a master musical artist on that instrument. It is the same for Bowen.

The body is either at-tension (attention), being focused on protecting the body, or it is relaxed and at-ease.

Chapter 8

Bowen Session Basics

Bowen is designed to be gentle and subtle, though strongly persuasive. Those who receive Bowen often feel their body involuntarily shifting or moving around slightly as tension begins to release and the energy of the body begins to open and flow and find its proper path again. Often they laugh, sigh, yawn, and in most cases, drop off into a very deep state of relaxation, while healing takes place from within.

Bowen works best as a stand-alone therapy. Meaning it is to be used alone without the use or interference of any other kind of therapy or treatment during at least the initial 5 sessions. These excluded therapies include acupressure, acupuncture, chiropractic, physical or physiotherapy, massage, reflexology, shiatsu, or any other kind of physical manipulation that is more forceful or invasive than Bowen. Anything more invasive than the gentle touch of Bowen is not to be used. Bowen makes changes in the body on a core level. The body needs time to respond, make changes, and complete healing from the inside out, without influence from outside sources.

Note: Bowen Practitioners, unless they are medically qualified, do not suggest or recommend that someone refrain from medical or other assistance they may need. We do, however, suggest that the individual do what they think is best for their body. For any medication-related questions, people are asked to consult with their pharmacist and/or primary care physician.

Repeated activation of the healing response and healing cycles using Bowen Moves over the course of a few sessions has a great tendency to increase the potency and influence of the healing mechanisms of the body, while also strengthening them at the same time. Bowen Moves or Procedures performed during subsequent sessions reinforces the information the body received during previous sessions, and at the same time, begins to address other issues the body is now up to handling. Most people, as previously mentioned, require an initial 3-5 sessions, spaced at 5-10 day intervals, 7 days being optimal.

Continuing this course of 3-5 sessions over the space of 3-5 weeks adds tremendously to the healing abilities of the body. These additional sessions help to widen the gap between prior health issues and optimal health by giving the body the information it needs, as well as the time to receive it. These sessions also expand on having the body work in its most optimal manner, advancing its reorganization and streamlining its functions allowing them more ease.

After performing a Move or series of specific Moves on an individual, the Practitioner incorporates a compulsory pause or break, which is very essential for Bowen to work properly. During the pause or "cooking time," the practitioner refrains from touching the body or performing any other Moves. They step away from the individual, preferably out of the room, for at least two minutes (longer for some very specific procedures) to allow *the body* to:

1. Receive the message sent
2. Begin to put the body and mind in a restful state
3. Allow the body both the time and space to heal from the inside out
4. Assist the body in releasing the effects of injuries or traumas

It is in the state of "cooking," as already explained, where the healing begins. Each Bowen Move causes multiple interactions to take place within the body and requires time for the brain to assimilate and decipher the information before it can allow changes to occur. During rest, the body simply begins to readjust and make the needed changes for optimal function and performance. Rest, not sleep, is the true pre-requisite for healing the body and mind.

Generally the initial treatment may take approx 30 – 60 minutes. In more complex cases, where the session needs to be very straightforward and specific, the session may just be 15 minutes or less. These shorter sessions that address the body more directly for very specific concerns are most common after the second or third session.

For 3-5 days following a session, the body will continue to unwind, untorque and change, as though it received a session. In most cases, when the Bowen session is over, is actually when Bowen begins its best work. Because of this, some of the greatest healing and health restoration take place during this period *after* the session.

Many who receive Bowen share experiences of dramatic and profound changes that occur 3, 4 or even 5 days after a session. It is very common for an individual to initially come in with a long list of ailments and conditions, sometimes 3-4 pages long, and very regularly 50% of their list will disappear within 7 days after their first Bowen session. For the maximum healing to begin to take place in the body, it is highly recommended those who receive Bowen complete the initial 3-5 sessions.

Because Bowen is so simple, a long drawn-out medical history including current medications the person is taking isn't really needed. Although knowledge of past physical, mental, and emotional traumas proves helpful, what is most important is what is happening with the person today. To Practitioners who understand how Bowen works, time is better invested performing Bowen on the individual than long drawn-out stories and histories of what used to be. The way that Bowen works with the body, the body will always give the accurate information as to what is really taking place in the body that is relevant to the session.

ASSESSMENT

Bowen uses simple, straightforward, and easy-to-observe assessment techniques that give an instant and accurate account of where the body is and what it needs. More experienced Practitioners can do a simple full-body assessment prior to performing a session on an individual, by asking questions and keenly observing their overall posture, facial tension, expression, body movement, breathing and body language. Most sessions also use short, simple, specific assessments throughout the session to assess whether the individual may need a particular procedure. Most of the time, assessments are being made through the feedback given by the body as the Practitioner performs Bowen directly on the person.

BASIC SESSION

In a Bowen session Practitioners may slightly vary in their approach, partly based on their understanding of the work and/or their prior profession or training. Some of the common elements include:

- The session is almost always performed on a twin size bed or massage-type table. It *can* be performed nearly anywhere and in any position that is comfortable for the recipient

- The work is usually performed through loose-fitting clothing after belts, wallets and pocket items are removed. It is not necessary to remove jewelry, although many people do remove it. If tight-fitting clothing is worn by the recipient in an area that needs to be addressed, the Practitioner will often have the person change into something more suitable, or cover the table with draping sheets, then ask the person to dress down, leaving underclothes on, and then slip between the sheets for the session. This may be necessary especially when direct skin contact is needed to perform a Procedure correctly, which is uncommon but sometimes necessary.

- After some form of interview and assessment to more fully understand what the needs of the individual are, the practitioner will have the person lie down, usually prone (face-down), in a position that is comfortable for them. The Practitioner will then begin to perform classic "Bowen Moves" across a few muscles and tendons, classically beginning with the Lower Back Procedure.

- At certain points during the session, the Practitioner will stop and leave the person to relax for a couple of minutes or so. The Practitioner actually leaving the room for short periods *is part of the session,* so those receiving Bowen for the first time should not be alarmed The person may begin to feel their body change around or they may become drowsy during the first two or three "rest periods" and begin to fall asleep. This is perfectly normal and natural. Dropping off into a restful state is indicative of the release of accumulated tension.

- The session usually begins in the waist or hip area and progresses down the legs, then up the back to the shoulders and neck, then to the mid-back region of the body before having the person turn supine (face up). If only the mid-region or the upper portion of the body is to be addressed during the session, the lower portion of the body may not be addressed at all.

- After the person has turned onto their back, a few more Moves may be performed to address other areas of the body or to access a different angle on sections that were already addressed. After completion of the session on the table, the person will be asked to sit up. After a few moments, another set of Moves may be performed to complete the session. The person will then be asked to step down with their weight distributed evenly on both feet. This begins to set the work and begins reprogramming symmetry back into weight-bearing structures. As the session completes, the person is reminded of the post-session protocols of drinking lots of water, walking every day, no hot or cold baths, etc., and the Practitioner advises when the optimum time for a return visit would be, according to the changes in the body from the first session and the Practitioner's observations of how the person's body has taken the first session.

• The Practitioner custom-designs the Bowen session for each individual. Those Practitioners who have developed skills of awareness of what is happening in the body often have a greater ability to observe what the body is telling them, which can also reduce the number of sessions that a person may need. A beginning student or beginning Practitioner more often than not has a very high rate of success if Moves are performed as taught.

During any session, the body provides tell-tale signs as to what is happening. A few of these signs include; the body heating up or becoming cold, producing mid- to high-range temperature variances that can be noticeably felt, the proverbial involuntary shifting or twitching of muscles, changes in skin color, tingling throughout the musculature, palms, or soles of the feet is common. Rarely, a sense of nausea, sweating, or feeling cold may occur during a session. Commonly these signs begin to occur right before the recipient of the session drops into a very deep meditative state of rest. These very distinct and unique clues offer the Practitioner a front row seat into what state the body is in, what it needs to enable itself to heal, how the body is responding, and when the session is over as well. When these or other remarkable changes occur, the Practitioner will begin to check for what is called "Flux." "Flux" is a state or condition that indicates the body is on the verge of becoming over-stimulated. Flux is a clear sign that the body has had enough for the day.

INTERMEDIATE LEVEL SESSION

An intermediate level Bowen session usually begins on the second visit after the body has been initially opened by the BRM's performed on the first visit. In nearly every case, the practitioner can straightforwardly note changes that have taken place in the body since the last session, and begin to see where they are to start for the session. Most times, the Practitioner will ask how the person is feeling, what came up for them the past week, and if anything did, they will usually ask how they felt during the changes and how long it lasted. These are also clues to where the body is and what may need to be addressed in the session in order to more specifically address the body in a particular area or region. Infrequently clients may return for their second visit and comment that they have not felt, seen, or noticed any changes,\; however, because they are in their body constantly, they may not feel or even notice the change that took place because it was so subtle over a period of time. The practitioner can, nearly always, observe changes that have clearly transpired since that prior week.

An intermediate session can and may again include the BRM's either singularly or as a whole, with the appropriate waiting times, or the session may just include the minimal BRM requirements to open and set up the body for other particular Procedures later in the session. If the session only includes one or two Procedures, it is important to understand that this fine-tuned session is being designed to directly affect a very specific region, condition, or pain. In this case, the session will be structured in order to focus *all* of the body's energies and resources toward a specific pain or health issue. Most practitioners find that the greatest physical changes commonly occur between the second and fourth visits, and deeper level changes after that.

ADVANCED LEVEL SESSION

Practitioners rely on *the body* to tell them where it is and what it needs. It is not necessarily what the recipient "liked last session," what worked last session or a couple of sessions ago, what worked "last year," or a specific Procedure a person "enjoys receiving."

During an advanced session, it is usually the opposite of what most people think. Most people think that because the session will include "Advanced Procedures," that more work will be performed. Actually it will be the opposite. Remember, "less is best" with Bowen, so less may actually be performed.

An advanced session will very specifically address only one issue that is usually "hanging on" or one that hasn't been eliminated yet. The great thing about an advanced session is that although very little work is performed, HUGE and extensive changes throughout the entire body and mind are commonly the result. Receiving an advanced session is usually a rare occasion because generally the basic and intermediate procedures do the job just fine to eliminate what was there. The advanced work is not very common and is a *very* precise set of one or two Moves that directly address a very specific ailment or pain that basic or intermediate Procedures did not handle. Many advanced Procedures include longer "waiting times."

Occasionally, those who receive advanced work comment, "You only did one or two things. Is the charge still the same?" to which I ask, "If your automobile was not functioning properly and you drove it to a mechanic who only took 15 minutes to change a simple fan belt and got you back on the road again, would you question what the mechanic did or what it cost?

Of course the answer is no. The problem was fixed, you are back on the road again swiftly, and it did not take much time at all. In this case, the mechanic took care of a problem that needed attention and did what was necessary to bring the car back into good working order. An experienced and competent mechanic will also quickly yet carefully check other areas of the vehicle, using both sight and sound to further inspect other needs the vehicle may have. The mechanic may suggest coming in at a future date for further repair or preventative maintenance.

Bowen Practitioners apply similar work practices. They do not need to perform five or ten procedures on the body, when just one or two will do to address what is going on. He or she commonly performs advanced procedures singly, only after the initial BRM and intermediate work have been completed on previous visits. Advanced work addresses deeper or more chronic conditions that still exist, but only after the proper groundwork was properly laid. Advanced work is capable of producing unheard of results almost instantaneously in as little as one to two minutes in nearly every case.

The application of an advanced coccyx procedure, for example, often works in the same manner as rebooting a computer, which resets the whole machine, top to bottom.

NON-RESPONSE TO BOWEN

Bowen can be counted on like clockwork to dependably reset the body, help restore it back to optimal health and successfully remove pain. However, if the expected results are not achieved after a few sessions, the Practitioner will review the Procedures used, and question the individual to determine if unsatisfactory results have occurred because the person receiving Bowen has been doing something that continues an uncooperative patterning or cycle. Uncooperative or negative patterning includes; incorrect posture, badly worn-down shoes, heel lifts, the application of heat and/or ice after a session, lifting very heavy objects, lifting and twisting, the use of magnets on the body, over-training while exercising, ergonomically incorrect seating and/or arm and hand positioning, the habitual crossing of the legs, or a myriad of other concerns.

Practitioners look to see if there is something occurring which is impeding normal progress of Bowen sessions. An example of this is individuals with Repetitive Stress Injury or Carpal Tunnel Syndrome continue typing 18,000-30,000 bits of information per hour into a computer, eight hours a day and who have no desire to change jobs. In such a case as this, the body was not designed for such excessive abuse. In other rare cases, the person doesn't want to get well, because the illness or injury satisfies some deep need.

Psychotropic medication or drugs also interfere with Bowen, because the synapses in the brain do not work properly because of the chemicals used in the medication are so strong they significantly alter brain function.

In some rare cases, there is something happening either in the body or in the brain that inhibits the workings within the body to such a degree that even Bowen is prohibited from working. In other rare cases there is something physically awry which needs to be addressed using surgery or other means.

A Bowen Practitioner will always give their best shot at it. I have seen a handful of cases where Bowen began working, and it did for a while, then it just stopped working. A few months later, usually within the 3 – 9 month range, the person either called or came in to report that, even though they stopped having Bowen sessions some months ago, they still felt something was changing very slowly. And then one day they woke up and the pain or ailment was simply gone. In these few cases, the persons also reported that they did not seek out or do any other treatment because as far as they were concerned they had done everything else prior to Bowen, and Bowen was their "last resort."

REMOVING THE LAYERS

Bowen peels off layers of pain and disorders, like the layers of an onion. This sometimes occurs days after a session, as the body sorts itself out in order to restore and heal areas which have needed help for quite some time. Occasionally, as the layers begin to be removed and releasing of prolonged pain and tension begins, it unveils other aches and discomfort that were masked by increased pain tolerance. Another way discomfort can increase is from releasing overused muscles that have been compensating for pre-Bowen long-term misalignment. When other aches and discomfort unveil themselves, it is clearly a sign of progress.

In most cases when this occurs, the person is able to more specifically pin-point areas and relates them to prior injuries or traumas. Bowen Practitioners love it when that happens, because the conditions that are surfacing are the body's ways of saying, in essence, "fix me next." The Practitioner can then directly address those areas, addressing older issues that have been set in for decades, in many cases. By addressing these old issues, the body on its own reverses and eliminates old patterns, one by one, until the core issue(s) which started the initial condition or pain/spasm cycle surfaces.

POST-SESSION WORDS OF WISDOM

Post Bowen session protocol primarily consists of drinking plenty of water and physically moving for a couple of minutes every half an hour for the remainder of the day after a session, or until the person has a chance to go to sleep. Keeping the body in motion enhances the session by maintaining and sustaining muscle flexibility which helps move toxins that may be stirred up in the body, while helping the body to realign and supporting continued muscle re-tensioning. Movement also helps the body so it doesn't stay in one position, getting the body to think that a specific position is going to be the norm. After a Bowen session, the body is actually in a neutral position and it has to reset its positioning. Without movement, the muscles can tighten and not fully provide the body its fullest result. The muscles need to move occasionally, while the body rebalances and resets.

After a Bowen session, it is best to drink at least around two quarts/liters of water a day for the next few days. The elimination of coffee from the normal daily routine also helps immensely as well. Additionally, it is advised that the person refrain from alcohol consumption for approximately a 24-hour-period following a session, when the body is very open and highly responsive. We have found that those who consume alcohol after a session need very little to greatly affect them.

Because Bowen is notorious for initiating the detoxification processes in the body while it begins to self-correct its problems, and dormant toxins which have built-up in the body may begin to release. This is truly a vital occurrence, as the detoxification activates cleansing processes in the kidney, liver and gallbladder. The movement and subsequent removal of toxins from the body can bring about some discomforts in the body. What is best is to drink a lot of water, if this happens, and go for a 20 minute walk or do some gentle exercise to get and keep the toxins moving, and it is nothing to worry about. If you have any questions about what is happening with your body after a session, call your Bowen Practitioner and they can help you understand what is happening.

After a Bowen session, rest is best. By rest, I don't mean staying home from work and catching up on the yard work, gardening, cleaning and organizing the house or garage, but actual *rest*. Refraining from hot or cold baths, hot or cold showers, whirlpools, hot packs, heating pads, cold packs, ice treatments, or any kind of magnetic apparatus (i.e. insoles, wrist or body bands, mattresses, pillows, or beds) is also advisable. Warm baths or showers are recommended. In other words, take good care of yourself.

Chapter 9

The Bowen Practitioner

The challenge for the Practitioner is not in just learning the Moves, but consists of much more than that. Learning to skillfully and accurately read the body, knowing and understanding how and where to perform each specific Move, knowing when to use a particular procedure to create the desired result (and when not to use it), how much is the exact amount of pressure to use on a person for that day, in each specific location on the body, and the speed of the Move are just some of what a Practitioner needs to know to be successful. Beside these, honing communication and people skills are also necessary abilities, in order to be able to relate to people who are in pain and ill health.

The role of the Practitioner in Bowen is straightforward. To perfect the Practitioner's skills requires many hundreds, even thousands of hours of combined study and practice, together with performing Bowen on many people who present a wide range of conditions and disorders. Even then, skillful Bowen Practitioners are constantly refining their skills and techniques, expanding their knowledge of how the body works, and how Bowen works with the body, as well as how the body responds to specific Procedures. In-depth experience and continuing education separates the professional Bowen Practitioner from the part-time one who just occasionally works with someone. Learning Bowen is only the beginning. The practitioner must increase their proficiency level through study, practice, and examinations long after they complete the core Bowen curriculum.

Practitioners agree that the true learning of Bowen begins after they pass the final accreditation examination. Many Bowen professionals find that it takes many years of experience to obtain an in-depth idea of how Bowen really works. It also takes hours of seminar attendance, study, and ultra-fine tuning of skills to discover how Bowen truly affects the body's healing mechanisms in such a profound way. With Bowen, addressing health issues of others is simpler than most other healthcare professions, primarily because the body does most of the work thereby removing much of the mental and physical stress associated with a normal healthcare practice. A well-trained and experienced Practitioner can easily be performing Bowen on 4-6 people at a time, while being fully able to take very good care of each of them.

**Do the correct procedure for what the body presents,
and that's all, and the body *will* respond favorably.**

~ Ossie Rentsch ~

It is important for a Bowen Practitioner to:

1. Master knowledge of the body
2. Use the proper technique, accurate locations, pressure and speed
3. Properly apply Bowen on the body in a manner which can begin to effectively engage all levels, systems and organs
4. Know what to look for
5. Know how to properly communicate with the person receiving Bowen, so the recipient is able to understand what is occurring in their body
6. Tune in and listen to the body, letting *it* be the guide, especially in specific, rare, or non-response cases
7. Do "less is best"
8. Know when to stop the session
9. Know when to refer

> The practitioner is not God, although God is in and guiding the practitioner.

Healing actually begins when the Practitioner initially meets the person who comes for a session *and* accepts the person's overall condition on all levels. Starting out on this common ground assists both the Practitioner and recipient to begin at the same point. This accelerates the healing process. Remember, the Practitioner is only a facilitator.

Both the novice and experienced Bowen professional have the ability to achieve the same end results using Bowen (in most cases). A student of the work or newly accredited Practitioner, though not as highly skilled or experienced in the application of Bowen may, because of the focus and intent, achieve marvelous results.

Bowen can be performed using the "grenade approach," meaning the work is performed close to, but not quite on, the specific location on the person's body, when the Moves are performed well but not perfect. The results of the grenade approach work primarily in a mechanical fashion on the body. Mechanically addressing just the physical aspect of the body leaves the mental and emotional aspect relatively untouched. More experienced Practitioners do the best work when they use what I call "the laser approach." They perform the correct procedure in the precise location for that person's body. They can intuitively address the problem using the least number of procedures to obtain the desired result.

The accuracy of the location where the Move is applied, combined with the proper application of the Move, significantly magnifies the results and elevates the level and rate at which you release the energy of the body and mind. Using this laser-like Bowen approach, the body rapidly peels off layers of signs, symptoms, conditions and disorders and increases the healing capacity at a much deeper level.

Bowen is truly an art form. The art comes from learning when and how to do enough to *heal*, but not enough to *overload* the body. Too much Bowen negates the work that has already been done. The right amount of work with the right amount of pressure using the correct procedure(s) produces the correct response. That is the art.

For example, coaching is an art in and of itself. The coach of an athletic team knows what to look for and what to do to assist an athlete to reach his or her optimum potential, individually, to help them bring the best to the team. The Bowen Practitioner can do much the same to assist health and healing. He or she just coaches the body along – the messages tell the body what to do. It is up to the athlete or the body to respond to the coaching. It is not up to the coach to perform; though it is the coach or practitioner's responsibility to discover what works best. The key is to communicate the message directly and with clarity.

When the correct Procedure is chosen by the Practitioner to address what is taking place in the body and the Moves are performed on the body in the proper manner, the brain receives the crystal-clear information very directly and it rapidly initiates a reflexive healing response. However, when the correct Procedure is chosen by the Practitioner and the Moves are performed gently yet improperly (not precisely and crisply) the brain receives only partial information which it is not clear or powerful. In these cases, a reflexive healing response is initiated, though it is not as effective as it could be. However, in these cases, the body <u>does</u> respond anyway, although not as comprehensively. In subsequent sessions, if the body is addressed in the same way, using the same Procedures, more often than not the body, will in the end, fully respond, though it may take it a little while longer for it to get there. This is one of the reasons why Bowen can be so effective, even for beginning students.

If the correct Procedure is chosen and the Moves are performed too hard and/or too fast, the body still has the ability to favorably respond to some degree, because <u>some</u> of the information that was given, is usable. In these cases, the brain has to sift through and sort what is offensive to the body and what is useable. This can undoubtedly interfere with the healing mechanisms to some degree, I believe, because although the brain and body are given the correct information, the input is too strong or harsh and it causes the body to first go "on the defensive." The strength of the correct information that is given is disproportional to the level of reactive defense the body naturally and automatically will go into to, to first protect itself.

If the Procedure chosen by the Practitioner is not the correct one <u>that the body</u> <u>needs</u> to address the specific condition or pain on its own, it will usually produce very minimal, if any, results and in most cases the condition or pain will simply not begin to correct itself. On the same note, the body <u>will</u>, however, use whatever it *can* use of the Procedure that *was* performed, to address multiple other issues that are present in the body that also need to be addressed. In this case, the Practitioner must re-evaluate and re-assess what the body is calling for to see what *it* needs to properly address the initial condition or pain. After re-evaluation and re-assessment, another Procedure may be chosen and performed. However, this may not be true in every case. Sometimes after the re-assessment, the Practitioner is certain that the correct Procedure was chosen and the body just needs time to make changes and respond.

RECEIVING BOWEN

The age, condition, and overall health of the individual must be taken into consideration, to a degree, when Bowen is performed. Because Bowen, when performed properly, cannot harm someone, a newly-born-baby, the aged, and the feeble and infirm can be successfully worked with good results. A Practitioner can perform Bowen on a growing child and an athlete in training more intensively, using Bowen Advanced Procedures, because their bodies are in better shape and they have a large tendency to respond extremely well. In nearly every case, the growing child and conditioned athlete need fewer sessions. Athletes are like fine-tuned machines, they often obtain greater and faster results than the average adult.

As far as athletics are concerned, Bowen is actually "the athlete's secret and trainer's dream." It is the athlete's secret because it naturally enhances performance, stamina and focus. It is a trainer's dream because it can *very* quickly help put an athlete back in the game with amazing results. One Practitioner on a training staff can greatly enhance the efficiency of an athletic training department. Athletic medical staff and trainers who have witnessed the wonders of Bowen for their athletes, truly swear by it. They often invite competent and experienced Bowen Practitioners to assist them in the care of their athletes because it makes their job much, much easier.

> In most cases, 92 - 95% of the time, when an athlete is injured and they receive a Bowen "quick fix," they can return back to their sport, game or event in as little as two to five minutes, at 80 – 100%! What is THAT worth to *any* professional, Olympic, or collegiate team?

Bowen has been very successfully used to naturally enhance the performance of athletes to a <u>great</u> extent. After receiving Bowen, performed in a *very* specific way that gets the body to "let go," while stimulating it at the same time, many Olympic hopefuls and top collegiate and high school athletes have *by far* out-performed their personal best, ever. It doesn't matter what sport the athlete is in: track and field, bi-athlete, tri-athlete, marathon and ultra-marathon, football, golf, baseball, basketball, fencing, wrestling, rugby, rowing, swimming, tennis, cycling, motocross, skateboarding, snow and water skiing/boarding, etc., all who have received Bowen very quickly recognize Bowen's ability to enhance their performance and increase their focus and energy level as well. Athletes who receive Bowen from "sports specific" trained Practitioners respond VERY well. There is a very specific protocol that must be adhered to in order for an athlete to perform at their peak.

Regularly-trained Bowen Practitioners *have not* been specifically trained for sports. Many years of personal experience performing Bowen on top athletes has proven that, performing Bowen in the normal "relaxing manner" on athletes prior to or during a game or event is usually unfavorable, as it makes them want to just sit on the sidelines and relax. Performing "regular Bowen" on athletes during any time *other* than "game time" works very well, if performed with the correct timing (referring to a certain number of days prior to a game or event).

Athletes respond <u>very</u> quickly to Bowen and for them "quick fixes" work very well, especially right before, or during a game or event. A quick fix is a very short session that quickly addresses only one or two primary concerns, and in many cases the athlete can remain standing or can sit in a chair. A quick fix generally only takes only 30 seconds to 2 minutes, so the athlete can be back in the game, in or very near top form, in almost no time! In most cases, 92 - 95% of the time, when an athlete is injured and they receive a Bowen quick fix, they can return back to their sport, game or event in as little as two to five minutes, at 80 – 100%!   What is THAT worth to *any* professional, Olympic, or collegiate team?

Athletic trainers find that Bowen is extraordinarily effective in quickly handling sprains, strains, muscle pulls, and muscle soreness or tension due to injury or overwork. They have also found that Bowen also greatly reduces vulnerability to injury while accelerates healing time. This, of course, is as long as there is no muscle tear, fracture, or laceration. In most cases, if an athlete moderately sprains an ankle or strains a muscle, they can immediately be addressed and returned to their event with little or no pain, swelling, or discomfort, *at all!*

What is best, is for an athlete to first receive a complete session or two prior to game time, in order to open and address the entire body. However, because they are in such great condition, in most cases quick fixes will work extremely well for them even if there is not time for them to receive a complete session, although the quick fix may not fully "hold" for a long period of time.

Many athletes who have suffered from past injuries that have "hung on for a long time and never seemed to go away," have received a couple of sessions and the long-term effects of pain and stiffness simply disappeared.

Nearly every athlete who has received Bowen finds that:

- Their state of mind and ability to focus is greatly enhanced

- They receive immediate decrease or total elimination of pain after injury

- They notice a huge increase in strength, ease, and fluidity of motion

- They experience significantly enhanced and sustained athletic performance

Coaches who have witnessed the affects of Bowen on their athletes *know* that it gives them a huge competitive edge. Coaches who know about Bowen really encourage their athletes to receive regular sessions to keep them in optimal condition.

"Bowen is a true relief from pain. Healing without surgery is very important to athletes. Bowen has greatly benefited our athletes in the Sacramento State University Football program."

> **~ John Volek ~**
> **Former Head Football Coach, Sacramento State University**

AGE

The age of a person who is receiving Bowen is basically irrelevant, as age does not seem to interfere whatsoever in achieving the desired results. Age does not seem have any particular reflection or play any part on the number of sessions a person may need, except in cases of infants or children, who tend to respond and heal *much* faster and who require much less work to be performed on them to attain the desired results. For example, a newborn 1 ½ days old normally does not require a full BRM session, nor do they need the normal two-minute waiting times between Procedures.   The reason is that the infant's energy level is so high and their body is in such a hyper state of change and transition that just the mere momentary interruption of the energy flow in their body is enough to make a significant difference in the brain/body response. Although a more complete session can be given to adolescents, the same is generally true that they require much less work up to the age of puberty, when significant changes take place in the body so that it responds more like an adult-aged body.

Elderly and semi-immobile individuals vary in the number of sessions they may need, primarily depending on the overall health and condition of their body. In most cases, they will require Bowen to be performed with a lesser amount of pressure, or their bodies may no longer respond as quickly to healing and so a few more Bowen sessions can be required to produce the results Bowen makes available for them. However, I have seen individuals close to 100 years old respond as well, if not better than most middle-aged persons, and I have also seen those who are nearing the century mark require a few more sessions than normal as well. In general, the muscle tone is less in more mature adults. The skin and muscle tissue of these individuals may be sensitive to the touch, so it is best for Bowen Practitioners to treat them with "kid gloves."

EXPECTANT MOTHERS, BABIES, AND CHILDREN

One of the greatest gifts that can be given an expectant mother is a series of Bowen sessions throughout the pregnancy and most assuredly right after the birth of a child.   Expectant mothers who regularly receive Bowen sessions during this highly shifting time in their body can often handle the pregnancy *and* the birthing process more calmly with much greater ease and less discomfort.   Because a woman's body is changing so rapidly during pregnancy and especially near the time of delivery, she will need to receive Bowen, initially once a week for the first 3 – 5 visits, and then as needed after that. The closer to delivery time the woman is, especially the day or two prior, her needs for Bowen may increase.   During labor, some Bowen may be given as frequently as necessary as the body begins its wondrous changes in order to give birth.

Mothers who have received Bowen during their pregnancy always comment that they have found that their child tends to be significantly calmer, more at ease, confident, and harmonious than other children who have not had that opportunity. It is because the child incidentally received Bowen when the mother received her session, by being in the womb.

Rick Minnery, a highly respected and well-known mid-wife and experienced Bowen Practitioner and Bowen Instructor from England, shares many personal experiences related to the great results he has seen with expectant and nursing mothers, newborn infants and children. He regularly teaches classes and shares his knowledge at national and international conferences. At the 2001 European Bowen Conference in Cypress (Mediterranean), and 2004 Bowen Association of Australia International Conference in Geelong, Australia, Rick held classes for Bowen Practitioners to teach them how to properly and readily resolve many problems surrounding pregnancy, birth and baby using Bowen.

Many Practitioners, including myself, have performed Bowen on newborn infants as well as on the mothers, literally right after the little ones have arrived out of the womb. We have all witnessed the profound effects Bowen has on both newborn and mother. Doctors, nurses, and midwives who are present are amazed at what they see happen and how quickly both mother and child respond. Babies respond extremely well to Bowen the moment after they are born. Their tiny bodies respond so quickly that performing only a minimal amount of Bowen right after the birthing process works great to help erase some of the "birth trauma" and gets them ready for the adventure of life ahead.

At the **Bowen Healing System**™ Centers, we offer a free Bowen session as a celebrated birthday gift to both mother and newborn baby sometime after the little is ready to come visit us. It is a gift we freely give to the communities we serve.

Toddlers and children also respond very well to Bowen, and generally only need 1-2 sessions for most ailments. Young children who experience recurring ear infections, asthma, ADD or ADHD, bedwetting, or constipation, for example, respond very rapidly and extremely well to Bowen.

Scope of Practice

Skillful Bowen Practitioners can be viewed as the keyboard operators who know and understand what keys to use and when to use them, in order to initiate the body's healing.

Professor Malcolm Stemp, Oxford University, says, **"Any natural therapy *must* obey the first law of natural cure, which is that the body must be treated as a whole without reference to named diseases."**

Bowen Practitioners address the whole body to assist the restoration of health and removal of pain and trauma, using a gentle and caring touch without reference to any named condition or disease. They address the body in a way that consequently addresses every condition that exists within the body at once. Bowen Practitioners <u>do not</u> diagnose, prescribe, treat any specific condition or disease, or ask individuals to alter refrain from taking medication. They are taught to these are best left to the medical profession. Practitioners use Bowen only as a means to reset the body to heal itself while *allowing the body to self-diagnose.* When necessary, Bowen Practitioners will inform individuals that they need to seek help from medical or specialized healthcare professionals.

BOWEN AND ITS USE WITH OTHER THERAPIES

If other therapies are incorporated with Bowen during the initial 3-5 visits, they tend to erase the direct Bowen work that has done. After the initial Bowen treatment regimen, a healthcare practitioner can introduce other therapies on an alternating weekly schedule. This is very effective for severe, chronic conditions. Bowen is and can be used as a complementary approach that enhances other therapies. It does not interfere with medical care.

AS A FIRST AID

Bowen very often works wonders as an immediate first-responder for heart attacks, stroke, choking, insect bites and stings, joint dislocation, acute pain, sprains, strains, sports injuries, and accidents. It can be used as an emergency alternative for CPR, in certain cases, and can alleviate shock in as little as 10 to 15 seconds.

FOR BACK PAIN

Continual muscle spasms eventually lead to the compression of spinal discs, which in turn causes either herniation or rupture of these discs and creating intense pain. This compression or herniation of the disc(s) caused by multiple layered muscle spasms can be eliminated or greatly reduced through Bowen.

A *Newsweek* article on back pain states that back-fusion surgery was initially designed for serious instability or deformities of the spine. Over the years, the number of fusion surgeries has drastically increased due to technological advances in medicine, surgery and new procedures *in hope that the back pain and problems will disappear.* Many surgeries do produce good results, although sometimes the procedures don't work. The article further explains that chiropractic is currently the most widely-accepted non-surgical alternative treatment for back pain. It involves manipulation of the spine, *which obviously can create some risks.*

The article also notes that massage has the ability to help knead out persistent pain, at least temporarily. One physical therapist reports that he uses massage to loosen muscles and increase blood flow. He states that the massage he gives as a physical therapist is not a spa-like experience. He uses an electrical vibrator to distract clients from the pain of his fingers pushing into their muscles. "You've got to get in deep to break loose the spasms."

> *I beg to differ!* Bowen can successfully achieve great results, almost instantly, in nearly every instance - using very light touch. The pain goes away in nearly every case!

The article also reports that acupuncture doesn't produce instant results either. It stimulates the release of feel-good endorphins. It does not provide instant relief, but does have a cumulative effect. The article also reports conventional doctors as saying, "If it makes you feel better, go for it."

Dr. Richard Deyo, a University of Washington professor of medicine and health writing in The New England Journal of Medicine, February 2004, stresses that sometimes a well-performed fusion does little for pain. His view is that back pain "is a part of living and being a human being."

> *Because Bowen can be used successfully in most cases,* **I beg to differ!** *I have seen case after case where the person was suffering from severe pain, wanting to do anything to make it go away – even surgery – and a relative or friend recommended Bowen. After just a few sessions they either disregarded their prior thoughts about surgery and/or canceled the surgery altogether.*

Harvard University is spearheading a NIH-funded (National Institute of Health) pilot program with a goal to see if there is a more efficient, multidisciplinary way to attack serious back problems and make it cost-effective.

Dr. Carragee and others at Harvard believe that the answer to back pain has as much to do with the mind as it does with the body. The study found that *the best predictor of pain was not how bad the defect looked but the patient's psychological distress.* It also found that depression and anxiety have long been linked to pain.

Dr. John Sarno, at the NYU Medical Center's Rusk Institute of Rehabilitation Medicine, believes that almost all back pain is rooted in bottled-up emotions. He explains how repressed rage over a parent's divorce, sexual abuse, trouble at work, and other problems can stress the body, leading to a mild oxygen deprivation, which he says will eventually emerge as muscle spasm, nerve dysfunction, numbness, and pain. He believes that recovery begins with recognizing the connection between the mind and the body. "Pain is created by the brain to make sure the rage doesn't come out. It protects you by giving you something physical to pay attention to instead."

Doctors now actively look for simpler, more effective ways to treat one of the most vexing problems in medicine, back pain. Dr. David Eisenberg at Harvard Medical School's Osher Institute states, "We've come to the point where we have to think out-of-the-box. The time is now…What we need are bold new ways to think about the spine."

Many Western and alternative approaches often assist the body *or* mind to continue movement through some stages of healing, but often fall short because they only affect one aspect of the entire healing process and do not address the body/mind as a whole.

One unique factor which sets Bowen apart from other therapies is that it is administered with a very light touch. For those with skin and muscle sensitivities, a surrogate can be used on their behalf of the person. As the surrogate lightly touches the person who needs to receive Bowen and Bowen is performed on the surrogate, both receive a session. This works well for a person having a stroke, a child who does not want to be touched, or a person hospitalized with serious or life-threatening injuries.

Misunderstanding occurs with those determined to find a cure for a specific symptom or condition. This leads to invasive measures inflicted or forcefully administered by individuals or groups that chase symptoms and treat after-the-fact conditions. This rarely leads to the return of optimal health. Treating symptoms often leads to a greater and more rapid decline in health.

Bowen directly and more accurately addresses the body from this perspective far better than any other healing modality in the world. Bowen facilitates the release of the interference caused by the initial incident. It removes layers of symptoms and disorders, until it finds and addresses the core issues. Bowen works extremely well for those people who want results and for those are searching for alternatives to symptom medication.

Bowen Facts

The advantages of using Bowen are:

- **That Bowen is consistent and effective in nearly every case**
- **Bowen is superior to other therapies or treatments**
- **The body is treated as a whole**
- **The body knows what to heal first**

- The source or origin can be addressed
- Bowen is most effective in treating a very wide variety of conditions simultaneously
- Bowen is natural, gentle and relaxing
- The body gives great feedback
- The body re-aligns itself with no forceful manipulations
- Infants achieve remarkable results
- Bowen is by far the best natural approach to health and healing
- Bowen is a quantum leap forward in complementary and alternative healthcare and maintenance
- Bowen proves itself as an advanced healing system
- It has the ability to help eliminate chronic sicknesses that do not respond to allopathic treatment
- It opens the body and allows the body's own wisdom to take over
- The high success rate of Bowen continues to defy commonly-held notions of Western medicine

Bowen is by far a more efficient and natural way to create the desired inner calmness without harmful side effects that synthetic drugs often have on the body.

Many healthcare professionals worldwide report that Bowen can and does rapidly address the body to heal, while considerably reducing rehabilitation time for most injuries and traumas.

Why Bowen?
Because Bowen works!

"This is _exactly_ what I have been looking for!"

Bowen directly and more accurately addresses the body from its perspective far greater than any other healing modality in the world. Bowen facilitates the release of the interference caused by the initial incident, by opening the body and allowing it to remove the layers of symptoms, conditions, disorders, and dysfunctions on its own, until the original or core issue is found and addressed.

Bowen works extremely well for those people who want results and for those who are searching for alternatives to medication of symptoms.

The difference between God and a doctor is that God _knows_ he's <u>not</u> a doctor!

Bowen is "Healing for the 21st Century" and beyond

Natural medicine has played a major role in the survival and enhancement of the health and healing of humans and animals for many millenniums. Currently, practitioners from all kinds of therapies and approaches as well as Western medical and alternative professionals respond with enthusiasm that Bowen thoroughly compliments and enhances other treatments. Osteopaths, naturopaths, chiropractors, physiotherapists, physical, sports, massage therapists and many other professional therapists diligently learn and use Bowen in their practices.

Bowen occupies a very key lead position in the frontier of complementary and alternative healthcare. Because of its uniqueness, simplicity, and consistency in addressing a wide range of health-related concerns, *Bowen ought to be looked upon as its own separate and distinct therapeutic modality* as it does not fit in or under osteopathic, chiropractic, physical therapy, or massage classifications.

Chapter 10

Discoveries, Theories

It generally takes 21 days to form a new habit in the body and the brain. The same can be said for how the body generally works with Bowen for those who have had lingering or long-term health problems or pain. In Bowen, one of the goals is to establish a series of healing habits and patterns throughout the entire body and brain that overpower, and then eventually defeat, the old pain/spasm or trauma/shock cycles, or ways the body is used to being so that they disappear, restoring optimal health and healing.

A theory that exists in the world is that it takes a minimum of 1 month of proper care and treatment for every year a person has had a specific condition, in order to restore the body back to good and proper health. What has been discovered with Bowen is that it can take as little as one session, and 7 days following, to set the body right again.

Another way to clarify what happens in the body with Bowen is to compare it to some degree to a radio or television station. The brain is the broadcasting system, which sends signals using different frequencies. The receptor sites throughout the body receive the signals and then respond. If the brain sends a signal and the body doesn't receive it and does not return a signal, the brain then searches neuropathically to find an open pathway or channel in order to insure delivery. If it doesn't find a suitable new path, the body has the ability to take over and compensate, use and even, at times, create new neuropathways in order for the body to get what it needs.

In cases where moderate-to-severe injury has occurred, where too many signals travel down one path primarily because the injury or trauma has damaged or restricted the pathway to some degree, the neuropathway becomes congested like rush-hour traffic. When the pathway becomes overloaded, the body tends to go into a mild form of shock to protect itself.

This mild form of shock can remain in the body for decades. Severe injury or trauma or too much energy traveling on these pathways can also block or shut them down for some time. When a pathway closes or is restricted, it keeps the brain from sending or receiving signals throughout the body, sometimes causing it into a much deeper level of shock. Medical professionals have been taught the importance of getting a person out of shock, as the consequences can be severe damage to body and/or brain, or even death. Because performing the first two Moves on the lower back region activates the CNS, ANS, and institutes the awakening of systems, re-igniting the healing mechanisms and getting people out of shock so quickly, these two Moves could be taught to people world-wide, similar to the Heimlich Maneuver or CPR as an additional "first responder" action.

REMOVING TOXINS

Bowen works superbly and naturally as a therapeutic agent that detoxifies body tissues by re-hydrating the cells and improving cellular nutrition. This greatly magnifies the elimination of impurities and toxins from the body, down to the cellular level. Occasionally, these toxins can be naturally pushed through the skin during the session, producing strong, foul-smelling odors that permeate the room. Toxins can include medications, drugs, alcohol, chemicals, environmental toxins, pollutants, food additives, and more. If this occurs, it is best to drink plenty of water and go on a walk. It is not harmful in any way, it's just a normal process of the body that was naturally sped up a bit to help the body to heal faster.

REVERSE PIEZOELECTRIC THEORY

In addressing the body as Bowen does, causing the muscle-stretch-reflex to temporarily reverse itself to clear tension from the muscles and surrounding area, I theorize that piezoelectrically something similar is happening in the body as well.

When a Bowen Move is performed properly, the muscles and fascia are slightly stretched, separating both adhered muscle fibers and fascia. When the muscles release themselves and snap back into its normal groove they fit into, the sudden release causes a surge or wave, sending out impulses. This, I theorize, sets off the piezoelectric aspects of the nervous system in a unique manner that is quite different from what the body considers to be normal. When the surge is released and pressure is applied to the underside of the skin, it creates friction. A combination of friction and force between the layers of the skin and the fascia tissue stimulate both the peripheral and central nervous systems, physically and electrically, setting off and increasing a charge in the body's energy field as well. Setting off the charge throughout the body and from the outer layers of the skin indeed affects the whole body and the body as a whole, because the remainder of the body exists within the skin.

Metaphysical

Balanced, flowing and rhythmic energy in the body displays itself as health and well-being, as the whole works together with ease in synchronicity. In other words, the body is connected as a whole. On the other hand, energy that is deficient, in excess, or not free-flowing in the body displays it as an unwell or ill-at-ease state. Blocked energy in the body has a huge tendency to cause disharmony throughout the whole body, mind and energetic field, directly affecting the entire essence or being of a person, or that which many call spirit. This causes a desynchronized or chaotic vibrational state, in which the individual parts of the body, mind, energy and spirit act separately as disconnected energies or frequencies.

Re-opening the body, mind, energy, and spirit back to balance naturally causes release. This release commonly unravels numerous volumes of past thoughts, feelings and hopes that are neither related to, nor beneficial to, the present, often causing ill health and dis-ease. Releasing what has been holding the individual in ill health can bring back unresolved events or issues that have been long forgotten. Releasing these unresolved events or issues instantly frees one from the past, opening creativity, laughter, love, mental and spiritual awareness. This awareness is one of the key components of IntraPersonal Metamorphosis or "Awakening from Within" which can occur when one's health is fully being restored. Synchronization and harmonization of body, mind, energy and spirit helps to bring forth IntraPersonal Metamorphosis. When the awakening from within occurs, detrimental psychological behaviors commonly right themselves.

THEORY OF FIRST TRAUMA

In the complex inner-workings of the brain and the body, there is a link between the conscious and subconscious minds and past traumas. Bowen subtly, yet directly, has a way that can disconnect or remove these links and trigger the subconscious mind to release the influences of old traumas on the body. The body and mind often remains focused, to some degree, to the places where the body holds the injuries or traumas using the set up neuronal patterns. Physical pains return because the memories of physical traumas are stored in the fascia tissue and as the body cycles through its elimination cycles, it also stirs things up.

Emotional pains return because the brain stores emotional traumas in the amygdala (an almond shaped structure in the brain) and the stored feelings can re-trigger at ANY time. Even though an injury or trauma happened many years ago, the old pain spasm cycle still has not been erased. In one case, the third Bowen session completely eliminated a pain the person had suffered within his foot over 61 years prior, when he stepped on a nail at 11 years old. In another case, a Bowen session eliminated a person's 82 years of suffering from a very severe post-birth trauma.

The memory of trauma remains because it is deeply imprinted in the amygdale for emotional trauma, primarily in the fascia tissue for physical trauma, and in the brain for mental trauma. Sights, sounds, smells, tastes, and feelings can trigger a relapse of the body into states of moderate to severe tension, spasm, and emotional or mental pain. The subconscious mind remembers every minute detail of every incident experienced, and responds accordingly when re-triggered, causing/re-creating reactive physical spasm or pain, or mental or emotional suffering. Continual re-triggering of these reactionary patterns produces severe wear and tear on the body as a whole.

Old patterns not erased begin to accumulate, one pain/spasm cycle, one issue on top of another, gathering layer after layer. These layers slowly reduce the body's efficiency, offsetting the synchronization of the systems, causing other signs, symptoms, and conditions to appear.

First Trauma

Because what I commonly and consistently observe and have personally witnessed myself with my own body, I theorize that Bowen has the very effective ability to remove older and more recent "first trauma" patterning from the body. "First trauma" is term I've given to the first or initial trauma actually received by the body that becomes the source, the keystone keeping the entire series of pain/spasm and mental/emotional cycles recurring in the body. It is the aspect that is remembered first and therefore has the deepest attachment to the body. In most cases, it is not the one that the person is able to recollect, because the event happened so quickly and at the same time many of the areas of the body were impacted *almost* simultaneously, meaning within milliseconds of each other.

Physical, mental, and emotional trauma each have very individual aspects that can influence very different areas of the body. However at times they can display themselves in the body as more similar than dissimilar, because the physical, mental, and emotional aspects of the body are so strongly interconnected and can be difficult to actually separate. One area cannot be affected without causing some measure of an effect on the others. Where the first _actual_ trauma was or which was the first area that was affected may be very difficult to discover, unless it can be recalled.

What is meant by the "first actual trauma" is the first one the body received or the one the mind energetically picked up on before the rest of the body or mind was impacted. For example, with the crash–test-dummies in slow motion on television, the car first collides with the obstacle and starts to crush, and then the head begins to snap forward, immediately followed by the rest of the body because of inertia. The air bag bursts open and fully inflates right before the head contacts the airbag, etc. What is meant by the "first actual trauma" in this case could be one of three things. It could be the head beginning to snap forward if the impact was not expected, or it could be the body attempting to tighten in order to brace for the impact when it was expected (i.e. the hands gripping extremely tight or the feet naturally trying to push through the floor board) or it could be the body sensing that something was going to happen and it began to "self brace" on its own long before the effects of the impact could actually be felt by the person.

Because the body is very aware and is constantly and naturally on guard to "protect," very often it will instinctively sense something milliseconds before it actually happens. When I inquire into a person's overall health before performing Bowen on them, the inquiry deepens when they disclose that they have had an accident of *any* kind. Very often through deeper inquiry, I find that what people share is actually a huge acknowledgment of how the body/mind works on more profound levels. When asked, "What did you sense or feel right before the accident happened?," many people readily report that they knew, just a split second before the accident happened, that they knew it was going to happen, though they didn't actually see it happening. Also in nearly every case, they say something to the effect of, "…and my body (or neck, or back, or arm, or leg, etc.) tightened up right before the impact was felt. It is as though the body somehow *knew* it was going to happen."

EXAMPLES OF FIRST TRAUMA

Many years ago when I first started Bowen, The first person that came to me was a gentleman in his mid-fifties who, 11 years before I met him, had 750 pounds of material fall off a forklift and land on him, immediately crushing him to the ground. Doctors did their best to put his severely injured and traumatized body back together again. I performed Bowen on him and when I finished the Ankle Procedure, his whole body miraculously began to change before my eyes. The severe ankle trauma he had suffered during the accident which had taken the first blow or trauma as the body was crushed to the floor with the weight of the material so many years ago, was finally released, allowing his body to instantly change its course. In this case, the body immediately began to revert back to essentially how it was just prior to the accident.

In another case, a top senior collegiate football player was carried off the field in the first few minutes of the game yelling and screaming about the extreme pain in his knee right. He had had surgery on the same knee during the previous off-season to repair ligament tears. The medical doctors told him that he would have to wait until half time for them to take a better look. He was infuriated. He wanted to return to play NOW. In tears he signaled for me to come over. "Is there anything *you* can do?" he cried. "It's my senior year and I want to play."

I performed the first two Moves on his low back and his knee pain disappeared almost instantly. He jumped up and begged the doctors to check his knee again. They made him run at different speeds, quick turns, stops and starts, squats, and leg kicks. The medical staff agreed to allow him back in the game. He played the entire game and afterwards he said to me "That is the best game I have played to date. Thanks."

The next Monday, I overheard several training staff members commenting about what had happened. They saw the injury take place and heard the medical staff tell him he had to wait. They observed that I had done *almost nothing*, but he returned to the game about 5 minutes later.

"What did you do to Richard?" they all asked. "Just the first two Moves on his lower back." I replied with reservation. "After you did what you did, the pain was gone instantly and there was no inflammation, at all!" they said, looking <u>very</u> surprised. "It's just the way Bowen naturally works, as long as there is no fracture, tear, or laceration. I didn't see how it happened, I just saw him being carried to the sidelines," I said. "What happened," one of them continued, "was that Richard had tackled the opposing player with the ball, and another player tackled Richard from behind. During the tackle he received, his right leg was forcefully cranked out to the side, severely twisting his knee. About the same time, he also took a helmet to his lower back. It was so similar to the hit he took in a game last year that I swore it was a replay."

Afterwards that day, I spoke with Richard and asked him a few questions. He said, "The hit I took Saturday felt just like the one I took last year that took me out for the rest of the season, except it hurt a lot more the second time. I flashed back to what happened last year, and then I thought…Well, THIS season is over. When they carried me off the field and I was screaming in pain, it felt like it happened all over again, just like last year. I *didn't want* the season to be over; it was just the first game of the season. Sitting on the sidelines, my body felt strange and somewhat different than how it felt after the hit last year. When the doctors told me I had to wait until halftime, I went ballistic. The game just started and I wanted them to do something. When they told me again that I had to wait, I looked for you. You really didn't do much, just a couple of those Bowen things. Immediately I felt a huge shift in my body and somehow I knew I was going to be just fine. After relentlessly asking the doctors to check me out, they finally agreed. Thank you. I don't know what you did, but I feel great, even today, and my knee isn't even uncomfortable or tender at all."

Immediately after I performed the first two "master key" Moves on Richard, I saw his body let go, and change. What I believe happened was that the Moves released both the new and the old trauma that caused the body to go into the imprinted pain/spasm cycle. For weeks on end, the college medical staff examined Richard's knee and scratched their heads in amazement.

In another case, a 38-year-old male Marathon runner experienced excruciating pain every time he received a bump or light blow to either one of his knees, which happened occasionally when he played with his children. Every time either knee was hit, no matter how lightly, the excruciating pain always came. And as always, a few minutes would pass and the pain would be gone – until the next time. His doctors couldn't find anything wrong. They told him his knees were in excellent condition for his age, especially considering that he was a top marathon runner.

He had previously undergone hypnotherapy to try to recall the details of an injury he sustained as a youngster. At 6 years old, he was kneeling in the back of the family station wagon when his mother slammed on the brakes to avoid another auto. He slid from the back of the car and smashed his nose and face on the metal bar that encased the seat he slid into. The impact gave him an immediate concussion and broke his nose.

Many years later, he came to Bowen and the initial sessions brought some relief. One day, the Psoas Procedure was performed on him during a session. Immediately, he instantly recalled the accident and burst into tears. "I saw the whole thing in slow motion. I remembered the smells, the brightness of the sun, the clothes that my mother, brother and sisters were wearing. I remembered the food I was eating while I sat in the back of the car, and I remember its taste too. I saw myself kneeling in the back of the car. *I remember feeling the extreme pain in my knees. They were forcefully driven over the exposed full-length hinge in the back part of the station wagon. I attempted to pull myself up in reaction to the pain, just milliseconds before my face and nose hit the bar on the back of the seat. I recall that I woke up in the hospital emergency room. I told my parents and the doctor how much my knees hurt. I remember that the told me,* 'No - your knees do not hurt. Your nose is broken, your face is swollen, and your eyes are back and blue.' *But, to be honest with you, my nose or face never has hurt.*"

This individual reported that *two wonderful things* came out of that session. The first was that later that day, he played football with his two young boys, and one of them hit him with a pro-style tackle on the side of the knee and knocked him to the ground. He sat there and cried with joy. The pain was finally gone and has never returned. The second was he knew back then that he was right, that his knees did hurt, and he was able to totally recall the accident, AS THOUGH IT JUST HAPPENED, and that he recalled every last part of it.

In another amazing personal case that took place two years ago in while I was in Australia, Anne Schubert, a Bowtech Instructor and one of the very first persons to ever learn Bowen from Ossie and Elaine some 25 years ago, suggested that she perform "just the first two lower back Bowen Moves to see what would happen." I was up to it, as I always want to personally experience the different facets that Bowen has to offer. Anne performed the two Moves then left the room.

In the past, I have *always* had some kind of challenges breathing. Whenever I would breathe, it just seemed like it took so much effort. As long as I could remember, since very early childhood, it seemed like it always took a lot of effort to breathe. Although it never hampered anything I did, including running marathons well under 3 hours, I occasionally visited a doctor from time to time to see if there was something they could find.

Of course, I have had Bowen sessions many times before. This time though, I wanted to see what would happen if I only received the first two lower back Moves, and nothing else. I was allowed to "just lie on the table for a while and get in touch with what is happening in my body and what was coming up for me as I laid there." Anne very carefully and quietly entered and exited the room every 10 minutes or so to check on my progress.

This is what happened: At first, I felt my body begin to tingle, starting in my lower back and sacral region and began to move down my legs, first on the left, then the right. A few minutes later, it shot up my back then slowly moved down my arms into my hands, beginning with my left. A minute or so later, a little sharp pain shot up my right arm from the hand, and I instantly recalled a fall I had taken around 4 years ago where I slipped off a ladder from about 3 feet up, and used my right hand and arm to break my fall. My hand and arm heated up and then began to taper off and cool down.

After my arm cooled down, I felt a rush move from the right side of my face over the top of my head, to the left side. It then suddenly shot to the TMJ or the right side, quickly heated up then shot to the left TMJ. I then began to feel pressure increase on the left side, it then intensified, and as quickly as it came, it just disappeared. After that, I began to feel pressure from behind my heart, on the back side. The pressure moved slowly from behind my heart to the topside of the heart and began to quickly increase and intensify. All of a sudden, it became difficult to breathe, my chest started severely hurting in the upper left chest region. Then instantly, I recalled an incident that happened when I was around 1 ½ years old.

I totally saw in my minds' eye and recalled the entire incident like a movie on a screen in front of me. What I recalled was that I was outside with my cousins, playing with them in the snow on a sled. My father had taken the two-runner sled and fabricated a back on it with rails for the young children to hold on to, and I was riding in that sled.

One cousin would push me on the sidewalk from the back, running as fast as he could, then he would let go and I would slide until I stopped. The other cousin would then quickly spun me around, push me from the back as fast as *he* could, let go and I would slide until I stopped again, get spun around, etc., over and over again. I was laughing, getting bumped and spun around.

Then one of the cousins slipped as he was pushing me, and the sled went up on one runner. It quickly shot off to the right, into the street, and my chest slammed full force into the back bumper of a parked car, followed by my face. (Remember, cars in the 1960's did not have plastic bumpers, only those solid chrome ones that do not dent) Immediately my entire body became very hot and my hands clammy. My entire body began to shake a little for a couple of minutes and then, all of a sudden, it was as though a huge heavy weight was lifted off my chest. At the same instant, vertebrae in my back adjusted, and my whole body became limp.

I had *never* been that relaxed in my life, and I began taking huge deep breaths that I could never take before. It was truly amazing, such an enormous release from just two Moves. Bowen never ceases to amaze me, and once again, I was shown the miraculous power of Bowen at work, firsthand. I was only on the table for around 20 minutes. Because the depth of the release was so tremendous, I laid down for a couple of hours and went into a very deep restful state.

From that day forth, my life has been entirely changed. My double vision has improved, I can breathe much better, I am definitely more relaxed, and my body is not constantly on "high alert" anymore.

I know these are typical results witnessed by other Bowen Practitioners, as well. Whenever Instructors, Practitioners, or Students of Bowen gather, countless powerful and truly life-changing accounts of this magnitude are exchanged.

PROPOSAL

I propose that, one of the reasons why it can take more than a few Bowen sessions to address a particular concern, in some cases (i.e. especially those that are difficult, very long-term, severe, or complex), is that many layers of interwoven and compressed neuronal patterning must first be removed or replaced in order to address the body in such a way that it can revive the healing response. Peeling off the layers of patterning may take some time as the brain/body connection begins to revive and re-establish itself throughout the body.

I do assert that the unique reflexive muscular relaxation response that Bowen stimulates through the muscle stretch reflex is extremely powerful and in most cases, that it is completely opposite of most other therapies or approaches and what they do. Also, I assert that Bowen, unlike any other approach, has the ability to slice through multiple layers of neuronal patterning very quickly to allow the body to address core issues in such a way that often causes "instant" changes to occur in the body.

Chapter 11

Crisis or Healing ?

Crisis: a crucial turning point or critical moment - any decisive or significant change in the course of a disease, favorable or unfavorable

In the Chinese language, *the same word used for both danger and opportunity*

Healing: the restoration of health through a remedy or cure

    A healing crisis can or may cause a person some temporary discomfort, as the body unravels, untorques, retraces, or encourages its own way back to balance as it cleanses itself in the process. *It is the body's way* of eliminating toxins and waste that have "set in," from various systems, organs, and tissues throughout the entire body. A healing crisis may involve the different levels of the body. Each level generally includes a few indicators of which degree of crisis an individual may experience.
    The following are varying degrees of crisis including some of the indicators.

    ≈ Mild Crisis – Cleansing

            Increased urination
            Looser stools than usual
            Slight stomach ache
            Restlessness
            Uneasiness
            Clammy hands or feet

    ≈ Moderate Crisis – Deeper Cleansing
            Slight diarrhea
            Muscle or joint discomfort
            Headache
            Pressure in head
            Emotional unrest and releasing
            Sleepiness
            Moodiness

≈ Severe Crisis – Detoxification

> Extreme heating up of the body
> Annoying to intense body and/or joint discomfort or pain
> Profuse sweating
> Migraine
> Deep emotional releasing or cleansing
> Vomiting
> Unwarranted and unfriendly mood swings
> Bouts of anger
> Deep sleep for periods of up to 3 days

Present or past drug or alcohol users may be more likely to experience cleansing. It can and may present itself as a state of drunkenness as a more in-depth organ detoxification takes place in the body. Severe forms of crisis are rare and occur *only when and if* the body needs to aggressively detoxify itself, prior to and in order to jump-start healing system, by abruptly flushing toxins and waste. In these cases, a weary or sluggish organ or system is usually triggered to rapidly come back to life to quickly assist in the body's rebalancing.

If any of these apparent "detoxification" symptoms occur, call your Bowen Practitioner. In most cases, you will be directed to increase your intake of purified or distilled water and take at least a twenty (20) minute walks, if you are able. Distilled water is best when receiving Bowen, because distilled water is just water, with nothing in it. It is pure water, no chemicals, no additives. It can actually help accelerate the removal of toxins from the body.

A healing crisis, though it may be an unpleasant experience. is actually one of the most worthwhile, natural, and beneficial confrontations your body may ever experience. As the body awakens from a deep slumbering state, it can often immediately trigger intense healing and repair.

During and after a healing crisis, the body rapidly bounces back, and rebalances and re-acclimatizes itself to the renewed state of health, well-being and healing. Healing crises are rare, and can in most cases be avoided. Practitioners are always instructed to pay close attention to the indications that the body is being overworked.

A healing crisis is simply the body's way of taking on all it can, to change at one time. It truly is not something that is bad, although it can be uncomfortable to go through sometimes. What I know and understand of a healing crisis is that it is truly something great that the body is doing to cleanse and help itself.

Producing a healing crisis is *__not__* the desired or sought after response in Bowen. The object is to give the body only what it is able to handle on a given day.

Chapter 12

In the words of others

Shared knowledge adds to the knowledge base and supports the whole.

If a healing method is not working, it simply is not working...***go find a solution***...don't just try something that may add to or cause more problems than those that currently exist.

The simplest solution is often the best

Any doctor who has gone through medical school who <u>does not</u> believe in alternative or complementary approaches to healthcare, went through medical school with their eyes closed
~ Dr. Sherry M.D. ~

The September 2004 issue of AARP *Bulletin* includes a profile of a highly successful Georgia consultant pharmacist, who specializes in telling people what prescription drugs and over-the-counter medications they <u>shouldn't</u> be taking. As one of the pioneers in this field, he has seen the rise of overmedication of seniors since 1968. In this article he shares that "almost 100 percent" of the people he sees are taking too many prescription drugs and/or the wrong drugs altogether, for their condition(s). His estimates are consistent with numerous research studies. A new study, for example, published in the *Archives of Internal Medicine* found the 20 percent of patients ages 65 and older were prescribed "at least one drug that should always be avoided" by elderly people and that most seniors are prescribed several of these kinds of drugs.

Virtually every prescription drug comes with an extensively long list of side effects, and although many are "only" annoying, a shocking high percentage of the side effects are deadly.

Dr. Andrew Weil, MD, a physician who practices natural and preventative medicine, has advanced the integration of alternative and complimentary therapies with Western medicine. In the January-February edition of <u>Utne</u> in the *Focus: Health and Wellness section*, Dr. Weil states that "Western medicine needs to rediscover the body's mysterious ability to heal." In his words, most doctors do not provide "common sense medicine"

Dr Weil also says: "I think that's sad that science and medicine have separated themselves from nature. This separation has enormous consequences for our society because, fundamentally, healing is a natural process. If you want to understand healing, you must develop a feeling for the ways of nature...*and the way that the body is designed to naturally work.* Instead, medical training today isolates people from nature...*and the natural healing abilities of the body.* (Italics added for an additional personal insight to what I believe he was talking about.) "I get reports from around the world of supposedly incurable conditions being cured. These reports testify to the human capacity, to heal. Yet many medical doctors do not believe the human body can repair itself…I believe that modern medicine is a big piece of the logjam that keeps the world going in a destructive direction. If we could change medicine, I believe we would see positive change in many other areas of our society and in the world at large. In my view, integrative medicine is a step in the right direction."

He also says "I have a colleague who periodically writes articles about the dangers of herbal teas, warning that, sooner or later, those who use herbal products are going to be poisoned. Most scientific rhetoric is not that overt, but the underlying message is that nature is fundamentally wild, dangerous, and unpredictable, whereas modern pharmaceuticals are safe. That message is especially annoying because it's actually the other way around, and I say that as a doctor who often has to deal with the casualties of pharmaceutical science."

He goes on to say "Conversely, conventional medicine causes a lot of harm in its preference for chemical drugs that are strong and fast acting, and this is the single greatest black mark against it. There are emergencies where it's nice to have a drug that works quickly, but those situations are rare. Nevertheless, most medicine is geared toward treating all illness as a crisis. Sooner or later (the patient) is going to experience an adverse drug reaction, which can be as mild as hives and as major as death and permanent disability."

Dr. Weil stresses that integrative and alternative healthcare involves a partnership where patient and practitioner work together to address the multifaceted levels of true healing. He is also a huge supporter of natural therapies that work with the musculo-skeletal system to alleviate pain and promote health.

In the same Utne article, Dr. Weil explains that Chinese and Western medicine are based on very different concepts regarding health, illness and healing. The Chinese emphasize prevention, whereas in Western medicine, preventative medicine deals primarily with immunization and public sanitation – these are important, but they are not the essence of prevention. The focus should be on teaching people to reduce the risks of disease, to reduce and handle stress and to nurture our nervous system.

He mentions that the superior Chinese medicine remedies are the ones that work for everything – the cure-alls, whereas Western medicine distrusts cure-alls and searches for those medicines that treat only one or two specific conditions or diseases.

In the January 31-February 7, 2005 issue of U.S. News & World Report – Special Health Issue ***"Who Needs Doctors? Your future physician might not be an M.D. – and you may be better off"*** gives a near-future picture of healthcare. The magazine asks the question "Who will take care of you?" The magazine predicts that nurses and other new healers will help fill the widening gap between doctors, because many doctors have retreated from patient care. Those left are so overworked they have trouble filling the need. The system no longer works for the doctor or the patient.

Dr. Donald Novey (2000:371-380), writing in the Clinician's Complete Reference to Complementary and Alternative Medicine, presents information written by Patrik Rousselot, a native Frenchman and a former International Senior Bowen Instructor. Patnik briefly explains how Bowen is applied and used on the body. It includes research and studies in progress. Rousselot includes a long list of conditions, disorders, and symptoms that this therapy alone effectively addresses.

...Bowen challenges belief systems with the experience of minimal stimulus invoking such a powerful healing response. As Gene Dobkin puts it, "The magic of Bowen is not so much that it works, but that it works doing so little."

Little statistical or clinical information exists as to how Bowen assists the release of energy blockages, leading to the healing of the mind and spirit, called "IntraPersonal Metamorphosis" (IPM) or the awakening from within. Energetic releasing and changing occurs during the course of a normal Bowen session.

Heart surgeon, Dr. Mehmet Oz, MD, in his article "Healing With An Open Mind'–points out that a surgeon learns to trust the wisdom of other medical traditions. He is well aware of the effect stress has on the body. Depression can cause immune cells to stop functioning normally and increases the risk of infection. Studies show that it can take more than just high-tech solutions to bolster a patient's healing ability and in certain cases, even save his or her life.

Dr. Oz says, "I entered medicine with the naive belief that we (doctors and medical specialists) knew everything we needed to know to cure the sick. I believe that high-technology solutions would close the few remaining gaps in our healing arsenal. My specialty, heart surgery, was a spectacular example of this modern success story. After all, if the heart literally breaks, we can replace it with a new one – the ultimate fix. But patients have taught me that there is more to healing than what doctors find in textbooks and technology."

"I began to understand that the answers to wellness frequently lie with the patients themselves. Patients often know intuitively what will help them get well – and the responsiveness of a medical team can be essential to their healing...eventually, my search for healing took me beyond modern Western medicine...even something as simple as aromas can aid the healing processes. Indeed, aromas can reduce nausea, block infections, and alter heart rate and blood-pressure."

"The clues to full health are hidden throughout the world in many healing traditions. It is up to each of us to navigate our own path to wellness."

The "bodywise" section of the July 2004, "*O   The Oprah Magazine,*" includes a quick look into Bowen as an innovative body therapy as a place to turn to when you are tense. This section, gives an extremely brief explanation of Bowen and includes that it can be "used to treat shoulder, back and neck pain, plus headaches, postural problems, and repetitive strain injuries". As Bowen becomes more mainstream, many others who are influential will readily give credence to what Bowen can do.

In her book, <u>Hands of Light,</u> Barbara Ann Brennan (1988:23) states:

It is time to stop invalidating experience that lies outside our Newtonian way of thinking and broaden our framework of reality.

Recently the country's mindset began to change from letting medical professionals tell us what to think and do regarding our bodies, to one of learning to find out what works best for us. This change has instilled a strong desire to understand not only how the body works, but also how to restore and keep it healthy, and strong inclination to avoid chemical substances that may do more harm than good.

Energetic Bodywork, by Rita J. McNamara, (1998:xi-xii) adds:

> **We are witnessing a tremendous resurgence of interest in ancient forms and systems, searching for old/new ways to know ourselves. We gently brush off the artifacts and pore over the manuscripts and scrolls, hoping to find the answer, the way to step into the future with some sense of grace and purpose. It is as though, in the crossing over the psychic threshold of the year 2000, we feel the need to reach back into our dimmest past and take all the grandmothers and grandfathers with us. The burgeoning "new age" has generated countless trends, philosophies, cults, foods, gimmicks, and diets. Most of it is designed to "put us in touch with ourselves." Many are now learning to equate physical or emotional problems with a lack of grace or spiritual balance. We have forgotten that Job's trials were the means to his evolution, his dialogue with the divine.**

The body, mind, and spirit are inseparable, yet they independently work together for the greater good of the whole being.

THE BODY

The body has an intricate and often instant-feedback system that allows us to recognize what we are creating in our lives. We often choose not to be aware of what is taking place and give more importance to what we "think" we have to do. **The body mirrors our lives and is a great indicator to the status of what is needed for optimal health.** In her book, Minding the Body, Mending the Mind, Joan Borysenko Ph.D. (1988:85), shares her personal experience of the benefits of having a migraine headache and how it serves a useful purpose.

Borysenko writes:

> **"It was the only legitimate way to get any rest and not have to produce for a while. A migraine headache takes precedence over anything that may need to be done and ... it is the only way my body knew to release all the tension I had stored. A migraine always felt like a storm to me. When it was over, I lay limp, washed totally clean, and totally relaxed. Too bad that my body had to fight itself to death and then lie exhausted in order to let go. Many of us do the same thing with pain and other illnesses and anxieties. The mind/body has incredible wisdom. It will seek whatever way it can, at the least possible cost, to bring us into a state of regulation if we do not do it on our own."**

In this instance, rest was one needed factor to release stored tensions. Often the lack of energy, pain, signs, symptoms, conditions, and disorders of the body are the body's way of telling us to slow down. As we continue pushing beyond our limits, our ability to keep up becomes weaker. Acute, temporary conditions arise that may lead to chronic conditions.

Borysenko (1988:20-21) also states that:

> **"The acute stresses of life produce temporary physiological responses from which the body recovers. It's the chronic stresses ...that are the real challenge to healing which can upset our endocrine balance, elevating the immuno-suppressant hormone cortisol**

and destroying its natural diurnal rhythm...and also deplete the brain of the vital neurotransmitter norepinephrine, the chemical in our brain that is necessary for feelings of happiness and contentment."

We often push beyond the *stop zone* because of what we think we have to be or do. Our lack of awareness, our worry, tension, or stress, often leads to the breakdown of normal bodily function. Most people push themselves until their bodies stop them with pain, dysfunction, or disease. Schwartz (1990), in <u>Repression and Dissociation</u> reveals that stress may contribute to diminished health. When individuals ignore key cognitive-emotional feedback, it *retards communication between the subsystems*.

This creates organ sluggishness and an imbalance within the body. This imbalance attacks whole systems leading to de-synchronization and a partial function loss. This inability to sustain optimal health and well-being creates pain and disorders. Impaired systems often create a lack of energy and mental acuity. If not repaired they can bring on major crises and deadly disease. Trauma and surgery can also reduce optimal capacity.

Dr. Dora Kunz (1982) observed that a natural autonomous rhythm occurs in the body when we have a vital healthy field. She explains that each organ in the body has its own corresponding energetic rhythm and that the different rhythms interact. Within a healthy individual, the rhythms transfer quite easily from one organ to another. She also concluded that perceived rhythm *as well as* the energy levels are changed following surgical procedures. This blocks energy and reduces organ function.

BODY/MIND AND AWAKENING THE SPIRIT

Healing transfers energy. The definition of emotion is energy in motion. A<u>ny</u> change made in the body occurs on an emotional level. Rita J. McNamara (1998), in <u>Energetic Bodywork</u>, explains that an individual receiving a treatment (that begins to change the energies in the body) will often experience revealing emotional sensations, which sometimes briefly allow the person to relive a past emotional episode.

This often releases startling images and feelings. These releases often take the form of yawning, or stretching. Some moderate releases include feelings of sadness, fear, depression, crying, nausea, headaches, or laughter. High-level releases may occur as heart felt misery, rage, hate, guilt, shame, screaming or yelling, vomiting, uncontrolled shaking, crying, laughing, or fainting.

Psychiatrist Dr. Wilhelm Reich studied the relationship of disturbances of the energy flow in the human body to physical and psychological illness. He discovered that the unconscious blockages in the natural energy flow produce negative mental and emotional states. Releasing these energy blocks clears the negative mental and emotional states. Dr. Reich found that the blockage releases clear the negative states and change an individual's physical, mental, and emotional well-being. This underpins the Bowen concept.

Dr. Weil (1995), author of <u>Spontaneous Healing</u>, explains how restrictions within the healing systems can be the result pf physical and emotional past traumas. He also believes that most digestive problems are rooted in stress. This means that the lack of energy due to overwork, overexertion, lack of rest and sleep greatly diminishes the immune system and affects the whole body and mind.

Dr. Weil explains that changing attitudes causes a rebirth and a new beginning. We can produce this rebirth with activities that induce states of relaxation. The inner wisdom of the body is obscured by inattention through stress, fear, doubt, and worry.

Borysenko asserts that activities that induce a relaxed state of mind ultimately restore inner listening, allowing us to make the best choices. This brings true peace of mind. Satisfying desires does not bring pleasure. Even-mindedness is not a necessary condition for happiness. True peace of mind is an opportunity to live fully and consciously.

Albert Einstein stated: **"The striving for such achievement is in itself a part of liberation and a *foundation for inner security*."** (italics added)

Borysenko (1988:26):"**We can reach an internal balance point where the mind becomes still. In this state of stillness, the physiology shifts into the relaxation response. Negative conditioning circuits are derailed, and the mind is open to the formation of more productive habits, creating new circuits that activate your inner healing potential.**"

Mind wellness plays an integral part in the process. Dr. Weil's "The Role of the Mind in Healing" summarizes the spiritual awakening that often occurs when an individual submits body and mind to a higher power.

In an emergency room, a calm patient is far more likely to survive than a hysterical one with a similar injury. Calmness governs healing, and the quality of life. In Quantum Healing, Deepak Chopra, MD. (1989), states that the body has the innate ability to heal itself by bringing the body into a restful state that builds the foundation for healing. He further explains that the most important precondition for curing any disorder is total, deep relaxation. Chopra suggests that the body knows how to maintain balance unless thrown off by disease. If you want to restore the body's own healing ability, you must do everything possible to bring it back into balance.

He also affirms that individuals often feel a force inside themselves that extends beyond their personal boundaries. The awareness of this force creates a leap in consciousness and an ability to remain at a higher consciousness level. This is the key that unlocks the door to the true self and true healing. People don't undertake inner healing because they don't have the understanding to do it. This ability springs from a core level so deep that you cannot go any deeper. It is at this core, he has determined, that miraculous healing exists.

The Touch of Healing by Alice Burmeister (1997) presents atypical transformational experiences of others who have received alternative treatments in the Japanese healing art form "Jin Shin Jyutsu." Burmeister (1997:13-14,25-26) writes that:

"Virtually all traditional healing systems...are founded on the principle that in order to heal the body, the person must strengthen and harmonize the flow of life energy within.

Our health or harmony depends upon the free and even distribution of this life energy throughout our body, mind, and spirit. When the stress and strain of daily living disrupts the movement of life energy, our mind, body, and spirit are all affected.

Not only do we succumb to worry, fear, anger, sadness, and pretensions, but we increase our tendency to become ill or "out of balance." Harmonizing particular depths of energy of our being provides a direct foundation for the next, and each one is responsible for a specific set of functions within the body, mind, and spirit. When energy circulates easily and abundantly, body, mind, and spirit are all nourished. But when the flow becomes blocked, constricted, or stagnant, disharmony results."

Burmeister also reveals that turning on the "safety locks," which act like switches in the body, restores health, and emotional equilibrium. It also releases emotions, pain and discomforts, and eliminates the causes of both chronic and acute conditions. Turning on these switches often reverses conditions that have been pronounced incurable. This reawakens the awareness of Universal life energy. Dr. Andrew Weil (1995) writes that this energy is the same energy that Chinese doctors call qi (chi) or Universal life energy. He explains that most people experience this as warmth or tingling or subtle vibration, which directs attention toward the spiritual pole of existence.

An increase in the rate of this energy has a great tendency to uplift, renew, recharge, inspire, and turn thoughts to higher purposes. Weil believes that the way we breathe reflects and influences the state of the nervous system. To harmonize body, mind, and spirit with the Universal cosmic energy in concentrated form, we must first become aware of what is taking place and make necessary changes. Through the practice of awareness and listening, our awareness will attract the healing and internal relaxation that often occurs as part of a spiritual awakening.

Weil's expanded concept of True Health includes body, mind, and spirit. He believes that society will make a quantum leap in true healing potential as the connectedness is understood and accepted. He says it is necessary to find and use simple methods of healing that take advantage of our own healing potential.

Dr. Weil (1995) expounds that the challenge of healing is to discover how to turn on the right switches to activate the processes. Bowen comes forth as a simple and unique method to meet this challenge.

FIBROMYALGIA

The October 1999 edition of the PREVENTION MAGAZINE "Say No to Pain the Way the Experts Do" reveals Bowen as a "TRIED AND TRUE method that is a remedy for those suffering with fibromyalgia." Says Cambridge naturopath Bradley Bongiovanni, N.D, "It's helpful in reducing pain and spasm in people who can only tolerate a light touch,"

MATHEMATICS

In his Massachusetts Institute of Technology (MIT), Masters Thesis, "*A Mathematical Model of the Stretch Reflex in Human Muscle Systems,*" James Charles Houk, Jr., uses a mathematical approach to study, ascertain and give mathematical explanation to the stretch reflex of the human body and how it works. This thesis examines "the functional properties of the more peripheral components of muscular control systems" while also giving "insights which lend to the problems of voluntary control and servo-analysis of the stretch reflex…". Most of what is written and explained in this thesis may be far too complicated for those who are not mathematicians or engineers. This thesis, I believe, offers insights and a form of general mathematical proof of how the highly variable and complex muscular control system works as an engineering control system for the body. In essence, it can be viewed to offer sound proof that Bowen works mathematically.

Chapter 13

Cases

To ensure privacy and confidentiality, the names have been changed in the following cases, though the primary facts in each case and the results remain unchanged. As everyone is an individual, the case histories included are illustrations of a few benefits that Bowen has been able to produce.

CASE 1

Marge, in her mid seventies, had very few health related complaints. Her main issue was the stiffness that she felt early in the morning.

An initial assessment revealed that she was active, her muscle tone was good, and she was in good health for her age. There was slight muscle tension of the pelvic region, knees, and back; therefore, only a few sessions would be necessary. Her initial session consisted of the BRM and the kidney procedure.

Her response to the initial session was one of relaxation and "feeling good all over." Her next session was the inclusion of the pelvic and knee procedures. She felt so good that she felt no need to return. This was the response we wanted to achieve.

Three months later she returned. She could hardly walk and her right knee was swollen. Marge explained the following: "I don't remember doing anything to that knee but when I woke, it just puffed up and hurt terribly." Questioning her about her activities revealed that she had been gardening, preparing her spring flowers for planting and that she had been kneeling and sitting sideways on the ground with her ankles tucked under or near her buttocks. An assessment clearly showed a high pain level in the knee. The knee was red and inflamed, and had a minimal range of motion.

Her session that day consisted only of the lower back and knee procedures. We applied the knee procedure lightly so as not disturb the knee. I returned after a few minutes to check Marge's condition. She mentioned that her leg felt a little better but it still hurt. As I stood back, observing the position of her body on the session table, her knee jumped up about five inches from the table and I heard a single "pop" from her right knee. Within five minutes the inflammation was drastically reduced and Marge found that her knee was "as good as new."

CASE 2

Jim was involved in a variety of sports from motorcycle and automobile racing to track and field, baseball, basketball, and football. He played them all, intensely. Though highly athletic and on a rigorous daily workout schedule, he was always in pain. His shoulders and neck gave him the greatest problem.

We had him fill out a client information form and did an initial assessment. We found nothing out of the ordinary. His muscles were bulky and tense from daily workouts, but his body's ranges of motion and flexibility were above normal. We treated him using the BRM, kidney, and shoulder procedures. Afterwards he felt more relaxed and the pain in his neck and shoulder subsided.

During the next week, he continued to work out and felt only slight differences in his neck and shoulders. The next session consisted of the BRM, coccyx, pelvic, the Temporal Mandibular Joint (TMJ), and other more advanced neck and shoulder procedures. This increased his level of relaxation.

The third day after session brought a new series of neck and shoulder stiffness, The assessment showed a slight movement of the pain and stiffness toward the back of his neck. The session involved repeating the BRM, coccyx, pelvic, advanced TMJ, and even more advanced neck and shoulder procedures. This, again significantly reduced the pain. .

During this week, Jim called to ask if there was something else that I could do because, even though the pain subsided initially, it had returned with vengeance. His neck was stiff and felt locked.

I had done everything that I knew to do. I had him lie down on the session table with his head facing me. I told him that I had done all the procedures that I had been taught. I explained to him that I was going to let him rest on the table while I focused on his body. Asking the Higher Source, I was led to do a very different procedure behind his head. This procedure, which took a little over five minutes, was different from anything I had been taught.

The very second I removed my hands from behind his head, a tremendous wave swept him from the top of his head to the bottom of his feet shaking him nearly off the table. This startled both of us. A few short moments later, his body went limp and dropped into a deep state of rest for approximately 10 minutes. Upon rising he said he had never felt better and the neck and shoulder pain were completely gone.

I have treated him for other minor athletic injuries but, to this day, even though he plays college football, he has yet to experience any pain or neck discomfort.

CASE 3

Harry, in his mid-forties, came to the clinic for a "general tune-up." Initial assessment showed that although he smoked cigarettes, his general health was good. He had suffered a slight fall 3 years ago and just wanted to make sure he was balanced. The assessment showed torque in the pelvic region and right ankle tension. His initial session consisted of the BRM and the ankle procedure. His response was one of " general relaxation."

His next session consisted of the BRM and the asthma procedure. He responded, saying, "I am relaxed and can breathe easier." The third session consisted of an advanced procedure between the shoulder blades and the North, East, and West shoulder procedures, to which he responded, "Wow, it's as though a huge weight was taken off my shoulders."

Three weeks later Harry called to say, "I don't know what you did, but after nearly 25 years, I had the sudden urge to quit smoking." Harry hasn't smoked a cigarette since.

CASE 4

Susie, in her late forties, came to the clinic with complaints of allergies to many plants, animal dander, wool, and perfume. Her initial assessment revealed a high level of torque in the region between her knees and lower neck, tension between her shoulder blades, and excessive torque in the ribcage. She revealed that she was thrown off a horse at age 16, landed on her back on uneven ground, and suffered a mild concussion. I asked when she first began to smoke. She replied just before her 17th birthday.

Susie's initial session consisted of the BRM, knee, and asthma procedures. Her response was one of general overall relaxation.

Her next assessment revealed an abnormal tilting of her head forward and to the right. Her session consisted of the BRM, kidney, advanced neck, and TMJ procedures. Upon arising, Susie felt light-headed and dizzy. She lay back down. and I covered her up to give her body time to process the changes.

The next week revealed chest and ribcage discomfort and extreme coccyx pain with deviation of the coccyx to the right. Her session consisted of the advanced chest pain and coccyx procedures. I covered her with a blanket again and made her comfortable using pillows. This time her body went into a very deep restful state. After 90 minutes. I helped her to her feet. Her face glowed. She said, "I feel great! I feel like I was asleep for 100 years and it was wonderful!"

Susie called a month later to thank the staff. She had quit smoking after her last session.

CASE 5

Van, a college football player suffered a severe knee injury which caused a tear in the ligaments and the muscles behind the right knee. The injury had been surgically repaired during off-season. After the surgery, I treated him using the BRM and other advanced procedures to assist healing. He wanted to be in the best possible shape at the beginning of the season.

Performing Bowen for a college athlete led to the opportunity to be on the sidelines for Van's first football game of the year. In the opening quarter they carried Van off the field in excruciating pain, holding the back of his right knee. The college physician told Van to take off his pads, saying he would take a better look at the injury at half time.

Van looked at me and asked "Can you fix it?" I responded by performing the first two Moves of the Lower Back Procedure. The physician looked at me in disgust and walked away. But in a few minutes Van donned his pads and resumed to play at roughly 85 to 90 % capacity. .

What had just occurred startled both physicians. Even I was amazed. I asked the student trainer if he saw how Van was injured. "Yes I did. Van was hit in the lower back with a helmet as his right leg was torqued back in a strange position."

This made sense. The body, namely the brain, remembers first trauma and locks that pain pattern into the brain's files. When you unlock the first trauma, other pains that may have occurred even milliseconds after the initial trauma are often immediately be released and magically disappear.

CASE 6

Vicki and her husband had tried unsuccessfully to have children for nearly five years. They had been treated by infertility specialists and had previously tried fertility medications. They read literature on the subject, tried Chinese medicine, herbal combinations, and yoga.

In a previous visit, Vicki's brother asked if there was anything that Bowen could do. I assured him that Bowen had an outstanding track record in that area. When the sister and brother-in-law arrived, I explained the course of action and summarized the time frames and instructions that needed to be followed strictly.

We filled out the client information and gave an initial assessment   The assessment revealed that Vicki's pelvic region was torqued, her rib cage was compressed, her coccyx deviated to the left, and her diaphragm unbalanced.

We treated Vicki initially using the BRM and releasing the psoas region. Vicki commented that she felt relaxed. We scheduled the next session for seven days later, but she was unable to come back for almost three weeks. She also canceled the next appointment because she caught the flu. We rescheduled for the following week.

Vicki called the day before her appointment and said she had just found out that she was expecting a baby! Both she and her husband were ecstatic. Case in point. Bowen worked quickly when everything else fell short.

We also treated Vicki during her pregnancy which helps makes the pregnancy favorable for the expecting mother. Later, she gave birth to a healthy little boy, Alex, who has also received Bowen sessions, namely to erase the effects of birth trauma and to help his body function .

CASE 7

Millie, in her mid eighties, came to the clinic with a myriad of small difficulties. She was concerned that she felt she was going to live a lot longer than she had anticipated. Her body had all "these aches and pains" going back to childhood.

The initial assessment revealed just a few areas of tension. Her first session consisted of the BRM and the kidney procedure. Her response was "I feel good!"

The next visit showed slight improvement. We used the BRM to treat her as well as the asthma and knee procedures. On Millie's third visit she showed remarkable improvement and lessening tension. Not really knowing how to proceed, I asked numerous questions regarding her diet, elimination, exercise, and sleeping habits. Nothing she was doing seemed detrimental to healthy living.

I was on the verge of canceling any further session when I was directed from within to treat her in this session, using opposite procedures that really did not make any sense together. I listened and proceeded. The two procedures were the coccyx procedure for left deviation, though there was no discernible discomfort or deviation of the coccyx in any direction, and a very advanced rarely used procedure that addresses the occiput region, or base of the skull.

Admittedly I did not know what the results would be because both procedures ware extreme. We gave Millie pillows and covered her with a blanket. Within 2 minutes she slipped into a restful sleep. When she woke up she looked as flexible as a rag doll and her face looked 25 years younger. I asked Millie what she was feeling. She responded, "My God, this is the best I have ever felt in over eighty years. I feel as though my birth trauma was finally erased. That is the only way I can explain it. What a spectacular difference!"

CASES OF BODY AND MIND

CASE 8

Larry came to be treated for a variety of aches and conditions. His complaints included low and mid-back pain, asthma, neck tension, shoulder pain and pain between the shoulder blades, kidney region aches, insomnia, and the inability to concentrate for moderate to long periods of time.

The initial assessment showed an intermediate level of pelvic torque, restricted movement in both shoulders and neck, slight swelling in the right kidney region, and a deviation of the coccyx to the right.

This session consisted of the BRM, with the addition of the kidney and asthma procedures. After the session, Larry said that he felt relaxed and that he could breathe better. We set the next appointment for seven days later.

During the week, Larry noticed an improved ability to breathe, a reduction in pain near the kidney region, and less tension in the neck and upper back. He said that during the week, "I slept like a baby." A pain showed up in his right knee that he had not felt for four or five years. He also mentioned that he did not write this on the initial client information form. It was a work injury that had occurred about eight years earlier that severely injured his knee and kept him out of work for a long time.

A short assessment showed a deviation of the coccyx to the right, less restriction in the neck and shoulder areas, and tension of the hamstring muscles and intermediate pelvic torque. The second session consisted of the BRM, with an addition of the hamstring, coccyx, knee, and intermediate level shoulder procedures.

During the session, Larry went into a very deep state of rest and snored loudly. The torque in his pelvic region lessened and he became slightly dizzy for a few moments upon sitting up. After the session, Larry immediately reported that his neck and shoulder pain were drastically reduced and his back no longer ached. He said he felt as though he were standing straighter and taller.

The days between appointments brought significant changes. In Larry's own words, "This last week was like a roller coaster ride. My body experienced different pains. My mind got a little uneasy and I became anxious for about a half a day. Also I noticed that I slept much better."

The next assessment showed that his pelvic region, though showed a significant torque toward his right knee more prominently than before. Also he had a region of torque in his chest region that had not been there before. His coccyx was centered, stable, and pain free. Upon mentioning these differences, Larry announced that he had forgotten about an accident he had when he was younger, which did some extensive damage to his chest and ribs.

This session covered the pelvic and chest regions and the right knee. When we finished the treatment of the chest region, Larry immediately started a short tear-filled emotional release. This brought forth the feelings he had had after the accident that injured his chest and ribs. He remembered being in so much pain that he did not know if he would live through it. At the time, he had wished his life would end. After the emotional release, he felt free on the physical, mental, and emotional levels.

The next week clearly brought unique changes. He said, "I noticed that I was much more relaxed at work. I just handled what came along. Life seemed so much easier and freer. My hemorrhoids are disappearing. What is surprising is that I am losing the weight that I haven't been able to take off for years."

After the fourth session, Larry's pelvic region balanced. He had become increasingly aware of what people were really saying without saying it and what they really felt inside. He was able to not only read it in their eyes, but he knew exactly what it was that they were trying to hide from others

CASE 9

Rick was in an accident when he was five years old. Although his face and head were badly injured, his eyes swollen shut, and his nose broken, he remembers telling his parents and the doctors how much his knees hurt. But they kept saying there was nothing wrong with his knees. From that time forward, whenever someone touched his knees, he would immediately drop to the ground, curl up in a ball, and cry in agonizing pain.

At age 37, Rick experienced weekly headaches. The initial assessment showed that there was excessive torque in the pelvic region, coccyx deviation, rib rotation plus chest torque and full body tension.

We treated him using the BRM and the kidney procedure. The session relieved some excess tension. His second session consisted of the BRM, hamstring, asthma, coccyx, and pelvic procedures.

His body settled into a more profound state of relaxation combined with deeper breathing. He also had reduced pelvic torque, and remarkably less body tension. The next seven days brought a variety of changes. His ability to focus and concentrate became more acute and his energy level increased rapidly, although the pain in his low back and both knees was still there.

The assessment on his next visit showed an increase in loridosis in the lumbar region and a continuation of the pelvic torque. We treated him using the BRM and the psoas procedure. After completion of the psoas procedure, Rick immediately went into a state of profound emotional release. His body shook uncontrollably, he became chilled, and he cried out as if in immense pain.

We covered him with a blanket to contain his energy and within one minute his body went limp and he fell into a deep sleep. Forty-five minutes later he woke up and begin to describe his experience. He said. "I saw what happened before, during, and after my accident, as if it had just happened. I saw my mother slam on the brakes to avoid what would have been a terrible accident.

I was in the back of the station wagon, kneeling on the cold metallic surface that covered the storage area below, playing with a little yellow dump truck. As the car screeched to a halt, my body rocketed forward toward the back seat which was surrounded by a thick metal protection bar. Milliseconds before my nose and face hit the metal portion on the back seat, my knees, with all the weight of my body on them, scraped deeply across the exposed storage compartment metal hinge that extended the full width of the car. I knew that my knees were injured though the doctor and my parents kept telling me that my knees didn't hurt but my face did. Amazing!"

Later that week, Rick telephoned to say that as he was playing football with his boys, one of them forcefully ran into his knees to tackle him. Normally a blow to the knees would put him out of commission for a couple of days, but, much to his surprise, it did not even phase him. No pain, no shock no dropping to the ground. He also reported that his headaches "just disappeared."

CASE 10

Debbie, in her late forties, came to the clinic with the notion that because she was always sick there was nothing anyone could do for her. She insisted that she would always remain this way. She came in because her friend told her that Bowen was better than any massage she had ever received. Our initial assessment revealed all kinds of disorders, pains, tension, and stresses. Her body wanted to constantly assume the fetal position.

The initial session included just the basic BRM and kidney procedure. Instinct told me that there was more going on than the eye could see. Her response to the session was, "I feel OK."

Debbie's next visit included an assessment that showed no deviation of the coccyx nor pain or discomfort in the skull, face, neck, chest, or abdominal regions. Her session consisted of the BRM, as well as asthma and pelvic procedures. We used these procedures with the intent to remove or generate any signs of physical or sexual abuse the brain might be concealing. The only noticeable response was that of an increase in the depth and frequency of her breathing, to which her response was that she "only felt slightly frightened and uncomfortable, but ok."

154

The next week did not reveal anything different from what she had been experiencing in the past. Her next visit revealed extreme tension in the abdominal, chest, and back regions. She had little ability to focus that day and felt uneasy. We treated her with a series of procedures that have been known to occasionally release emotions. The session consisted of the coccyx, pelvic, TMJ, kidney, asthma, and chest procedures, with their accompanying waiting periods. Near the end of the session I asked her, "Who terrorized you?" to which she readily replied, "No one that I know of."

Before the session ended I again asked, "Who terrorized you?" and added, "I sense it happened when you were twenty-eight years old. " Her eyes widened, her mouth dropped to the floor, and she exclaimed, "At college, I was stalked by a man whom I had seen on campus a couple of times before and who wanted me. One night he called and told me that he was coming to get me. Moments later someone walked up the gravel driveway. It was dark. I was petrified and grabbed, a broom handle to fight to the death. Steps came closer and now this person was walking on the porch toward the door.

In a panic, I stopped breathing. I literally wet my pants and couldn't move. There was a knock on the door and I couldn't have screamed if I had tried. The only thing I could think of was to get near the window to jump out if someone came crashing in. I looked to see where this person was and saw a personal friend standing by the door. I ran to the door, let him in and told him all the things that just took place. I shook violently from panic and fright. We called the police and they arrested the stalker who was on his way to my place." Huge tears of relief gushed down her face. Debbie shared that "I feel alive and finally free."

CASE 11

Sabrina had been experiencing severe migraines so her chiropractor referred her to the clinic. We followed normal procedure and gave her an initial assessment. We found mid, upper back, neck, wrist, elbow, and low back tension--nothing out of the ordinary for a secretary.

Her first session consisted of the BRM, kidney, elbow and wrist procedures. After the session she talked about the calming feeling she experienced, along with a lightness in her body.

The week following the first session proved to be calm and relaxed. Her next assessment clearly showed that her coccyx was curved, like a hook, back into her body, and that her buttock muscles were holding a great deal of tension. Sabrina was treated using the BRM, advanced coccyx, and pelvic procedures. Nearing the final stages of the session, I discerned that her problem was at or near the base of the skull. I performed the skull release procedure and sensed that she had experienced severe head trauma at age two. She hadn't mentioned this in our conversations.

Upon completing the procedure, Sabrina's whole body shook violently from head to toe. She then began laughing as though from the bottom of her soul. Within ten seconds, she began to cry uncontrollably and her body shook violently for about five minutes. As a practitioner I have never seen such tears, the emotion that backed them, and the violent manner in which her body shook .

I shared with Sabrina what I had experienced. The insight included seeing her suffer severe head trauma around the age of two. She questioned my words and did not recall such an event. Then suddenly she cried, "Yes! How did you know? When I was two I was jumping on the bed with my dad and I bumped into him and went sailing off directly onto the top of my head. I was knocked out cold. My dad thought he had killed me." She then shared that the release she just experienced was the release of the pain that *she* took away from her father.

CASES OF BODY, MIND, AND SPIRIT

CASE 12

Patera came to the clinic to be treated for right shoulder pain, headaches and neck and shoulder tension. Her right shoulder lacked a full range of motion; it was at only 71 percent. Tension existed between the shoulder blades and in the lower back, neck, knees, ankles, a slight pelvic torque to the left, and a deviation of the coccyx to the left were found during the initial assessment. The initial session consisted of the BRM, with the addition of the kidney, knee, and frozen shoulder procedures. After the session, Patera said that she felt relaxed. Her shoulder, now had nearly 100 percent full range of motion. When walking, she noticed a freer feeling in her knees.

At the next appointment seven days later, Patera mentioned that about the sixth day after the session, the tension began to return to her shoulder and neck. She also noticed more tension in the left ankle.

A short assessment revealed that her coccyx deviated to the left, her shoulder was at 92 percent of full range, the pelvic continued torqued to the left, and her left ankle was noticeably more tense than in the previous week. The second session consisted of the BRM, with an addition of the coccyx, pelvic, ankle and frozen shoulder procedures.

During the course of the second session, Patera's body went into a very deep state of rest and her body temperature rose. We covered her with a blanket to contain her energy and let her rest. We attempted to wake her at 5 minute intervals over a 20-minute period but couldn't. Being in a deeply relaxed state of rest, her body encountered a mild, yet healthy healing crisis and began a healing cycle from deep within.

Upon arising Patera was visibly relaxed. Her voice sounded much deeper and her pelvis was almost fully realigned. Patera stated, "I haven't felt this good in many, many years and from what I can tell, at this point, my shoulder pain is completely gone. I feel as if there was a small current of electricity flowing through my ankle." The range of motion in her shoulder was now 100 percent.

The next few days her body began a detoxing process. She experienced a case of diarrhea for the first two days, a mild headache for the first three days, and her emotions went on a wild roller coaster ride. She vomited once toward the end of the week and her body just wanted to rest. This is a case of an intermediate level healing crisis.

The next session included the BRM, hamstring, kidney, psoas, and TMJ procedures. These procedures brought her pelvis into full alignment. She also had a newfound sense of balance in her body and mind. When she arrived at the clinic for the next session she was almost unrecognizable. She looked as though she had had a major face-lift. Her face shined brightly and she looked fifteen years younger.

I commented on the noticeable changes. . Her own explanation goes as follows: "I thought my life was doing just fine. I knew that I needed to make a few changes but it is like I have been given a new life. Things that used to bother me don't even phase me now. Life seems so new, so interesting and so motivating. It is as though I am awakening from within.

156

I met Lorraine and her two children, ages 5 and 7, during a volunteer services project the clinic supports. I noticed that she was physically, mentally, and emotionally abusive to her children. During a break, Lorraine told me how horribly tough life had been for the past two years and how so many of her friends just walked away after they learned that her husband, Tom committed suicide. Lorraine and her children looked like the walking dead. They couldn't smile. Their faces were worn and gray, their body language looked like someone had dumped the cares of the world on them.

I have seen people on their deathbed who looked better than Lorraine and her children. I suggested that Lorraine come in to visit the Bowen clinic. The initial assessment of their bodies showed excessive tension in the neck, shoulder, chest and back regions. All three had abnormal, shallow breathing patterns. The initial session consisted of the BRM, with the addition of the kidney and respiratory procedures for each of them. All three said they felt much more relaxed.

Their next six appointments began to unfurl layers of trauma and stress unimaginable for children their ages. Lorraine showed only slight decreases in stress. The eighth visit caught everyone, including myself, by surprise. During the middle of the session, the daughter, who had previously been asleep, sat straight up and began screaming at the top of her lungs, "I WANT MY DADDY!!!" This sudden outburst of extreme agony-filled pain and emotion overwhelmed everyone in the clinic. After this passed, she softly whimpered, "I want my mommy." Lorraine and her son also received a session that day.

During the following week both Lorraine and her son experienced similar outbursts of agony and emotion. On their next visit all three were hardly recognizable. It was as though everything had changed. Their bodies acted alive again, their minds were keen and sharp, and their spirits high. Since that time, their whole lives have completely changed. They have moved to another state and have started a new life.

Heal the body. Heal the mind. Awaken the spirit that is within.

CASES METAPHYSICAL

CASE 16, 17, and 18

There have been three separate cases where individuals in good general health, had out-of-body experiences while receiving Bowen sessions. The only similarity in the three separate cases lies in the fact that the out-of-body experience took place just moments after we performed the coccyx procedure.

Two individuals shared feelings of joy, expressing sincere gratitude for the experience. The third shared knowledge that the spirit is not part of the body. She said she did not want any more sessions and did not want to experience such a sensation again.

DISTANCE HEALING

CASE 19

While my part-time Bowen practice was growing, I worked for a prominent organic food packaging company. One day, the wife of Tom, one of the mechanics, was involved in a tragic nighttime traffic accident in which she had run over and killed a young man. Apparently in shock, the young man just walked right out into the oncoming traffic traveling at 65 mph.

Upon learning that his wife had killed someone, Tom went into a deep state of trauma and shock. Being a devout religious man he believed that she was going to be thrust into hell. .

Normally, this man was very active, doing many things simultaneously. After this tragedy, he took time off work to be with his family but he remained in a state of constant stupor. It was as though the life within him was disappearing.

Other veteran Bowen practitioners had said that this work could be done at a distance, in other words, energetically. Wondering what I could do for Tom, I decided to give distance healing a try.

I did a full-scale session as if he were right in front of me. After I finished, I thought nothing of it. The next day he dropped by his workplace and his fellow employees were totally shocked at the substantial change that had taken place. He was no longer in a stupor. He was grounded, centered, calm, and very at ease with himself.

In response to his supervisor's incredulity at Tom's amazing change, Tom said, "A very strange thing happened to me. While I was driving home yesterday after stopping I felt as though some force, or energy was penetrating my whole body. A large portion of the worry, fear, and doubt that I experienced just vanished. I feel that everything will be all right. I don't know how to explain it. I just know inside that it will be OK."

CASE 20

Tara came to see if we could help with the pelvic muscle spasms she experienced almost every day. About two years before coming to the clinic, she had suffered a very severe accident that crushed her pelvis. It had been broken in 28 places and the doctors overseeing her recovery told her she would never walk again.

She ignored the doctor's pessimistic outlook and took her first baby steps 30 days after the accident. When she came to the clinic, she had extreme levels of torque in and around the pelvic region and moderate to extreme bouts with painful re-occurring spasms. Treating her on a weekly basis proved helpful. Because her situation in life changed, she moved a few hours away into the mountains. One day she called to request the name of a Bowen practitioner near her hometown. We found that the closest practitioner was about 75 miles away and that our clinic was about the same distance. She asked how she could do something without driving that distance. I briefly mentioned a couple of cases in which distance healing had worked successfully. She nearly begged that I do this for her. I told her that I would hang up the phone and give her a distance session as soon as time permitted. Focus was a main point of distance work. She agreed. Later that day I focused a full session in my mind, including additional procedures for the conditions that currently presented themselves. Approximately one hour after the session she called to acknowledge that her pain had disappeared while she was resting.

Susan, a young teenager, was very active in sports, music, and life in general. Though she was active, her life was unsettled primarily due to the death of her grandfather.

I called the family approximately 18 months after the first session. Talking to her mother, I learned that Susan had had a nervous breakdown just two weeks previously. She wasn't doing too well. When I hung up the phone, I decided to give distance healing a turn to see if it could once again do its miraculous work.

Focusing within, I pictured Susan in my mind receiving a full session. Seven days later I repeated this process. One week later, I called to check on her. Her mother answered the phone and said to me, "You know, the strangest of all things happened. Right after you called, Susan started doing better and began to stabilize. We took her to the doctor and much to his surprise he said that Susan was making the quickest, most remarkable, and miraculous comeback that he had ever witnessed." Previous to this long-range attempt at distance healing, I had only done work within a 75-mile radius of my location. This was more than 2,000 miles away!

OTHER NOTABLE CASES

As we have seen, Bowen can be used in cases of accidents, strokes, heart attacks, and nearly every emergency situation. It is simple first aid that has been extremely effective in severe cases where medical personnel are not present. It greatly assists victims and in most cases quickly helps them recover from shock. Medical circles affirm that more people die from shock than from the actual accident.

CASE 22

While attending a fun event with my children, some of the other children began playing a game of chase. Soon many children were running in all directions in a small-enclosed area. Two children collided head on and one of them broke a tooth near the root. He began screaming and doubled over in agonizing pain. I ran up to the child and gently applied the first two Moves of the Lower Back Procedure. Within 12 to 15 seconds, the child's body calmed down, the pain greatly subsided, and he was able to find the broken tooth. After 2 minutes he turned to me and gave me the most sincere "Thank you, mister," I have ever received. After that, his parents took a relatively sedate child to the dentist.

CASE 23

A 75-year-old woman, who was having her hair styled, suddenly felt strange sensations in her body. A nurse noticed what was taking place and immediately stepped forward to assist. I was nearby, saw the commotion, and went to see if I could help. Suddenly this aged woman's face began to droop on the right side and the nurse exclaimed under her breath, "My God, she is having a stroke." I told the nurse to place her hand on this woman's shoulder and I proceeded to do one single Bowen Move on the nurse's neck. Upon doing the Move, the nurse's body jolted and within 15 seconds, the elderly lady who was experiencing the stroke calmed, her face lifted back up, and color began to return to her face. The nurse turned to me and said, "I have seen some pretty interesting things in my days as a nurse, but this was miraculous. What did you do?" By the time the paramedics arrived it was all over. The woman was taken to a nearby hospital and diagnosed by the doctors as having suffered a very light stroke and was released the next day.

CASE 24

A 45-year-old man came as a referral from his daughter. Three different physicians told him he needed both knees replaced. After the first Bowen session he received significant relief. After 7 visits he said, "I feel young again. My right knee has never been better and my left is, I'd say 95%." I haven't seen him since.

OTHER BRIEF CASES

A very young man had long standing hip problems. One month after the initial series of session he said it seemed as though it was going to flair up again, the ach started to return, but after about 20 minutes of session, it just disappeared and has never returned again.

BOWEN AND CONCUSSION

Bowen has been successfully used to help quickly and safely restore concussion victims back to normal. There are hundreds of thousands of sports induced concussions that occur annually let alone the many hundreds of thousands of fall and injury related concussions that also occur every year. Personally, I have experienced wonderful success for concussion cases for athletic and non-athletic injuries using strictly Bowen.

Craig Mattimoe, a Neuromuscular Therapist and Bowen Practitioner working in the athletic field in the San Francisco Bay area, also used Bowen to safely restore these individuals back to normal. He has documented many cases relating to Post-Concussion Syndrome (PCS). Craig has named Bowen for the use of concussions PCS-Accelerated Resolution Therapy or AR – Accelerated Recovery.

His study and research in field trials have yielded 33 consecutive safe and rapid restoration recoveries out of 33 cases. This is truly a remarkable and unprecedented accomplishment in the absence of any approved medical remedy, allopathic or alternative.

An excerpt from his website, www.concussions.info, is used with Craig's written permission and is as follows:

"The 33 cases were consensus representations of all three concussion grades: 1 (mild), 2 (moderate) and 3 (severe). Using the American Academy and Neurology concussion grading scale, there were no mild grade 1 cases. Of the 33 cases, 20 athletes or 60.6% were moderate grade 2 cases and 13 athletes or 39.4% were severe grade 3 cases.

Following the application of PCS-Resolution Therapy *(Bowen for concussions)* each of the 33 cases routinely resolved, with 30 of the 33 (90.9%) being symptom-free in 72 hours or less following *one* 45-minute rebalancing session.

Twenty-seven of thirty PCS cases (89.9%) were medically cleared to resume play immediately following post-session reevaluation by team physicians or trainers. The lengthiest and most physiologically challenging case (migraine headache history) of the 33 required just 12 days to become asymptomatic and achieve medical clearance to return to play.

Although the differential in recovery rates of all 33 cases is almost negligible, grade 2 cases have thus far required slightly more post-session recovery time. The symptomatic common denominator seems to be post-traumatic amnesia.

All 33 athletes safely returned to contact sports without ill effects... Given the astounding numbers of sports-induced concussion cases *and* the conspicuous absence of any prescribed remedy for post-concussion syndrome from any of the diverse arenas of medicine, the emergence of a potentially- effective protocol is a truly inspiring development.

Therapeutic recoveries of "repeat" concussion cases appear equally effective and nearly indistinguishable from "first-time" PCS recoveries, both of which also compare favorable to "limited" history recoveries (1 or 2 prior concussions). In essence, the effectiveness of Accelerated Recovery PCS recoveries appears wholly uninfluenced by the prior existence, number or severity of previous concussions.

Accelerated Recovery's potentially- groundbreaking results (a 33- case pilot study) are currently being rewritten (at journal request) for re-submission and peer-reviewed medical journal publication."

For those who are interested, there is more information about Bowen on Craig's website. Also included are many testimonials. These findings support and give enormous hope to those who are looking for help with PCS and mild traumatic brain injury. When publication of these findings is available, we will offer website links

NOT SO SUCCESSFUL CASES

One man who fell off a ladder and fractured his shoulder came for Bowen to restore the range of motion. For three weeks there was progress. Then progress stopped, I suggested that he go see his doctor to get an MRI or X-ray. Sure enough there was a bone impinging shoulder movement. After he had the chip removed he came in again for two sessions and within two weeks the shoulder range was fully restored.

One woman was having great success with Bowen and was progressing very rapidly. She then decided she didn't need to be well because her family members would take care of her, so she stopped treatment and halted her progress.

The ordinary doctor is interested mostly in the study of disease.
The nature curist is interested more in the study of health.
His real interest begins where that of the ordinary doctor ends.
Gandhi 1869-1948

Chapter 14

Some call them miracles

Time and time again Bowen proves pivotal in helping people who have endured many years of intense pain and suffering to become pain-free.

NOTE: This chapter includes a few of the testimonials we received from those who have undergone Bowen sessions. Testimonies of this kind are commonplace for Bowen Practitioners.

When my youngest son Winston was five years old, he severely dislocated his right knee while skiing. His leg turned 180° backward. I performed the first two Bowen Moves on his low back to get him out of shock. By the time I removed his skis, he had stopped screaming from the pain. I performed <u>one single Move</u> over the top of his knee and within 30 seconds his leg spun around and went back into place.

Two and one-half minutes later, Winston stood up and started to run around. I told him to sit down until the ski patrol arrived. When they came, they checked him out and cleared him to go. There was never any swelling or bruising associated with his injury, I believe, due to the fact that I applied Bowen immediately. To this day, Winston has never had any problems with that knee.

Raymond Augustyniak

In 1992 I was hospitalized with pneumonia and almost died. During my two-week hospitalization they diagnosed me with AIDS. I was discharged with 97% of my immune system destroyed by the HIV / AIDS virus. Since then I have had numerous opportunistic infections and chronic health problems. My viral load, which measures the concentration of the virus in my blood, had always been high. After 3 Bowen treatments in 2004, my viral load became undetectable for the first time in 12 years. I also have renewed strength and energy. I credit my improved health to those Bowen treatments and encourage others with HIV and AIDS to consider Bowen...

G. H. III   Sacramento, California

My first Bowen session was an incredible experience. I have endured pain in my left eye for years and after treatment it became pain free. My face suddenly relaxed about three hours after the session.

I got off medication after about two and one half weeks of Bowen treatment. After the third session, my body changed dramatically and began an unwinding process. The pain in my lower back and spine disappeared.

Bowen has turned my life around. If someone would have told me I would feel this good after just a few sessions, I would not have believed them. I AM a believer now!!!

Tina

Approximately four years ago, sciatica had me reeling in extreme pain. It eventually subsided and I forgot about it. In April 2001, it struck again. This time the pain increased. I took pain medication. Two days later, when I had a flight scheduled, the nagging pain still bothered me.

I went to a spa at the hotel to receive a hot rock massage. This gave me temporary relief. Later that evening the pain struck again, this time crippling me, I could only take ten steps at a time.

I returned home and made an appointment with my physician who diagnosed my pain as acute sciatica. He referred me to an orthopedist, who after a series of tests, said I had a pinched sciatic nerve. He scheduled me for physical therapy once a week for the next three months. He also gave me Vicodin and Motrin 800 for the severe pain.

The problem subsided, though I wasn't 100 percent. I felt better and continued running on the treadmill keeping a weary eye on my problem. On October 4th, I experienced intense pain after an airline flight. I could hardly walk without having to stop and massage my leg to obtain relief. I made an appointment with my doctor again.

This time he suggested a chiropractor. In the meantime he requested an MRI for my back. If I didn't find satisfaction with the chiropractor he would schedule surgery.

My physician indicated that I probably had deteriorated the nucleus around my L5 region. I was told that recovery would take approximately two to three months.

I went to the first chiropractor, at $45 per visit. He indicated I would need at least a year of maintenance visits. At that point I sought a chiropractor that my insurance would cover. He told me that the treatment would be painful for a minute with relief following.

It was excruciating, far greater than the original pain! I could hardly walk and he told me to return the next day for a follow-up. Next day he popped my back and the pain partially subsided. He told me that I wouldn't be able to run again. I'm an active runner and need to exercise to keep my weight down.

I was taking Vicodin® with the Motrin 800® four times a day for pain relief. It was still hard sleeping with the nagging pain, I looked forward to surgery.

During this time I received a phone call from a friend who told me about Bowen. I'm a skeptic but I was at my wits end and ready to try anything. .

I made an appointment with Raymond Augustyniak of the Bowen Healing System center in January 2002. I arrived in severe pain; I could hardly walk ten steps without spasms. Raymond told me to lie face down on the table while he worked on me. I could barely lie in that position without going into the fetal position. I expected a massage with no results. He explained that the body was like a house and when a circuit breaker trips the power off you need to reset it. After an injury, your body shuts down to protect it from further injury. He said all he was going to do was to reset the circuit breakers.

The therapy lasted a little over an hour. After that, he asked me to walk to the front of the office and back. I got off the table and couldn't believe I didn't have any pain. This was incredible. Raymond told me he wanted to see me three more times over the next three weeks. I asked him, "Is that all?" He stated that when he was finished with me I should be 100 percent.

I returned the following week and felt about 85 percent. By the third appointment I was 100 percent and I went to the fourth appointment because it felt good knowing I was rid of my pain and all medications.

I told my doctor the following month that I no longer needed surgery. He couldn't believe that in just four visits I had recovered. I showed him by doing jumping jacks. I told him I wouldn't have believed it myself if it hadn't happened to me.

Now I tell everyone about Bowen. This is my testimonial to Bowen. It works! I can't say enough about it.

Frank R. - Sacramento, California

I never thought I would feel this good again! Life is so much more enjoyable without the gnawing pain. Thank you so much.

J. W. Weinhardt – Anchorage, Alaska

I wanted desperately to become pain-free, energetic and happy again after suffered a severe accident. I had a long list of debilitating and chronic disorders that kept me constantly fatigued and depressed. All my friends knew that I was searching for a solution that would end my struggles with pain and ill health. I wanted to stop all the medications I was taking for pain and get rid of the anti-depressants and lead a more balanced life naturally. One of my friends had heard about the miraculous effects Bowen has on people and she told me about it one day.

I went to receive my first session. I was amazed at the differences I began to feel happening in my body during the session. The changes that occurred from my sessions were definitely positive and to say that Bowen gave me my life back would be an understatement, from my point of view.

I now am medication free, living a life I thought I could never have. Thank you so much.

Chris T. - Sacramento, CA

Why struggle to get well by using other methods that *might* work when you can use Bowen first and get on with your life much quicker.

Scott K.

I had previously received numerous chiropractic, acupuncture, and reflexology treatments. After these, the pain increased and remained that way for many weeks.

Some doctors offered medication, (which I believe is only a temporary band-aid do not directly address or solve the problem). Others offered invasive surgical procedures.

Before receiving Bowen treatments I couldn't do the simple things such as writing, bending over, picking up a glass of water, getting out of bed, walking, driving a car, breathing, or standing without excruciating pain. At times I wished I would die. After the first treatment I <u>definitely</u> noticed a difference. Between the second and fifth treatments I experienced many pain-free moments. After receiving only 6 treatments the pain disappeared. <u>NO MORE EXCRUCIATING PAIN</u>!!! At times I feel sore or tired, but the eight years of intense pain is <u>gone</u>!

The work that Bowen does is miraculous. I am now celebrating my new life of joy and laughter because of this therapy.

Thank you so much.

J. Y., Elk Grove, CA

Dear Bowen Healing System,

A friend introduced me to your Bowen clinic. I was in agonizing pain from an accident, I didn't sleep well and I lacked energy most of the time. I received treatment from doctors and therapists over and over, but the relief did not last long. All told me that I should learn to live with my pain because of the accident and my age. Since I was 81 I hoped to at least manage the pain. I do not like to use medication and pain relievers.

My friend told me about some of the remarkable results at the Bowen clinic. I had not heard of it before, but I took his word for it.

I decided to do the initial 3-5 treatments to see if there was any value from them. . The treatments were affordable and if they relieved the pain it would be worth it.

To my amazement, I began to feel some strange sensations in my body from the very first They continued for the next few days after treatment. My body began getting warm almost immediately, like there was a heater inside. It felt like it was shifting or adjusting itself. You can't explain it until you experience it for yourself.

After the second treatment my body shifted some more and I slept deeply and felt rested for the first time in years. I lay on my back, something I had been unable to do since before my accident. The pain was also going away.

My energy had come back and the off-balance feeling I experienced had disappeared. I slept soundly and my mind chatter lessened.

The fourth treatment brought the most surprises. I relaxed during the treatment. Many of my pains and the twisted feeling went away. The next morning I received a phone call from a friend who asked me about Bowen. I found one of the brochures, and started reading it to her. A moment later I begin crying, I realized that I was reading without my glasses.

Bowen has not only released me from pain, it has literally changed my life! I refer all my family members and friends who have any kind of pain or discomfort to the Bowen clinic.

I thank you sincerely

Jerry T. Carmichael, California

I was introduced to Bowen just a few months ago. The Moves are gentle and non-invasive. They tend to address several body systems, fascia: neuromuscular, and lymphatic to name just a few. This treatment technique has changed how I approach acute and chronic musculoskeletal problems.

Herman M. - Physical Therapist

I cannot thank you enough! For years after living with an alcoholic and trying to recover from a rape, panic attacks, and menopausal stuff. I was a basket case. I couldn't function without getting sick or passing out. Your website introduced me to Bowen. Raymond talked to me on the phone and I began treatments with him the following week.
After a few treatments I can go to the office to receive treatments. I never thought I could leave my home again. The fear was too immense. After the first session I cried most of the night. I had not cried in years--and the healing began...
I'm beginning to live now, not just exist. Thank you!!!

Juneau- Fair Oaks, California

I had shoulder surgery at age 68. Since that time I have been unable to lift my hand above my waist. I did physical therapy to no avail and my doctor told me I would have to live this way the rest of my life. I like to cook and now had to do everything with my other hand. Not being able to reach the spices off the bottom shelf made life troublesome and time consuming.
My brother told me about the Bowen Healing System in California, so I flew out from Kansas City to give it a try. I received the first treatment and thought, "Well, he sure didn't do much."
Later that night, my brother asked how my shoulder was and to my amazement I was able to lift my arm high over my head! My brother and I sat there and cried for some time. I was so happy! I could cook again. I received a few more treatments before going home and flew out for a couple of treatments after I fell on an icy sidewalk. Once again, Bowen took away the stiffness and pain. What a blessing Bowen is!

Helen- Kansas City, Missouri

My baby was inconsolable for a little over a day. Being a new mother I didn't have a clue to what was going on with her. I called a dear friend and explained how she acted. She said, "It sounds like your baby has colic. I know right where to send you." She gave me the number to the Bowen clinic and I immediately called. Within 30 minutes I was at the clinic. Ten minutes later I walked out with a calm baby. They didn't charge for the treatment. I called my friend to tell her about the amazing experience. She said, "They took care of you, didn't they?" "They sure did."
Thank you ever so much for helping me and my baby.

Lindell K. – Folsom, California

Just a short note to say thank you. When my grandson's fencing coach told me about Bowen, I was skeptical. After dealing with constantly aching shoulder joints, knees, and headaches, I decided to give it a try. Western medicine had done nothing for us, so why not? I also took my grandson who had TMJ, headaches and a back problem

Your therapy was effective. Chris's headaches eased after the first visit and ceased completely by the end of our treatments. After my first visit I was able to swing my arms in a complete circle for the first time in a year! Since the follow-up visits I've been able to perform hard, physical labor in my yard and remodel my home. I have tired arms at night, but wake up feeling fresh and ready to go the next morning as though I had loafed the day before! (What a relief!) My body really does heal itself!

Since receiving Bowen treatments I am able to fully extend my arms, put equal weight on my knees, and bend over and reach forward. My bowling average has risen from 142 to 154! Recently I bowled a 215 – my highest score ever!!!

Everyone I sent you have seen great improvement and have thanked me numerous times for referring them (even my boss!)

Bowen has been a Godsend. I recommend the Bowen Healing System to anyone who has physical problems that just won't go away!

Sincerely,

Jeanie F. – Rancho Cordova, California

Our son underwent all kinds of tests for ADD and ADHD but his medications didn't seem to do anything. The doctor told us that Bowen was doing good things for children and adults with ADD and/or ADHD

The teachers dreaded having my son as a student as he was unmanageable and disruptive. I took him to the clinic and they were so relaxed with him. They did the treatment as I watched. It seemed like they weren't doing much to him. They told me that I should start seeing results within 3-4 weeks.

After the first treatment I noticed that he was a bit more peaceful and that he was even nice to his sister. I then took him to the clinic once a week. After the fourth treatment I was shocked! He was calm, talked quietly and slowly, and didn't interrupt me like he normally would.

Since then we have taken him off all medication and his grades have greatly improved. He gets along well with the kids in his class and is much more focused in everything he does. The teachers are grateful.

Miracles DO happen and Bowen DOES work.

Regina P. San Francisco, California

I heard about the Bowen Healing System from a radio program where Raymond shared the remarkable benefits that Bowen has achieved. I decided to see what Bowen could do. I had experienced allergy problems for 25 years. After a couple of Bowen treatments I found that my allergies lessened. After just a few more treatments I would judge my problem at about 2 on a scale of 1-10 with 10 being the worst. In the past it was in the 9-10 range. Bowen has been a Godsend. I no longer take medications for my allergies

I can't wait to see the results after a few more treatments!

Sincerely,

Frank H. - Antioch, California

I heard about Bowen from a friend but could not find a clinic close to my house. I flew from Tampa, Florida to the Bowen Healing System Center near Sacramento, California for my first three treatments. I had been in extreme pain for four years with fibromyalgia.

I was hoping for some kind of relief. I felt odd sensations in my body after the first visit and some of my pain went away. After the third session nearly all my pain disappeared and I keep getting better every day. I have no clue what it is or how it works, but I am grateful

Patricia – Miami, Florida

Shortly after I turned thirty – I'm now 34 – I developed what I thought were allergies. People told me that if I lived in Sacramento long enough this would happen. When the stuffy nose and sinus headaches started, I was sure they were allergy related and I would just have to live with them. A couple of years later I began getting what I thought to be migraines. They were accompanied by stabbing pain, sensitivity to sound and light, and nausea and vomiting.

My physician prescribed a myriad of medications that were occasionally effective, but the side effects, which included a racing heart and dry mouth, were awful. I had headaches that felt like they might be sinus related. I was referred to an allergist who ran several tests and concluded that I wasn't allergic to anything.

Suspecting a chronic sinus infection, he prescribed a cortizone nasal spray. The headaches went away for two weeks and then returned. A CAT scan revealed that I did have a chronic sinus infection, and this was the cause of the headaches. I took two different types of antibiotics for several weeks and had a week or two of relief but on the fifth week a lower grade headache returned.

Clearly the antibiotics were no longer working. While they weren't "migraine" headaches, the pain increased each day. I knew it was only a matter of time before the severe headaches returned. I couldn't concentrate at work. At night, I would go home exhausted.

A colleague referred me to the Bowen Healing System. I had five (Bowen) treatments, once a week, for five weeks. After the first treatment I felt such a difference that I quit taking the antibiotics. At each appointment, the practitioner dealt with a specific issue: sinus pressure, ear aches, and headaches He always had a recommendation to augment his treatment, including a cayenne pepper snuff, from Western Botanicals.

He also recommended lots of water, light exercise, and ginger tea. The treatments were relaxing and resulted in an overall sense of well being. By the fifth treatment I knew I was well on my way to being healthy without the need for painful surgery. I plan to continue occasional treatments for my personal maintenance. I am grateful for the results.

Jennifer M. - Sacramento, California

I worked as an industrial electrician for many years. I have suffered moderate to extreme back pain for nearly 27 years. I went through all kinds of therapies to find relief. This lasted a few days before the pain came back and never went away. Through the help of a friend I found your clinic. After just a couple of visits doing Bowen I feel like I am 35 again! It was worth the travel to get there.

Jacob B. – Las Vegas, Nevada

I have had severe allergies most of my adult life and became asthmatic in my 50's. . I always had my inhaler with me and used it nearly daily-- sometimes many times a day. I had excessive congestion in my nose and chest. I was referred to Bowen Healing System Center by a friend.

After treatments, my breathing became MUCH better. My congestion is completely gone; I can breathe freely for the first time in many years and don't use my inhaler anymore, This is the first time in 50 years that I don't have ANY allergies AT ALL and I quit taking all allergy pills!!! I can breathe perfectly through my nose. M chest is clear. I feel great. Doctors have told me that I would have to learn to live with my problems. Guess what? They were WRONG. THANK YOU VERY, VERY MUCH!

Sincerely
Catherine D.   Pittsburg, California

By my fifth treatment I knew I was well on my way to being healthy again, without the need for painful surgery.

Jennifer M. Woodland, California
Past chronic sinus sufferer

It feels great to finally feel good again! I haven't felt this well in 25 years. Thank God for Bowen.

Kim H. Missoula, Montana

I am a hair stylist who works long hours. I have had extreme pain in my neck, shoulders and especially my arms and hands. I was taking 18-20 Motrin and Aleve a day to help relieve the pain. After just one Bowen session I just took one aspirin the next day and haven't had to take anything since. I go in for a session once every couple of months to keep me healthy and feel good.

Tanya U. San Francisco, California

Since I suffered from extreme never-ending low back pain, my doctor scheduled me for back surgery. I went to the Bowen Healing System Center in the Sacramento, California area as a last resort in an attempt to avoid surgery. I have never believed in any kind of alternative therapy. I was skeptical to say the least.

My doctor and I were shocked. After four visits I was 100% pain free and fully recovered. Since then I have started working out and feel good. THANK YOU SO MUCH.

Frank R. – Houston, Texas

I'm 73 years old and have had ongoing chronic foot pain for 63 years because I stepped on a nail when I was 12. I went to the Bowen Healing System Center because a friend told me they could help. To my surprise, I became pain free after the third visit. I do not know what they do or how they do it. I am just grateful that it works!

Tom E. – Oakland, California

I wanted to drop you a note to thank you for the instant and terrific results from the single Bowen treatment I received in February 2001. I had very painful bone spurs which were the result of running back and forth for 8 to 12 hours a day on a concrete floor.

I unsuccessfully went the "foot doctor" route for many years. I might add, my mother arranged for a Bowen session in Boise, Idaho after one of your classes. She didn't share the details of the therapy she just asked me to "try it." I was skeptical, but willing to remain open to any "help" available.

The results were immediate and lasting. As I write this letter on May 14, 2001, I have had absolutely no pain whatsoever. I used to climb out of bed in the morning and hit the floor in pain. The day after the first treatment I was pain free and upon returning home to Salt Lake City I began to walk. I lost 20 pounds in three weeks and now walk 6-8 miles a day, pain free!

Thank you for applying this technique so skillfully and successfully. I truly appreciate all the changes it has enabled me to make in my life.

Margaret J. – Salt Lake City, Utah

I flew from Detroit, Michigan to Fair Oaks, California for Bowen treatment. In June 2002 I broke my right wrist which brought on a condition called RSDS (Reflex Sympathetic Dystrophy Syndrome). I had near constant pain and was unable to pick up, carry objects, or make a fist even after many months of physical therapy.

In the spring of 2003 I visited the Bowen Healing System Center and after just a couple of treatments, I was able to pick up objects. Most of the pain was gone.

Returning to Detroit, I checked in with my Orthopedic Surgeon. He was elated that I no longer had any pain and was able to carry objects. I also went back to my physical therapist, because I had an appointment set shortly after my return. He was shocked to see my progress and asked what I had done. I explained that I went to the Bowen Center and even though I couldn't explain what the did, it obviously worked.

He asked for the phone number for the clinic because he had NEVER seen anyone in my condition change so quickly. He said that it normally takes about one year to get the results I got after just a couple of treatments.

In June of 2003, I severely injured my left hamstring muscle experienced excruciating pain! First I went to my physical therapist for treatment, but after two weeks of treatment with no results, I returned to the Bowen Healing System Center. In great pain and on crutches I flew back to California. After a lengthy treatment of about 1½ hours, I walked out of the clinic without crutches and NO pain! The next day I went sightseeing in Yosemite National Park. I walked nearly five miles that day pain free.

I am thankful for the work you do at the Bowen Healing System Center. You have been a blessing in my life. Thank God for this form of alternative therapy. It is truly miraculous!

-and-

About 40 years ago I fell backwards over a rolled rug and landed on my tailbone. Since that time, whenever I would sit down I <u>always</u> had pain. Sometimes it was unbearable to the point that I would just stand. I had chiropractic care all through the years that helped my back for a short period of time but never helped the tailbone at all. I had the simple and gentle coccyx procedure performed on me while attending a Bowen class. I could not believe it – Whoa – Hoa! I had NO PAIN when I sat down and I became very emotional. The pain that was ALWAYS there was gone instantly. Bowen is a God sent blessing!

-and-

In July of 2004, I messed up my knee at work. I tried doctors and physical therapists for over six weeks with little change. I was about to go on a trip to China. I didn't know what to do because the China trip was going to require a lot of walking, yet I could hardly walk. I decided before the trip to fly out to California again. After two short visits I was 100%. I went back to my doctor and physical therapist and told them they needed to quit wasting people's time and money and that they needed to learn Bowen. My China trip went without a hitch, we walked miles climbing all the stairs and hills.

Thanks again and again,
Barbara H. – Hazel Park, Michigan

During my initial exam with a neurologist, I was diagnosed with a bulging, herniated disc between the 5th and 6th vertebrae in my neck that was pressing on my spinal cord, as shown by a MRI.

The recommended "remedy" was surgery to fuse discs and put in a metal plate by going through the front of my neck.

My symptoms were dizziness, feeling like I was going over backwards, pain in the left arm, shoulder, and neck area, and _very_ bad headaches.

I didn't want surgery, so I was referred to Bowen for a possible holistic approach to "cure".

I went for 4 treatments, 1 week apart for each visit. After 2 treatments, _all_ symptoms disappeared completely, but I continued with two more treatments, just in case.

I returned to the neurologist for a second MRI. The bone spur was _gone_, my body had absorbed it, and the compression was gone!

Healing had occurred using Bowen!

Thank you Tom Bowen and the universe!

Koni N. – Chico, California

After a Bowen session, I am very aware that the "barriers" I put out to protect me from other people and the world are gone. I happily observe that I'm just here in present time.

It's almost a dizzy kind of feeling, but with more awareness than usual. Bowen certainly works with and for the body.

J. V. – CPA

My wife and I suffered from chronic pain because of a car accident. We suffered from constant nagging pain and tension in our cervical, thoracic, and lower lumbar regions. I had heard about the Bowen Healing System Center and the work they did through a colleague. He commented that though he did not fully understand or comprehend, the results, his patients claimed they were miraculous. He asked me to look into it.

I called the clinic and asked a variety of in-depth questions. The information I received was both informative and convincing. After reading their website, my wife and I decided to fly out to California for treatment. We received a total of three treatments apiece. Each treatment successively removed gradations of pain and discomfort.

Even after having treatments, I am not able to explain what happens to the body when the practitioner performs their work. The only way I could explain it is that my body totally relaxes, tension lessens, and the pain just somehow disappears. Since our initial set of treatments we have not felt any pain or discomfort related to the accident.
Thank you.

Rich N. M.D. – Jacksonville, Florida

I am 72 years old and have been barely able to move my shoulder for the past four years. I needed help dressing, cleaning, and getting in the car. I went to the Bowen Clinic because my daughter had such good results. She told me I should go and see what they could do for my locked shoulder. I felt relaxed after the first treatment but my shoulder was still stuck. After the fourth treatment I had full use of it. Two weeks after that I put up 32 pounds of pickles. My shoulder works just fine, much thanks to the folks at the Bowen Healing System Center.

Della Z. – Fresno, California

I messed up both knees working as a contractor. The doctors told me I needed knee replacements in both knees, but because of my young age, I would have to wait at least 15-20 years before it could be done. If I didn't wait, I would have to have them replaced later in life. My daughter recommended the Bowen Healing System Center. I had my doubts that anyone could help. I went anyway and after 5 treatments my right knee returned to 100% and my left knee 95%. I told the people at the clinic that that was good enough for me. I know I'll be back if they bother me again. I talked to my doctor after the Bowen treatments and he was very amazed.
The body CAN really heal itself!

Butch B. – Reno, Nevada

I have been going to chiropractors for 20 years, lately, 3-4 times a week. After just one Bowen treatment I felt better than I ever had from the last 10 years of chiropractic treatment.

Lisa W. – Tracy, California

I heard about the Bowen Healing System Center from a tourist. They gave me the clinic's card and said that they believed it could help me with my chronic head and neck problems and the occipital neuralgia I had. I called and they assured me that the treatment would be beneficial. I booked a flight from my home in Hawaii and stayed with some friends while having my treatments.
Two weeks later the pain, tension and tingling sensations were completely gone. I am thoroughly impressed with what Bowen can do. Doctors in Hawaii gave me up long ago. They told me I had to learn to live with it. I am so glad that the tourist talked to me. It changed my life.
I've heard it said that the difference between God and a doctor is that God knows he's not a doctor!

Bob K. – Honolulu, Hawaii

I am 74 years old. Since 10, I have had back problems and headaches because of an accident. Since then I have progressively become worse. I have regularly gone to doctors, chiropractors, physical therapists, massage therapists and others trying to find someone who could help me with these problems. I've been told things like, "It's all in your mind," "I can't help you," "If this medication doesn't help come back and we will try another," "This will take years to fix," Since my very first appointment at the Bowen Healing System Center, I have been absolutely amazed. I have no words to describe the awesome changes that have taken place – no more pain – what a relief! There was no discomfort with the treatment either, what a joy.

H J E – Sacramento, California

My left big toe became swollen and painful and stayed that way for nearly five years. Most of the time I couldn't bend it and had to wear wide shoes, so it wouldn't hurt so much. The doctors said I had a bunion and they needed to perform surgery. I tried acupuncture and it seemed to help some.

I found out about Bowen from a lecture and demonstration given at the East-West Bookshop in Sacramento. I thought maybe I should try it, I've done everything else but surgery, and I certainly didn't want to do that. I had other friends that had bunion surgery and it didn't make their toes better. After a couple of visits the swelling went down and now the bunion is disappearing. I am doing what the practitioner has asked me to do. It is so simple. Why don't more doctors know about this?

Geri D. – Modesto, California

You really didn't do anything as far as I am concerned, just like you said. BUT I FEEL SO DIFFERENT! WOW!!! Bowen is phenomenal. Thank you so much!

Patricia M. – Seattle, Washington

My knees always hurt after the surgeries I had on them in the early 1960's. I could not find relief anywhere or with anything. Recently I had heart surgery and had been unable to breathe properly since. I received a couple of Bowen treatments. I feel young again. I can breathe! I just turned 72 and I can do things I haven't been able to do for decades. It's a miracle!

Ray A. – Chicago, Illinois

Returning home from work I developed a pain in the right side of my body. I lay down thinking it would go away. The pain increased to the point that I had to have my neighbor take me to the emergency room. They found that I had a 10 mm kidney stone – something that modern medicine can handle most of the time, relatively easy – pain medication, lots of water, pass or in my case blast the stone (lithotripsy, a procedure known also as extracorporeal shockwave lithotripsy – a procedure that uses sound waves delivered inside a water bath to pulverize kidney stones painlessly in the body) and pass the smaller stones.

Except, in my case I have a semi rare blood disorder called protein "S" deficiency. My blood clots at random unless I am on blood thinners 24/7. These conditions limit the medications and procedures doctors can use to help me maintain good health. Throughout the process, the blood condition kept rearing its ugly head.

Before it was finished, I had multiple blood clots in both legs, and my left lung. I also lost partial use of my left arm and hand. The more mobile I tried to become, the more the pain increased – until my body couldn't handle it anymore. Flashing lights and blackouts started occurring. My body was shutting down, I wasn't eating and I had lost 25 pounds in two weeks.

Doctors tried morphine (on top of all the other medications I was still on) to see if they could give me some relief. The morphine took the edge off giving me a small windows of time where I could function. I would do as much as possible until the next wave of pain hit and put me down for the count again. Luckily, I had a wonderful employer who allowed me to work on my schedule so I could continue to support my family. This went on for months, Doctors couldn't explain why I was in so much pain now that the blood clots were dissolved and I had passed the kidney stones.

I was then diagnosed with Fibromyalgia and had flu like body aches and pain 24/7. I was told that there was no cure or medication available at this time. I took classes on pain management and depression trying to understand and improve my quality of life. My friends and family tried to find solutions to improve my condition.

My brother put me contact with Raymond. The night of my first appointment I was wearing three layers of clothes, including a jacket. I walked hunched over. The pain was excruciating. My posture was that of an 80-year-old man.

I gave a brief description of my health issues and lay down on the table. Raymond didn't say much, just went to work on me with a series of light touches. I was thinking, well, even if this doesn't work at least it doesn't hurt anymore than when I came in.

The second session went about the same, but I could feel my body starting to relax for the first time in over a year. I didn't feel much change in the pain level, but my body became calm.

By the third session, I felt a reduction in pain. My body started to respond to these light touches. I was overwhelmed. I stood up at the end of the third session with tears in my eyes and turned and hugged Raymond. Thank you, thank you.

I started tapering off the medications, and by the seventh session I was off morphine completely. Doctors said there was no cure, but Bowen has proven otherwise.

It has been over a year and a half since that seventh session. I am working full-time and can do pretty much anything in moderation with only small amounts of occasional discomfort. I consider this "Normal" for a 43-year-old male.

Thank you Tom Bowen and Raymond for giving me back my quality of life.

Sincerely,

Ron K.

Chapter 15

The Effectiveness of Bowen

HOW EFFECTIVE IS BOWEN?

The increase of interest in Bowen and its effectiveness in addressing specific conditions has prompted the need for an increase in scientific research data and analysis to properly evaluate the effectiveness of the Bowen. **www.bowenhealingsystem.com** provides a link that includes current research findings.

A summary of findings and research that has been concluded, as well as known current research projects on the effectiveness of Bowen for the titled specific areas, are noted below.

FROZEN SHOULDER

Preliminary research reports that Bowen therapy may improve range of motion in patients with frozen shoulder. Additional studies are needed before a firm conclusion can be drawn.

The outcome of this study does show that Bowen was a *very* effective treatment, using only 3-6 visits, with individuals who possess a long-standing condition. Other prior studies conducted for treatment effectiveness on long-term frozen shoulder conditions using other forms of therapy resulted in much poorer outcomes.

Dr. Bernie Carter and Bowen Practitioners Rick Minnery and B. Clarke from England performed a recently published study on frozen shoulders on 20 participants at the Metropolitan University of Manchester (UK). This study involved 20 participants who had been diagnosed with frozen shoulder. They were treated using Bowen.

The participants of this study declared that a high level of satisfaction was received from Bowen sessions. By the conclusion of the treatment, full mobility (equivalent to the opposite and non-affected side) was regained by 70% of the participants of this study.

The remaining 30% of the participants showed significant improvement in shoulder mobility and function. A minor few within this latter group reported a present, low-level dull ache. At the conclusion of this study there were no reports of any severe, persistent or throbbing discomfort or pain present that existed before they received Bowen in this study.

Of the 20 active participants in this study, 6 participants received 5 treatments, 6 participants received 4 treatments and 8 participants received 3 treatments before the study was concluded.

The participants of this study were impressed by the results they received from Bowen and conveyed their commitment to using it in the future for therapy in case of reversion back to frozen shoulder symptoms, other aches or pains, or for any other condition where Bowen may once again prove successful. Each one agreed to recommend the Bowen to friends and family.

PAIN, TENSION AND STRESS

A study by Amy Norman, performed in at the University of North Carolina at Chapel Hill, Department of Physical Education, Exercise and Sport Science 1998, used a survey to compare practitioner and patient responses in evaluating the effectiveness of Bowen in the treatment of pain. The results concluded that the practitioners rated Bowen 85% effective for back pain with patients averaging 4.3 sessions, 88% effective for neck pain with patients averaging 4.5 sessions, 83% effective for stress & tension with patients averaging 4 sessions, 83% effective for other conditions with patients averaging 5.8 sessions and 80% effective for fibromyalgia with patients requiring longer treatments – depending on the degree of fibromyalgia symptoms.

The effectiveness of Bowen that was rated by patients was 85% for back pain, 80% for stress & tension, 95% for TMJ, 80% for hip pain and 75.6% for other conditions.

In my own clinical experience, the overall efficiency average for Bowen is 85-88%, depending on the location of the pain, the severity of the pain or discomfort, and the length of time the person has had the pain, with immediate relief experienced about 79% of the time; the average soars is even higher within 3-5 days following a session.

BLOOD CHEMISTRY

Dr. JoAnne Whitaker, MD used a darkfield, phase and fluorescent microscope to perform live cell analysis, to show significant blood chemistry changes that occur following Bowen treatment. The blood chemistry changes seen in Dr. Whitaker's research show substantial support and add confirmation to the substantiated claims received by patients who occasionally experience short-lived flu-like symptoms, i.e. a feeling of nausea, due to the detoxification processes that occur in the body that can last up to 5 days following a Bowen session.

These symptoms have not been found to occur in any specific pattern following any specific procedure that is performed or with any specific combinations or specific number session, i.e. first, second, third , etc.

It does add to the supporting evidence that Bowen does make significant changes throughout the entire body.

FIBROMYALGIA

Another study performed by Dr. Whitaker, MD showed optimistic affirmative effects of Bowen that is performed on patients diagnosed with fibromyalgia. In this study, each participant experienced varying degrees of relief, which lasted from a few days to over several weeks. The measurements of shifts in the Autonomic Nervous System by Heart Rate Variability studies fully complemented the clinical assessments.

EFFECTS OF BOWEN ON THE AUTONOMIC NERVOUS SYSTEM AND THE HEART

Another study conducted by Dr. Whitaker, MD, shows that Bowen directly affects the Autonomic Nervous System. In this study, Dr. Whitaker was able to show measurable changes in the rate and pattern in the Heart Rate Variability before and after treatment.

I have personally seen huge changes in heart rate, blood pressure and respiratory rate in people that were attached to monitors while in the hospital following severe trauma, whom I have performed Bowen on. As Bowen was performed on them and their bodies changed from a traumatized and "in mild shock" state to a more restful one, very significant changes were immediately noticed during the Bowen session. On these individuals, the Bowen session was performed either directly on the person or through a proxy who held their hand or other part of the body because of the severity or extent of their injuries. In each case I have personally witnessed, doctors have remarked regarding the rapidity of their recovery.

In one case, where an individual was involved in a multiple rollover vehicle accident, he suffered very severe injury on various parts of his body, including his skull and multiple fractures. Hospital staff performed CPR on him to bring him back to life earlier in the day. I received phone call from a friend of his significant other, right after the CPR was performed. I went directly to the hospital as soon as I was able. Though this person was in critical condition, I had his significant other place her hand on his and using her as a proxy, I performed Bowen on her.

As I performed Bowen, I watched the monitor that displayed very irregular heart and respiratory rates, even out and become steady and rhythmic. Those in the room visibly witnessed the person's body relax and sink into the bed as well as the changes that occurred on the monitor. Moments later, a nurse came into the room and looked at the monitor, she said, "Hm, now that is much better, he is finally beginning to show positive signs that his body is stabilizing."

In another case, a man was hit head on by a Jeep while he was riding his motorcycle, when the Jeep swerved into his lane at approximately 40 mph. He suffered many broken bones as well as other injuries and was already in stable condition when I arrived at the hospital. Because of the extent of his injuries, I used his friend, who is also a personal friend of mine, as a proxy to perform Bowen on him.

As Bowen was performed, his heart rate went from 87 to 58 beats per minute and his respiratory rate went from 22 to 8, as he deeply relaxed. As this man's mother was in the room, I asked her and my friend to watch the monitor before, during and after the Bowen session. They were amazed as they watched the monitor change throughout the session.

Cases such as these give greater credibility to the work Bowen does for the body and how it can be performed even on individuals in very serious cases.

PSYCHOLOGICAL EFFECTS

Ashley Pritchard, at the Melbourne, Australia, Swinburn University department of Psychophysiology, conducted a study that showed that Bowen was able to consistently reduce the participants' level of anxiety while enhancing their positive feelings. It was observed and noted that Bowen was successful in reducing anger, tension, fatigue, depression and confusion in these participants. In this study, objective measures were used to detect decreases in the heart rate and muscle tension linked to the participants' subjective sensations of relaxation.

TMJ

A research project has begun in Durango, CO by Dr. John Bauman, DDS on the relevant use of Bowen on TMJ abnormality. In this study, bite measurement, masseter muscle tension assessment using Bio Feedback and subjective symptoms were compared before and after treatment. So far in this study, in one third of the cases felt extraordinary relief in several of their symptoms immediately following the first Bowen session. 20 out of the 22 patients studied so far have shown evidence of significant improvement using the Bio Feedback assessment when compared to their beginning statistics.

MATERNITY RESEARCH

Rick Minnery, Midwife, Bowen Instructor and Practitioner, is currently conducting a long-term study on the value and effectiveness of Bowen for maternity patients. In this study, Rick is researching a variety of topics that pertain to expectant mothers. Some of these topics include the effectiveness of Bowen for:

- Reducing pre-natal morning sickness
- Reducing lower back pain during pregnancy
- Reducing heartburn during pregnancy
- Increasing relaxation during pregnancy and labor
- Reducing pain during labor
- Reducing length of laboring time
- Pre and post natal breast discomfort and problems (i.e. engorgement, mastitis, lactation, poor or excessive milk production)
- Post-natal problems such as perineal trauma

Other research studies are also being conducted as funding for Bowen research, necessary equipment and personnel is secured.

Early research gives very strong evidence that advocates Bowen as *very* beneficial for use in successful treatment of frozen shoulder, TMJ, Fibromyalgia, psychiatric disorders and job-related stress. Further study is warranted, of course, in these and other areas and for a vast number of other conditions, disorders and diseases as well.

Chapter 16

Equine Muscle Release Technique (EMRT) and Bowen for Animals

– The latter and greater portion of this chapter was written by Carol Bennett for use in this book with her permission –

Because Bowen has been found to be very effective for use on humans, animal lovers, in recent years, have taken the Bowen basic theory and principles and have adapted and applied them for use on animals, both large and small and have developed training courses for specifically for this use.

The first Equine Muscle Release Technique (EMRT) seminar was taught on a cool summer's morning (wintertime for those in the northern hemisphere) at the Astral Equestrian Centre in Cranebourne, Australia in the Victorian province February 14th, 1997.   Ossie Rentsch opened the proceedings on behalf of the Bowen Therapy Academy of Australia and welcomed all in attendance while also introducing the founder and developer of EMRT, Allison Goward. He extended the Academy's support for EMRT and the magnificent work Allison was doing on animals.

Allison Goward, (Australia) a registered Bowen Practitioner, developed EMRT, her interpretation of Bowen on horses, as a natural progression of the work she was performing on humans, united with her deep passion and in-depth training with horses. During the seven year developmental and refinement stages of EMRT, many amazing successes were achieved.

Allison's expertise in working with, and her dedication to, working on animals is second to none.   She is the leading expert in the world on the subject.   As minimum pre-requisite qualifications for attending any EMRT sanctioned course, each student must learn and regularly use the Bowtech and BTAA approved courses and be a Bowen Practitioner registered with the Bowen Therapy Academy of Australia who regularly uses Bowen for treating humans.   The EMRT approved course takes two years to complete.   Some of the reasoning for the extended coursework is:

- When working with animals, one must understand animal behavior, for their own safety and the safety of the animal they are treating

- To learn instinctive animal behavioral reactions – horses do rear, kick and bite, dogs and cats do attack

- To learn and use basic rules of safety

- One must to learn to read the situation as it is occurring, as animals cannot speak to share what is going on – though they rightfully and quickly give signs of all kinds and magnitudes

- To prevent an accident from ever happening with animals

Commonly, many championship horses and their owners, trainers and riders are treated in order to regain and maintain balance between owner, handlers and the horse. Astounding results are frequently experienced with these delightful and sensitive animals.

Since the inception of EMRT, other individuals have taken Allison Goward's lead and have developed other animal related courses. Touch Balancing® - Bowen for Animals. Cat and Canine Muscle Release Therapy (CCMRT), as well as are others are being offered worldwide.

People in Geelong, Australia still talk about the time when Tom Bowen was asked to treat a horse that suddenly became lame the day before the Geelong Cup (The Geelong Cup has the same prestige as the Kentucky Derby has in the U.S.) Tom was asked to at least take a look at the horse because it was doing very poorly and was about to be cut from the race. Tom did a few Bowen Moves on the horse and shrugged his shoulders and said, "That's all" and then left. The next day the horse won the race! I was in Geelong last year in 2004 during the week of the "Cup" as they call it, and overheard someone not associated with Bowtech® or Bowen talking about it. That is the third time I have heard the same story from three different people. Obviously there seems to be some truth to it.

Since the commencement of Bowen Therapy being performed on animals, animals and mammals of all kinds have been treated using this wonderful technique. Dogs, cats, tigers, lions, ligers (a cross between a tiger and lion), bears, wolves, coyotes, cows, snakes, reptiles, birds of all kinds, monkeys, dolphins and even elephants have been successfully treated, as well as many other kinds of animals too.

You may be thinking that it is odd that someone might even think of performing Bowen or any other therapy on snakes. Snakes used to supply venom for anti-venom purposes can go into a state of shock when they are "milked" of their venom. Often these snakes die from the shock and their life-saving venom is lost along with the snake. The costs involved with finding and securing the many rare or highly venomous species of snake are astronomical. Bowen performed on them has saved their lives as well as those who have needed the anti-venom.

Veterinarians regularly attend and support EMRT, Touch Balancing® - Bowen for Animals (Carol Bennett~U.S.) and CCMRT (Tina Spurling~ England) seminars in order to better treat their animal patients using natural means for the wide variety of health related issues and challenges they bring. Touch Balancing® - Bowen for Animals and CCMRT fully compliment each other in the work they are doing for animals worldwide.

Allison Goward began teaching Carol Bennett the intricacies of treating horses using Bowen around 1993. Since then, Carol has attended Allison's classes and has developed the Touch Balancing® - Bowen for Animals course and has treated a vast variety of animals and mammals of all kinds. She, along with Dr. Lynn Peck D.V.M., has also presented Animal Bowen® at the 2003 Annual Conference of the American Holistic Veterinary Medical Association

Carol Bennett wrote the remaining portion of this chapter for use in this book.

ANIMAL BOWEN®

The Touch Balancing® - Bowen for Animals Bowtech® Certified Course

As developed, taught, and written by Carol Bennett

The Bowen Technique applied correctly to the anatomy of each species is as dynamic for the animal's innate healing mechanisms as it is for humans. Animal Bowen® has been documented as to its application and use for the care and maintenance for animals since October of 1995. Its successes include animals large and small, domesticated and wild, those in competition, rehabilitation or suffering from injury, abuse, pain or illness; working animals, and loved companions. It is currently in use in veterinary clinics in the U.S. and Canada, as well as animal rehabilitation facilities, sanctuaries, and homes.

Animal Bowen® adds many benefits to the health and well-being of all animals. Simple sequences of light cross fiber strokes across muscles, applied precisely often bring about outstanding results in a very short period of time for most animal related issues. A complete treatment may consist of just a few Bowen Moves or a complete series of Moves depending on what the animal is in need of.

The use of the light touch, along with the effectiveness of performing even one or two moves, makes Animal Bowen® a minimally invasive, highly relaxing and low stress therapy that compliments conventional and alternative veterinary care. Pet owners can also easily learn to apply Animal Bowen® Moves through attending courses. They can then assist their own pets in between regular veterinary visits or in a crisis when a veterinarian may not be immediately available.

This simple technique is unique in that it is work you do *with* the animal, not *to* the animal. Rather than using a pre-determined or prescribed course of action, the practitioner observes the animal's muscle tension patterns through a series of assessments. The animal's physical and mental responses to the assessments are then used to determine the course of action or treatment. This approach engages both the animals' intelligence and its body's innate healing mechanisms.

Known benefits of Animal Bowen® therapy include improvements in general health by increasing lymph and blood circulation and tissue metabolism, thereby enhancing elimination of toxins and decreasing inflammation; relieving muscle spasm; improving muscle tone, improving flexibility and range of motion; and speeding rehabilitation from over-exertion, mental or physical injury, and illness or surgery. Bringing balance to the structural elements of the body also improves posture and enhances performance and stamina.

While this modality appears to help tremendously in the areas of injury and ailments, the contribution it makes to improve negative emotional states and behavior is without exception. One simple Move can reverse mistrust and fear in some animals; in others, it may take several full treatments to achieve the same result. Usually within several Moves the animal grasps that this is beneficial to them and they relax into their treatments just as we might relax when treating ourselves to a luxurious day at a spa.

The work is so gentle and non-invasive it can be applied to animals in traumatic situations after they have been thoroughly checked out by a veterinarian. Animal Bowen® is extremely effective at calming anxiety, fear, aggression and defensive behavior patterns. This allows the body to transition from a "fight or flight" state, to one of calm and repair, and accept further assessment and/or treatment.

The cat, for example, that finds insertion of an acupuncture needle distressing may readily accept an Animal Bowen® treatment. Animals readily accept this gentle approach that can make them well again. This is an important advantage of Animal Bowen.® An Animal Bowen® Move can be applied lightly at the hairline level, quickly and easily, and is often more effective than a deep or forceful manipulation or procedure that is common to most other alternative approaches. This allows the healing work to progress quickly even in animals that can barely tolerate only the gentlest contact. The results are often impressive, impacting both the overall physiological and mental/emotional states of the animal, as well as addressing specific difficulties and traumas at the same time.

Animals live in the same world we do. They suffer stress and stress-related disorders and illnesses. They ingest toxins from the environment just as we do. Their food sources are suffering from the same depleted soils and many are living their entire lives on processed foods supplemented only with synthetic nutrients. I have written and could write several more books on the subject of how the animals are being stripped of their vitality and longevity. It suffices to say that their bodies need the same support our human bodies do. They need whole food nutrition too. In this modern world, far removed from their natural life styles, animals also have a need to receive the wonderful benefits from alternative and complimentary therapies have to offer.

Since 1993, through my company, Spirit Symbols' Animal Connection Network™, I have worked towards one goal: To better the treatment of all living beings and to improve their experience of Life.

How does Animal Bowen® compliment that goal? One has only to look at this book to see how the human body functions, how Bowen contributes to its proper function and then realize that Life for beings skinned, furred, feathered, of scaled, basically functions the same way. The latissimus dorsi of a chicken attaches similarly to a cow's or a cat's, etc. The neuro-pathways, the lymphatic system, the digestive system, the respiratory system, the organs, the tissues and fascia in relationship to how Bowen is applied and works, are basically the same, whether for humans or animals.

Yes, there are differences in size and shape and function of the muscles, systems and organs; basically speaking, the relation to how the technique is applied and works, those differences are primarily relevant to locating the precise point at which to apply the Move its self. My (Carol Bennett) course for animals is structured to teach this very concept.

Animal Bowen® is not taught as, nor is meant to be, a replacement for veterinary care, but rather as an adjunct to it. Throughout its history I have continued to engage many veterinarians in the recognizing the diagnostic feed back loop all animals have. I have also encouraged them to document their experiences with it. Animal Bowen® is emerging as a very effective therapy. Dr. Lynn Peck, a veterinarian with alternative medicine as well as clinical research experience with animals, has been part of my instructor staff since 2003 as co-instructor for the Animal Bowen® Touch Balancing course.

Following is a note from Dr. Peck: "Although it has been 3 years since Carol introduced me to Animal Bowen® Touch Balancing, I feel that I have hardly scratched the surface of its usefulness in working with animals. I am now using it on most of the animals in my practice — sometimes as a primary therapy, sometimes as an adjunct — and I continue to be amazed and just shake my head in wonder (and at times, disbelief) at the amazingly consistent results that are achieved. How does one explain bio-mechanically regarding a dog with a ruptured cruciate ligament that walks out on all 4 legs minutes after a Bowen treatment, after being 3-legged lame for 2 weeks?...or how a dog who has always been extremely terrified of thunderstorms and human contact becomes completely relaxed and affectionate (to the point of jumping into the owner's arms for snuggling and giving kisses) after just 4 treatments? **This is a profound therapy!** I am delighted at the opportunity to be teaching with Carol, and I look forward to sharing Animal Bowen® Touch Balancing with others. I know that along the way my eyes, too, will be opened even more to the many applications for healing that it offers. ~ Lynn S. Peck, DVM, MS Florida

To learn more about Animal Bowen® - Touch Balancing visit the website at: www.animalconnectionnetwork.com. To learn about Bowen for horses visit the website: www.bowtech.com and click on EMRT (Equine Muscle Release Technique).

"A few clinical cases" by Dr. Lynn Peck:

1) 12 yr old female Greyhound with old fracture below right hock. Difficulty moving around, irritable to other dogs in household. Runs with difficulty, using a short, humped-back stride. Owners want to avoid using NSAIDs. Treated with Animal Bowen® only: 3 treatments 2 wks apart, and basic modification of diet to higher quality and some raw foods. After 1st treatment, moving better, playing more, lots of energy that held till next treatment. Improved each time; by third treatment was running and playing "like a puppy" with the other dogs; and no longer irritable. Eight months later, with no other treatment, still maintaining. Owners noted that this was the first summer she was not afraid of thunderstorms.

2) 8 (?) yr old Saddlebred mare, acute laminitis beginning 5 days previously. Very painful walking; on phenylbutazone (Bute). Animal Bowen® treatment begun, with extremely light contact on each move. About halfway through the basic 4 procedures mare indicated she had had enough, so treatment was stopped. Next morning: bright, obviously more comfortable, on only half the previous day's dose of Bute. After a second Animal Bowen® treatment that day addressing her front feet, mare walked off almost normally.

3) 13 yr old female domestic shorthair cat; left hip fractured in car accident so top of femur removed. As a result, left hind leg is shorter than right; cat walks with limp and back curved to left. Cat was feral until hit by car at 1 yr of age; always skittish and fearful of people other than owner. Would not accept Animal Bowen® treatment until done almost at "hairline" level. After first treatment last year, almost no trace of limping; back straight instead of curved. Has had several treatments since then; now has become very affectionate "lap cat" actively seeking to be petted and scratched. Braver with new people, especially children (used to hiss and run away on sight of them).

OTHER TESTIMONIES FROM ANIMAL LOVERS

I have a cat that had a very brutal and rough start from the beginning of its life. I received the cat as a kitten and it was so thin from abuse and no food that nearly all its hair was gone. The kitten could not walk straight; it would stumble all the time and walk into things all the time. After over a year of good nutrition and love the cat still had problems and would sometimes be a menace and terror around the house. I heard about Bowen and brought my cat to the office where she received treatment. After just one visit her whole demeanor changed. She was calm, friendly and nice to the other cats.

It only took two visits to the office to help her out. It was truly amazing and it sure has made my life so much easier as she now is well tempered.

Thanks.

Lori F. Fresno, California

I had Raymond come visit us at our home out in the country to perform Bowen on our dogs. Our dogs, we have six of them, fought almost constantly. They all had some problems of a physical nature from chasing or being attacked by the variety wild animals that live in the mountainous region where we live. We have had to take them to the veterinarian from time to time to have them put back together from their escapades in the wild. Let's just say that they all were in need of some help.

The wildest one, Jake, will not let anyone but family members near the house. He always needed to be tied up or put in his pen so he would not cause harm to visitors. He is a great protector of his area.

He had to be held down at the beginning of his first Bowen session so he would not attack. After receiving a couple of Bowen Moves, he quickly calmed down. After just a few more, he started licking Raymond's hand as if to thank him.

When his session was over he walked around the room a bit, went to his bowl and drank some water, as if he knew the Bowen water, walk and wait rule. He then came back and watched as the other dogs received their Bowen.

During the next week, surprisingly there was much less fighting between the dogs. When Raymond came the next time, Jake started barking, but in a different tone. It was as though he was happy to see Raymond again. When Raymond came into the house, Jake ran right up to him, stopped and then immediately sat down as if to say "I'm first – do me." Jake has NEVER done that to anyone.

After a couple of visits the dogs were playful like they were when they were just pups. What a change!

Rick F. Lake Tahoe, California

Chapter 17

Bowen Therapy Academy of Australia (BTAA), & Bowtech

By far, Bowen is the most advanced and powerful healing modality in the world today.

The goals of Bowtech are to:
- Develop and promote the practice of an interpretation of Tom Bowen's original work
- Sustain an instruction program for instructors and practitioners and instructors of Bowen worldwide
- Organize and encourage continued research and development of Bowen

Bowtech is committed to the competency, accreditation, and quality Bowen practitioners, instructors, and researchers.

The goals of BTAA and **Bowtech** are simple and straightforward ones. They are to produce high standard training curriculum for instructors while offering seminars that teach practitioners the proper use of the technique while at the same time presenting Bowen to the world. They assist in providing the training materials and seminars in order to provide highly skilled, competent, and qualified Bowen instructors and practitioners who use **Bowtech** ~ *The Original Bowen Technique*.

Registered instructors worldwide use an identical international training format to ensure consistency of instruction of the very same procedures and protocols that Tom Bowen used himself to treat clients. Practitioners who are qualified register with the Bowen Therapy Academy of Australia and the association or registry associated with their country. An instructor-training program is available to those who qualify.

Currently the BTAA/Bowtech seminars are approved as continuing education credits in the U.S.. These include CEU for the National College of Naturopathic Medicine, the Board of Chiropractic Examiners, and the Association of Naturopathic Physicians in the state of Oregon. The British branch of BTAA, Bowen Therapy Association United Kingdom (BTAUK), is an accepted member organization of the British Complementary Medical Association (BCMA).

As of this printing, BTAA currently spans 35 different countries and is expanding rapidly throughout the world. Currently there are over 60 instructors who teach **Bowtech** ~ *The Original Bowen Technique* worldwide.

Chapter 18

Prudence

There are a few therapeutic approaches out there that claim to contain Bowen or some portion of a rendition of Tom Bowen's work. These other approaches are not recognized by nor are their instructors registered with The Bowen Therapy Academy of Australia and Bowtech nor do they teach Tom Bowen's work as he developed it. Groups not directly affiliated with or Bowtech or BTAA are not sanctioned as such.

It is true that Bowen is effective in addressing many of the ailments that modern allopathic and alternative medicine fails to properly address or cure. It does not work for all of them, nor does it work in each and every case. Bowen is used to care for individuals. The results individuals will receive are dependent upon many factors that are outside the responsibility of the practitioner. Proper exercise, proper nutrition, and proper hydration are just a few of these factors, which can only be controlled by the individual receiving treatment.

Bowen can and should be used for severe conditions along with, but not in place of, more proven treatments.

Bowen has little power to address such issues as contagious skin diseases, malignant tumors, sexually transmitted diseases (STD), hemorrhages, blood vessel hardening, and many other serious illnesses and diseases. These are best left to modern medical science, which is far better equipped to treat these conditions and contain those that need containment.

LIMITATIONS

Limitations to what Bowen can do in assisting the healing process of the body do exist. One of the limiting factors to Bowen and other modalities is the client's unwillingness to be well. These individuals have a reason to remain ill that somehow serves their needs. In many of these kinds of cases Bowen simply does not work.

It is true that Bowen is very effective for scores of ailments that modern medicine fails to cure, but it does not work for all of them. The ailments from which Bowen can offer relief, are numerous, however it is less effective against sicknesses caused by serious irregularities of the organs.

Sicknesses clearly caused by bacteria, contagious diseases, and hemorrhaging, for example, are best left to modern medical science and technology, which is definitely better equipped to treat and offer protection where necessary.

Other limitations include not effectively treating fractures, torn muscle, ligament(s) or cartilage, lacerations, genetic and physical deformities, and nutritional deficiencies, among others.

Even though Bowen is extremely effective in addressing many conditions in the body, please understand that you are solely responsible for your own health. Use common sense. If you question whether to go to a Bowen Practitioner or doctor after an injury, trauma, or illness has occurred, by all means go see a doctor first. When emergency medical attention _is_ necessary, go to the emergency room.

After medical professionals have checked you, and if or when they say there is nothing they can do for you, then go visit a qualified and competent Bowen Practitioner. They will most certainly take care of you. If your condition is beyond our scope of practice then we will refer you back to medical professionals for further investigation of what is taking place in your body.

Bowen will not put doctors, or any other practitioner or therapist, for that matter, "out of business." All have their strengths. It may, though, increase their focus and attention to what they were taught to do best, which is to help people get well, and referring them to someone that can help them when the desired results are not achieved. All Bowen practitioners are taught to refer clients to other professionals, when necessary.

Other healthcare practitioners may also be able to give further advice in areas that Bowen Practitioners do not have proper credentials, i.e suggested changes to diet, posture and exercise regimes, in order to minimize the chances of re-injury, or re-occurrence of any specific condition.

Bowen is a very safe therapy, but it is not designed to be a substitute for medical advice or treatments recommended by a Medical Doctor. If you are in any doubt about any aspect of Bowen and how it may impact your current medical condition, please consult your Bowen practitioner. Bowen will work effectively alongside and in conjunction with normal allopathic (Western) medicine.

CONTRAINDICATION

Contraindication: a condition or factor that increases the risk involved in using a particular treatment, therapy, method or procedure.

Contraindications while using Bowen are few. They include performing, specifically, the Coccyx Procedure on a pregnant woman, performing the Breast Tenderness/Chest Procedure on those individuals with breast implants, and performing the TMJ procedure on someone who has had surgery for TMJ where bone was shaved or added to realign the bite or mating surfaces of the teeth.

RISK

Bowen has been proven safe by thousands of qualified practitioners world-wide. Bowen can be safely used on anyone regardless of age, condition, or medical diagnosis. The only risk is ridding people of pain and increasing their health and well-being on physical, mental, and emotional levels, which is actually no risk at all.

Bowen Practitioners do not make any claims regarding the effects Bowen has on cancer even though numerous individuals claim that Bowen has been the only single thing that they have done that has helped them increase their energy and stamina while they were overcoming their individual bout with cancer.

It is best to use common sense when an emergency or condition that is best left to medical personnel arises. After diagnosis has been made by medical personnel Bowen can often greatly assist in accelerating healing of the mind and body.

Common sense is not all that common.
~ Jed August ~

Chapter 19

Frequently asked Questions

This book would somehow be incomplete if it did not contain a chapter of FAQ's. By now you are asking yourself some very important questions, some of the questions and their answers are as follows:

Q – Does Bowen come from the tribes of the Australian Aborigines?

No. Tom Bowen originated and developed this system of whole body healing on his own.

Q - What are the primary objectives of Bowen?

Although the specific objectives vary greatly from one individual to the next, the primary objectives are to:

- Stimulate and activate the body's healing mechanisms to help the body to remember how to heal
- Eliminate pain
- Put the entire body *and* mind at rest – "letting go" – so it can use its energies and resources to heal itself
- Reduce or eliminate the high state of the "fight or flight response"
- Engage the body to restore itself back into its own perfect pattern of optimal health
- Return the body back to balance
- Reintegrate the communication systems between the body and the brain that have been broken down for some reason so the body can have clearer communication within itself

Q - How safe is Bowen, really?

In his prime, Tom Bowen treated nearly 13,000 patients per year, without incident. Since then, thousands of other Bowen practitioners have safely performed hundreds of thousands of Bowen sessions supporting Tom Bowen's claim of its safe use on anyone regardless of age or physical condition.   The extremely fit, to the sedentary or debilitated, can very safely receive Bowen sessions. When performed properly, this non-invasive approach is *very* safe and so gentle in its application that it can be used on anyone, in any stage of health, ailment, or illness, without the possibility of harm. Because of its gentle application, how it works with the body, and because its healing progresses in such a harmonious and mild manner, there is simply no possibility of harm when Bowen is performed in accordance with Bowtech and Bowen Therapy Academy of Australia (BTAA) standards.

Q – Does Bowen have any negative effects on the body?

There have been no reported cases of Bowen affecting the body in any kind of "negative" way, when Bowen is performed in accordance with Bowtech and Bowen Therapy Academy of Australia (BTAA) standards. Occasionally, though, temporary residual soreness from toxin releases in the body can occur, as structural alignment and system and overall body rebalancing begins. In cases that have had a long duration or the weakening of an area in the body, the changes which are instilled in the body from Bowen may show temporary signs of discomfort from the "rusty" area using a muscle or set of muscles which currently lack strength and stamina.

Q – Do I still need to take my medications while I am receiving Bowen sessions and what does it do for the medication I am now taking?

Bowen works to assist the body and therefore can enhance medication results. There are no known no negative interactions with medications. The long-term benefits that have been seen are that many people are able to reduce or eliminate the need for medication as a result of Bowen. Bowen practitioners **NEVER** suggest that anyone refrain from taking medication. That is between the person and their pharmacist and doctor.

Q – What makes Bowen so different compared to chiropractic, physical therapy, massage, or any other kind of work that is performed on the body?

Bowen is distinguished in its own category because of its gentleness, rapid effectiveness, low cost, and its ability to bring permanent relief, using only a very short number of sessions in nearly EVERY case. Also, the work is performed with the client lying on a comfortable table, fully-clothed, no oil is used, and they are encouraged to let go of life for a while and just relax.

Q -What can I expect after a Bowen session?

Everyone experiences something different. After a session some people feel energized in a way they haven't been in a LONG time, others feel a little lethargic or tired – the body's way of telling you to take it easy and to go take a nap. Honor whatever your body is "telling" you to do. Others feel calm and balanced, others relieved and stress-free and peaceful. Remember, your body is going to heal what IT knows is most important, first. Some even feel so different they say that it feels like they are walking in someone else's body. On rare occasions, people may momentarily feel a bit out of balance. For any of these we say: "GREAT, IT'S WORKING!" These displays are wonderful signs that show that your body is responding to Bowen. On rare occasion, some people experience "new areas" of tenderness, soreness, discomfort or even some level of pain in their body for a few days after a session. This too is GREAT! Muscles you haven't used for a long time didn't have a chance to go to the gym and work out for 8-12 weeks to get back into shape. They had to immediately start working after having been laid-off or not fully working for some time. When muscle compensations and poor postural or movement practices in the body begin to improve, some muscles and joints *will* have to work a little harder, whether they want to or not, as they recapture their correct function

Your body may also be re-tracing backwards through old injuries and traumas for some time as the body works its way back into balance. Your entire body is also releasing toxins and built-up waste products. It is really cleaning house! Muscles that have been held in contraction for some time do build up waste products and lactic acid. Bowen may have shaken your body up a bit, to begin moving these wastes out of the body and into the bloodstream, so you may experience feelings of having worked out or even those that feel like you have run a marathon. Drink more water and go on a walk.

Nearly everyone will feel some reduction of his or her pain or symptoms immediately following a session.

This is *very* common and happens in just about every case after a session. It is important to understand that Bowen is quite different in its approach in helping the body to fix itself and that all symptoms or pains may not "go away" after the first few sessions. It has taken years to get to the point where your body is and it may take some time to get it right again. Remember, we are peeling off the layers, not necessarily trying to take off huge chunks. It takes a bit of time, in most cases, to affect the deeper levels of the body. Concern your self with the progress that is happening and focus on the key that something good is happening.

If and when your body begins to detoxify or unwind, celebrate the fact that something *is* happening. Understand that your body may continue to change for 3-5 days after the session. Each day you body will often make significant physiological (structural), mental and emotional changes as it releases years or even decades of trauma and stress and the body's relationship to these factors of the past.

Some people feel they're slipping backwards after a few days.

On rare occasions, old traumas or injuries that have a long established pattern in the body can momentarily flare up. The body has held the pattern for some time and the old pattern is still the familiar –status quo- one it can first readily relate to. It also shows that Bowen did do something and that Bowen will work for you. Keep going, you are doing just fine!

Some people experience large evacuations of the bowel and urinary tract.

Once again, GREAT IT'S WORKING! Occasionally, people do experience huge releases from their digestive tract. The body has held tension, stress and trauma in the stomach, small and large intestines and the body has held onto fluids. Bowen gave the systems a signal to relax and "let go" and that is what it is doing. You may have to take many trips to the toilet for a couple of hours. Wonderful.

Q - What can Bowen "cure"?

In strictly a medical sense, Bowen must not be considered to 'cure' anything. With Bowen, the body is only given direct signals as information to engage the stimulation and activation of its own self-healing and self-balancing mechanisms trusting that the wisdom of the body will resolve whatever condition may exist. **It rarely fails us**.

Q – Will Bowen work to help long-term chronic problem?

Bowen will assist the body to restore its natural healthy balance even with a chronic problem. Chronic problems often respond more slowly as the body works to change a familiar unhealthy pattern to a new healthy one.

Q – How soon should I expect to feel some relief?

Instantaneous relief is common, sometimes within just the first few minutes during a session. In most cases, some level of relief occurs during or within a few short hours after a session. Results can come within the first week after the session. Again, 3-5 sessions spaced about a week apart are sufficient for most issues. These few visits are still a fraction of the number of visits in many other forms of care, not including savings of both time and money.

Q – Is Bowen for right for me?

Bowen has a long and successful track record helping people with an incredibly large assortment of problems and conditions.
Can it help you? Only by receiving a series of sessions can you really know. Be assured that you will know in a relatively short time whether it is helping you, as results speak for themselves.

Q – How long will it take for me to get better and how many sessions will it take?

If anyone could predict that...well, now that would truly be amazing. Because of the billions of possibilities that factor in and exist between humans and their ailments, it would be irresponsible to give a definite answer. I have seen seemingly difficult cases that mirror each other very precisely. One took only 2 sessions, the other 10. Generally, using most other natural or alternative methods it takes one month or treatment for every year that you have had the condition for the treatment to do any good at all. In nearly every case, Bowen works MUCH faster than this, usually only 3-5 sessions, generally 7 days apart, (in very rare cases more frequent sessions have been found to be very useful) will be all that is necessary to bring the body back into balance for most people.

Most conditions respond very rapidly to 3-5 sessions.
A more serious or chronic condition may take several sessions to begin seeing results and even longer to help the problem resolve. Some conditions are so long-term, extreme and complicated by age or other factors that a complete recovery will not happen. In these rare cases, ongoing treatment at regularly scheduled intervals is the only alternative.

Q - If this works so phenomenally well, why don't doctors, chiropractors, physical therapists and other healthcare professionals recommend or prescribe The Bowen system of healing as a regular course of accelerated recovery or treatment?

➢ Most healthcare professionals have neither heard of Bowen nor have they yet received personal treatment or know of someone that has received treatment.

➢ Bowen uncommon to mainstream medical reasoning – Although it is abstract, it is also very logical.

➢ Because of its relative newness to the world, most Bowen practitioners have a private practice out of their home and it is not yet mainstream.

➢ Only about 1% of all physicians include or offer natural or alternative treatments in their medical practice.

➢ Most doctors are taught to primarily use drugs and surgery by medical schools. Most medical schools are not familiar with alternative treatments and do not promote any treatment that isn't mainstream. This mind-set can linger for a doctor's entire career.

➢ The majority of doctors have very busy practices. They don't have the time to even keep up with the developments in their own respective fields, let alone new developments in the natural and alternative fields.

➢ Modern medicine is a business where "time is money." The average doctor now spends about 7 minutes with each client, which is not nearly enough time to deeply and thoroughly assess and almost instantly and correctly diagnose a condition, in most cases. Sad, although it's true.

➢ Doctors and other health care professionals work for HMO's and/or insurance companies. They receive a list of treatments that will be covered and paid for and any therapy that is not on the list generally will not be recommended.

➢ Most medical doctors are in a very conservative group; they usually "go by the book." Doctors fear malpractice suits if they deviate from normal and standard treatments or procedures. For this reason they commonly refer to and/or prescribe what is familiar to them. This may only be in their best interest and not in the best interest of the client in every case.

➢ There is strong pressure against anything that is unconventional. Physicians who favor alternative treatment run the risk of investigation and censure by medical review boards. The threat of losing their licenses keeps them in line. Very often peer pressure and the fear of ridicule from other doctors really discourages them from trying or doing anything outside of conventional medicine. The same goes for many other healthcare professionals who have been trained in medicine in many cases.

Q - So what can I do to play a part in telling my doctor or therapist that I believe that I found what I need to help me in my case?

Find a competent Bowen Practitioner in your area or state, go to them and receive a series of sessions. Then tell your doctor and/or therapist about the results. In nearly every case, they will see the rapid results and will be very curious to know what you have been doing. Better yet, invite your doctor and/ or therapist to go receive a couple of Bowen session so they can personally check it out for themselves.

Q – Is Bowen being used in hospitals and medical clinics?

Bowen is beginning to be recognized and used in hospitals and clinics in the U.S., Australia, Canada, and the U.K., in various countries throughout Europe and around the world. A hospital in North Carolina uses Bowen as a centerpiece for its multi-disciplinary treatment program.

Q - Will my insurance pay for Bowen sessions?

In cases where a doctor writes a prescription for Bowen, most insurance companies do pay. In cases where a doctor hasn't prescribed treatment, some insurance companies will pay for treatment, most will not – **yet**.

Q – Why don't insurance companies know about Bowen? From what you are saying, it could save them many millions of dollars every year.

There are two factors. One, substantial research hasn't been performed to "prove" all that Bowen can do, to convince them they can save loads of money; and two, the quantity of highly skilled Bowen Practitioners are few at the moment. We are working on both of these at this time.

Q - What is the cost for a Bowen session?

There is no standard price for sessions as practitioners charge individually and set their own price for Bowen, therefore session prices vary from $25 – $200 per session. $40 - $120 per session is most common. There are many factors that come in to play, location, region of the country, licensure requirements, among others.

Q – Why does Bowen work so effectively and succeed in many areas where other therapies or approaches don't or cannot even touch it?

Bowen is so highly effective for the body because opens the healing processes of the body and focuses them on what needs to be healed exactly where it is needed to facilitate speedy recovery to help the body eliminate pain, restore health, and recover lost function through regeneration.

Q – How does Bowen know where to work?

Actually, Bowen doesn't know where to work. Only the body does, however, the Moves performed on the body in their particular sequences, developed over much time, assist the body in awakening from its state of slumber or stupor and brings its attention to problems and alerts the body to the areas of highest priority so it can quickly and most efficiently focus its resources to get to work healing itself

Q – Why hasn't my body healed using therapies other than Bowen?

In most cases using other therapies, your body's pain cycle was just interrupted and not truly eliminated, or healing cycles have not been correctly stimulated or turned back on. Remember that the trauma, injury, overuse, stress or pain you have suffered from has "disconnected" your body from its healing and recovery functions, causing an ongoing imbalance in the body.

Q – Where are so few touches used and so little work performed during a Bowen session?

Bowen uses a "less is more" approach to healing the body. It is primarily because of the precision used in the application and location of each and every move. Bowen is more like a laser that goes directly to the point and part of the body that needs addressing, wherever it is coming from, no more, no less. It is the body that is doing most of the work. In other words, Bowen gets the greatest amount of work from each and every individual touch.

Q – Why does Bowen use so little pressure, in most cases, when the Moves are applied to the body?

Bowen uses such light pressure because it follows a very specific physiologic law of the body, the Arndt-Schulze law, which states the body responds more profoundly and positively to a low level stimulus than it does to a strong painful stimulus. Less really is more in the case of Bowen. It uses the least amount of work in search of achieving the greatest effect approach. i.e. you can use a twenty pound sledgehammer to turn on light switches in your home if you want to, but it's not necessary!

Q – Do all Bowen practitioners work in the same way?

Bowen practitioners who have been fully trained using Bowtech® and BTAA standards are taught to use great care and light touch to perform Bowen Moves. They have also been taught to use specific protocols to ensure the most effective Bowen is performed on every person. Practitioners who are accredited by and hold a current valid registration through Bowtech® follow strict ongoing educational requirements and stringent standards that require practitioner reviews.

Bowen practitioners who have been taught by sources other than those directly associated with Bowtech® do not have or follow such requirements. Many of these practitioners use much more pressure and perform much more work on the body than is needed, resulting in a much less effective session.

Q – What happened? It worked for a while.

    Great! The initial fact that it worked for a while means that your body responded and can heal using Bowen. There can be several reasons why the change or relief was temporary. The body may need a few reminders on how to reset itself and get back on the path to optimal health. KEEP GOING!

    The effects of a Bowen session begin during the session and continue working for 3 - 5 days after the session. Many of the greatest benefits experienced much after the session.

Q – Did anything really happen? I went to one session and I didn't feel much and I don't think Bowen did anything for me. What do you have to say for that?

    One session simply will not do it for most people. Receive at least 3-5 sessions for mild to moderate cases. For severe to extreme cases receive at least 5-8 sessions. We have seen cases where it took 6-8 sessions with not much happening then all of a sudden – BOOM – everything changed and the person shot back to good health almost instantly. **Sometimes it takes patience for Bowen to set in.** The bamboo tree seed is planted. It is fertilized and watered painstakingly for 5 years and not even one sign of a sprout. In the fifth year, as soon as you begin to see a sprout, it shoots up to 90 feet tall in SIX WEEKS! That is over 25 inches per day! Over 1 inch per hour! You can practically see it grow in front of your eyes!!! The tree had to first lay its foundational roots. **Sometimes the body needs to do that as well.**

    In most cases that there was seemingly no result, most people didn't follow the directions and did things they shouldn't have or they didn't do what they were asked to do (drink lots of water, go on a daily 20 minute walk if medically appropriate, refrain from coffee and alcohol, etc.) Also, humans have a wonderful ability to forget how bad something was once it's a little better.

    In the *extremely* rare case that nothing did happen, and there has been no change whatsoever and your Bowen practitioner has done all they could do for you, Bowen may not be right for you. The bottom line is that it simply does not work for everyone. The reason(s) why? We haven't found that out yet.

Q – I had some good results, but it seemed to stop working.

    First question, what are you doing or have you done to mess it up?

    I've had cases where people moved along great and then all of a sudden their progress stopped. In nearly every case, the person did something, like starting to exercise like a maniac; or they have had back problems for year and "Oh, I moved everything in my house and garage last weekend"; or " I have been running for a couple of months now, so I ran the marathon last weekend" or "I felt so good that my wife and I hiked up to the top of Mount Whitney (some **14,000 + feet**) We haven't hiked in years since I got hurt, so we decided to go again." HELLO... you can't do this to your bodies folks and expect it to not hurt again! Or their ergonomics at the desk at work is not good, for example. This is usually the case.

    At this point you really have to take responsibility for yourself. Your practitioner may have strong recommendations as to what you can do and could expect from further sessions. If you feel at this point that you are moving in the right direction and this is something you want to pursue, the choice is up to you.

Q – I've been going to Bowen for a while and don't know what I need to do or if I should continue.

If this is the case, communicate this with your practitioner and discuss what your next step or steps should be. Generally, a few sessions, the intervals between sessions should be stretching out, for example, from seven to ten to fourteen then to eighteen, twenty-one, twenty-four, twenty-eight days in between sessions. After this you should come in when your body "tells" you. Feel free to discuss any of this with your practitioner. You can discuss a further number of sessions or take it on a week-to-week basis, which ever you prefer.

Q – I have gone for my 5 sessions and I feel great! What should I do from here?

Great! Success again!!! We have your body back on track. From here you may discuss future sessions for preventive maintenance. It will always depend upon what _your_ body needs. It's different for everyone. You decide what works for you and what interval suits your schedule, stress levels, finances, etc. In traditional Chinese medicine, and in many other healing traditions in native cultures around the world, the minimum recommended maintenance for the body is at change of each season or four times per year.

Q – Will my problem return?

The problem may return in cases where muscle weakness and stamina are not addressed and where re-injury has occurred.
In all instances where client supports their recovery process with appropriate exercise and activity for their ability coupled with good nutrition and does their best to refrain from activities that will cause re-injury, **the likelihood of the problem returning is very low.**

Q – Can Bowen work with other forms of therapy or treatment?

Bowen is best used alone as a stand-alone procedure. There are ways to properly sequence Bowen with sufficient time allowed for Bowen to take effect while other treatments are received. Bowen works best alone.
Bowen can be effective with Physical Therapy, Chiropractic, Acupuncture, Massage, or Rolfing, on very rare occasions, although they DO NOT MIX WELL. What happens if any of these therapies are applied too soon before or after a Bowen session it can erase the effects of Bowen.

Q - I was told by doctors and specialists that I have to learn to live with the pain, can Bowen help?

I often tell people the impossible Bowen can do, the miraculous takes a little longer – sometimes. In other words and in most cases a definite and resounding YES! Many thousands of people have come to Bowen as a last resort after having been told, "You must live with your pain." **Bowen has a very high success rate** for cases such as these.

Q – I have cold hands and cold feet...can Bowen help?

In many cases, Yes! Restrictions in the neuro-pathways or in blood flow caused by tense or spasming muscles are often opened and released, thereby improving circulation of both.

Q - Are there any contraindications for the use of Bowen?

> **Contraindication: a condition or factor that increases the risk involved in using a particular treatment, therapy, method or procedure.**

Contraindications while using Bowen are few. They include:

1. Performing the coccyx procedure on a pregnant woman, as there may be the possibility of triggering premature labor - all other procedures are safe to apply during pregnancy

2. Performing the breast tenderness procedure on those individuals with breast implants; even though the breast tissue is slightly moved during this procedure to address the underlying tissue and the implant is not touched or contacted during this procedure, practitioners are taught that it is best to refrain from performing the procedure on individuals with implants

3. Performing the TMJ procedure on someone who has had surgery for TMJ where bone was shaved or added to realign the bite or mating surfaces of the teeth

4. Though not a contraindication, just a mere temporary discomfort, an occasional response to Bowen sessions may include body aches due to the body triggering its detoxification processes, which lasts for as little as 15 minutes to only a couple of days.

Q – Does Bowen have any negative affects on the body?

There have been no reported cases of Bowen affecting the body in any kind of "negative" way. Occasionally, temporary residual soreness from toxin releases in the body can occur as structural alignment and system and overall body rebalancing begins. In cases that have had a long duration or the weakening of an area in the body, the changes that are instilled in the body from Bowen may show temporary signs of discomfort in a "rusty" area from using a muscle or set of muscles that currently lack strength and stamina.

Q – Will I have to hurt more before I feel better after a Bowen session?

Pain and discomfort is not a part of Bowen and it doesn't cause pain to try to help relieve it.

Q – Are the effects of Bowen due to any kind of hypnotic suggestion?

No. The results that Bowen achieves are based on physical and mechanical mechanisms which signal the body to make much-needed changes to rebalance on its own. No other kind of suggestion or stimulus is needed.

Q - How long does a Bowen session take?

The length of a session varies and depends primarily on what your body needs that day _and_ what it can handle that day. When the body has absorbed about as much as it can handle for the session, there is no use in going beyond that point. Generally 30-45 minutes is needed. In some cases, sessions as short as 10 minutes is used for a "quick fix" or as long as 60 minutes or more may be needed to properly address what is happening in your body.

The shorter the session time, the more specific and direct the procedures are to address a particular issue to focus all of all the available resources of the body to a specific area or problem. A longer session doesn't necessarily give better therapeutic results.

Q - How do I know if I will receive a short or long session that day?

In most cases a practitioner will inform you if a shorter session is needed that day.

Q - Why is the cost the same for either a short or a long session?

For most practitioners, the session is more commonly priced "per session," not for the length of time you are on the table being treated.

EXAMPLE - When you take your automobile in for repair they charge the full hourly shop rate with a minimum charge of one hour in nearly every case. Even though you may just need an alternator replaced, it may take the mechanic only 15 minutes to remove two bolts while unloosening the belt, unclip one set of wires, remove the alternator, put in the new alternator, re-clip the wires, and tighten the two bolts and a belt. The charge will still be the minimum one-hour shop rate and your vehicle is as good as new again. The bottom line is what needed fixing was fixed and you are off again.

Q – Is it best for me to inform the practitioner that I have to leave by a specific time because of an appointment or commitment?

If you need to leave by a specific time, PLEASE inform the practitioner _before_ the beginning of your session. The practitioner may choose to allow your body to continue in a deep restful state for an extended length of time during the session to enhance the results.

Q – What if I have to get up and use the toilet during a session, will this mess up the session?

No, of course not. Do what your body is telling you to do. Listen to your body. If you need to eliminate, you need to eliminate.

Q – Is it OK if I talk during a session?

It is best if you refrain from talking during the session and help your body and mind to just let go of the world for a while.

Q – I have a little one that is quite rambunctious and I would like to bring him in for a session or two to help calm him down, but I'm afraid that he will disturb the others in the clinic.

Bring him in! That is what we have doors for. In most cases, once we perform a few Moves on him he'll be down for the count and you'll ask to learn how to do that!

Q – How soon can I get in for a Bowen session?

I can only speak for Bowen Healing System™ Center in this case. We pride ourselves in getting people in the same day. We have many rooms and tables available to meet demands. My knowledge of most other practitioners is that a session needs to be booked almost a week or two in advance.

Q – Can a family member or friend receive a session at the same time I come in for session?

I can only speak for Bowen Healing System™ Center again in this case. In the clinics we have multiple rooms. Some rooms have more than one table to accommodate multiple family members and friends together in the same room. Many other practitioners may only have only one or two treatment tables so it would be best to ask in advance.

Q – Do I have to be in the same room with my family member or friend when we receive a session?

The answer to this question is no. If you normally are treated in the same room as someone else, it is best to call ahead to make sure there is a room available and all the rooms aren't booked for that time slot.

Q – Can I just "walk in" for a session?

I can only speak for Bowen Healing System™ Centers where we have more rooms available. In most cases, definitely yes! It happens all the time. It is still best to call even 15 minutes ahead to tell them you are on your way. In cases where we are fully booked, we may ask a "veteran" client that is in a room that has more than one table if they would mind having company. In nearly every case, people do not mind because they know they will drop fast into a deep state of relaxation after the first couple of Moves are performed on them. They also know that they probably will not even know you are there in the room with them until they arise after the session.

Q – Do I have to take my clothes off to receive a session?

The answer is no. Removing a belt or loosening the trousers is all that is generally necessary. Some people like to take off all their jewelry, watches, wallets out of pockets, etc. and that is acceptable. In cases where people are wearing very tight jeans or a very tight dress, it would be best to remove the tight clothing without removing underclothes to receive the optimal session. In these rare occurrences, a top-draping sheet would be used to cover the person on the table and the Moves would then be performed through the sheet.

Q - How often does one have to return for another session? In other words, do I have to keep coming back over and over for treatment like in chiropractic?

Most people receive 3-5 sessions spaced 7 days apart. In more difficult cases more visits may be needed. After being re-balanced and restored back to good health, you will come back when your body tells you to. It may be once in three months, six months, one year, or in some cases, I have not treated people for over four years.

One day they call for a session. I may not see them again for another four years…to that I say "Great! We'll take care of you when _you_ need it."

Q – How will I know when my body will tell me when to come back for a session?

Very often it is very simple to know when to return for a session. After a fall, accident, or injury is definitely a very good time to return. The sooner you return, the quicker we can help you. In most cases though, it is when tension begins to return, or you start to feel fatigued, or you begin feeling not up-to-par, or you are feeling like you are getting sick, or your body and/or mind is out-of-balance.

Q – What if I just want to come in for regular maintenance once a month or just for a "tune-up" once every three months?

Great! If that is what your body needs, we definitely know it is much easier, for the both of us, to keep your body strong, healthy and well. Many in medicine (especially those in the ER), law enforcement, fire protection, and other high pressure professionals and blue collar workers have found that a Bowen session once every 30-45 days makes them feel great and on top of their game.

They come in for a variety of reasons. One has to do with releasing the high levels of pressure or physical labor they experience on the job. The next, it gives them an edge on work and life. Another, it gives them time to let go and get away from the cares of the world, to rest their bodies and minds during a session while listening to calming music, in a relaxing environment.

Understand, just like an automobile, your body needs regular maintenance to keep it running at peak performance. When you will have to come back for a "full body tune-up" so to speak may depend primarily on how much and how hard you drive yourself.

Q – Does Bowen work for preventative care?

Most certainly! It is, in my experience and opinion, by far the greatest healing modality in the world that can be used on anyone at anytime.

Q – Can Bowen do anything to help reduce my stress level?

Yes! Bowen reduces the effects of stress almost immediately. During sessions clients report sensations of calmness and the reversal of shallow breathing, rapid heart rate, and hypersensitivity common to stressed individuals. Using Bowen regularly, when your body needs it, lays the groundwork for a very healthy anti-stress regimen.

Q - I have panic attacks, what could Bowen do for that?

Bowen quite readily removes the issues that cause extreme anxiety and panic attacks. We have numerous cases where people have come in while having a panic attack and after their (single) session they are calm, serene and balanced again.

Q - I suffer terribly from seasonal allergies, like hay fever, could Bowen help me?

I can very confidently say _yes_ in answer to this question. Bowen has a very specific procedure that works extremely well for this. Very commonly people who have suffered many years with seasonal allergies find they do not suffer anymore after a course of treatment.

Q – I suffer from allergies that are not seasonal. Can Bowen help?

In most cases I can say Bowen can help very well for people with allergies. Some investigation into the actual causes may expose the origin of the allergies quite nicely. When that is discovered, the cure may not be too far away.

Q – My child is suffering from Autism. Is there anything that Bowen can do for them?

As far as Bowen is concerned, a few practitioners have reported positive changes in autistic individuals after Bowen sessions. Again, each case is different in magnitude and severity. Give Bowen a shot to see what it could do.

Q – I suffer from a disorder called Bi-polar. Can Bowen help me?

Bowen has been very successful in addressing Bi-Polar for most people who suffer with it.

Q – My son nearly died from a severe asthma attack. Could Bowen have been of any use to him or others who suffer from asthma?

YES, it could have! Bowen has a very specific respiratory procedure that directly addresses the respiratory system very quickly. In cases where people have arrived at the **Bowen Healing System™ Center** with a full-blown asthma attack, I have seen it stop in as little as 15 seconds.

I have had a case where one person collapsed out in front of the clinic because she could not breathe. I was immediately notified, ran outside with phone in hand, just in case I needed to call emergency personnel. **I performed one single Move on her. Within one minute the blue color on her face disappeared and her breathing was restored**. I did strongly suggest that she go to a doctor, which she did. They said they found nothing. In her case this had NEVER happened before. It came on instantly.

Later, she explained that she just happened to drive near the clinic on the way to the emergency room and she knew that she could not make it to the hospital. As she was a client of mine, she stopped in…hoping I could help her. In this case Bowen most certainly did. Will this ALWAYS be the case? I do not know.

In life threatening cases it is always best for the person to go to the emergency room. I have met a few people at the emergency room in cases such as this one.

When a person suffers from asthma attacks practitioners commonly show the person and their parent, spouse, sibling, or friend how to quickly perform one single Move. The Move they show them commonly stops an asthma attack in less than 30 seconds.

Q - My infant daughter has colic, could Bowen help her?

Yes! There are a couple of procedures that can very quickly be performed that will make parents and guardians VERY happy, just a couple of Moves that work extremely well.

Q – I have a child that is very irritable because they are teething. Can Bowen do anything for them?

I have seen Bowen work like magic in these cases, with parents and grandparents both saying Bowen is a Godsend.

Q - Is Bowen safe for my young granddaughter who just fell off her bicycle and hurt her neck and arm?

Bowen can be VERY effective in this case and nearly every other case of injury that just happened. *__If there are any cuts that need stitching, bleeding that won't stop, possible fracture, or signs of concussion, take her to the medical clinic or emergency room first.__* After she has been taken care of there, stop by on the way home for a mini-session for her. It will significantly accelerate the healing process.

Q- I do homeopathy, will Bowen work with that?

Bowen is commonly referred to as "the homeopathy of body therapies" and because of their many similarities and how they work with the body they are a great match and work very well together.

Q – I have been told that I will have to take medication and learn to live with the pain. Is there anything Bowen can do to help me?

Bowen has phenomenal results in many cases where doctors have told them "You will have to take medication for the rest of your life" or "You will have to learn to live with the pain." Bowen is successful in over 80% of these kinds of cases.

Q – I have breast implants. Is it OK for me to receive Bowen sessions?

Bowen sessions can be performed on someone who has breast implants; however, for the safety of the person with the implants, practitioners are instructed to *not* perform the Breast Tenderness Procedure on this person. Even though the procedure is designed to only address the lymphatic tissues which are underneath the breast tissue, without coming into contact with the implant itself, we feel it is best to refrain from any potential possibility of contacting the implant – however minute.

Q – Do all Bowen Practitioners work in the same way?

The practitioners who are accredited through and affiliated with the Bowen Therapy Academy of Australia (BTAA) and Bowtech, who constantly and consistently continue attending continuing education courses, do work in the same way. Other practitioners and/or groups which have broken away from, or are no longer a part of BTAA and Bowtech, perform something that is quite different, in nearly every case. The amount of pressure used to perform the work they do is usually heavier and much deeper, the sequence of the work altered, waiting times may not exist, and they commonly mix therapies together, among many other things in nearly every case.

Q – My mother just had a surgery. Should she get a Bowen treatment and if so, how soon?

Definitely, yes. The sooner the better, to assist in accelerated recovery and rehabilitation.

Q – I have a friend who is scheduled for surgery. Should they come in for a session before the surgery?

Definitely, yes. Bowen will help prepare the body for the intensity of the surgery, when surgery is needed. It can also assist in reducing complications through relaxing the body, so it can focus on healing.

Q – Will Bowen help me to recover after surgery?

When Bowen is administered after surgery, it goes to work to speed recovery by calming the body and focusing it on repair and healing.

Q – I have been diagnosed with Carpal Tunnel Syndrome. What can Bowen do for me?

Yes! There is a big difference between Repetitive Stress that inflames the carpal tunnel region and the actual Carpal Tunnel Syndrome.

There have been many cases where people have been scheduled for carpal tunnel surgery. After just a few sessions the person was free from pain. They found that the surgery was not needed because the pain was coming from a different part of the body. In these cases where there is just inflammation caused by something else, the pain was just showing up with carpal tunnel-related symptoms in the wrist area and it was not a case of true Carpal Tunnel Syndrome.

In persons having the true Carpal Tunnel Syndrome, a variety of conditions are occurring in the body to actually cause the closing of the tunnel, thereby pinching off nerves and other tissues causing a very painful condition. In these cases the surgery is necessary.

Bowen has been very successful in helping people avoid surgery when it is not necessary. Surgery should be the last resort. Even Chinese medicine states this. If surgery can be avoided using another approach, logic and common sense says--why not use it?

Q – I heard one of my friends mention that they felt some discomfort and soreness a day or so after a session. Could you please explain what is happening to them? Will that happen to me when I receive a session?

To this I say, "GREAT, it's working." In cases where a person has had a pain or condition for quite some time the body has a tendency to torque around the pain. In these cases the body has not properly used all the muscles it normally would because of the imbalance and instability that existed. During and for many days after a session the body will begin to realign itself.

Muscles that have not been used for sometime will not be as strong as they should be, and they commonly lack stamina because they haven't been properly used for a while. After a session these muscles will immediately be required to work in order to return the body back to proper balance.

This may cause some mild soreness as the muscles begin to get a "workout" to get back into shape. The best and easiest solution for this is to increase water intake _and_ go on a walk – for those who are able to. Increasing water intake and going on a walk will accomplish two things

It will re-hydrate the muscles and increases circulation which quickly decrease the muscular tenderness.

These occurrences are rare and the possibility of these happening to you is slim.

Q – After having a few Bowen sessions I feel great for the first time in years. How long will it last?

In nearly every case the condition will not return – UNLESS it was and is caused by something you are doing or omitting. If someone is working for a data entry company typing 18,000 units per hour 8 hours a day, for example, the possibility that a neck, shoulder, forearm and/or wrist condition that was released by Bowen sessions may very likely return. The reason for this is that the body was not designed for excessive and extreme constant repetitive motion.

If the muscles aren't strong and need to be strengthened and you are not exercising, your condition may very well return until you properly strengthen these muscles.

If it is a digestion-related issued that Bowen helped in resolving that is directly connected with proper diet, and if you are not eating or digesting food properly…it may return.

Q – After my first session Bowen gave me great relief, but it was just for a few days. Why did my body go back to where it was?

Because your body received relief I say, "GREAT we are on the right track and Bowen will do you well in your case!" Your body is used to being in the pain/spasm cycle and the brain is used to keeping it there. Re-patterning the brain and body through just a few more sessions should do the trick for you. Practitioners see this re-patterning happen all the time.

Q – I was told that Bowen can be used along with other therapies or treatments. Is this true?

It is best that Bowen is used alone to give the body time to receive the direct and subtle messages that were given to it and give the body time to respond and make changes. Any therapy that is more aggressive than Bowen has a tendency to negate the long-term structural and energetic affects Bowen has on the body. Mixing any therapy with Bowen is not recommended. Listen to your body.

But, I had a car (or work related) accident and my doctor and the insurance company wants me to do physical therapy and chiropractic, and maybe some acupuncture. Bowen works so much better for me. What should I do?

Have your doctor call the Bowen practitioner to discuss what is working best for you. Always follow the advice of your doctor and have your Bowen practitioner assist you with proper scheduling of your other appointments, so Bowen can have the greatest influence on your recovery.

Q – I was told that Bowen can cure anything in the body. Is this true?

No, this is not true. Bowen doesn't cure anything. The body does the curing. Bowen just sets up the body in such a way that the natural healing mechanisms deep within the body are turned on once again and turned on to the maximum capacity so that the body can use them.

Bowen can lay the groundwork or uncover the foundation upon which true optimal health stands.

Q - How do I find a qualified Bowen Practitioner nearest me?

Visit www.bowenhealingsystem.com or www.bowtech.com for more information.

Q - What does it take to learn to effectively perform Bowen sessions on others?

The answer is simple, **"How long did it take Tiger Woods to learn to play golf the way he does, or Michael Jordan to play basketball the way he does?** How long did it take for a doctor, dentist, musician, artist, attorney to learn what they do?" There is a difference between learning the mechanics of something, and really knowing and applying the intricacies of a specialized field. Constant learning and refinement is done by anyone who is a professional.

Generally though, it may take as little as 7 months to complete the initial Bowen course. There are no pre-requisites for attending the beginning module of training – known as Module 1. The study of anatomy, physiology, and other therapeutic skills formerly studied at universities, colleges, or other accredited schools can greatly enhance a student's study of Bowen and their ability as a practitioner.

Bowen may seem simple to learn, although it is difficult to perfect.

Q – If I want to learn Bowen, how can I find an instructor or have one teach Bowen in my local area?

Your best bet is to phone the instructor nearest you and find out what minimum class size is needed have them conduct a seminar. Visit **www.bowenhealingsystem.com** or **www.bowtech.com** for more training information.

Q – Can I combine Bowen with my exercise regimen?

For the greatest benefit, it is best to give your body a rest for about a day after receiving a Bowen session to give it time to respond more fully to the session. For highly trained athletes, Bowen can be performed, in a very specific way, with 30-60 minutes before a competitive event to elevate the athlete to peak performance and to greatly assist in injury prevention.

Q – Does Bowen work with Homeopathy?

Bowen and homeopathy are very similar in their approach to the body and therefore work *very* well together. Bowen has been called "the homeopathy of body therapies" because of its gentle application and dramatic results.

Q – Can I use my magnets after a Bowen session?

It has been discovered that the benefits of Bowen are without question affected in a negative way if magnets are used after a session. Remember, Bowen works on both physical and energetic levels simultaneously for many days following a session. The magnets, as a outside source, artificially draw blood to an area, as blood has high iron content, and magnets naturally attract iron and therefore can attract more blood to an area than the body actually needs.

Magnets are also an outside energy source that artificially stimulates an area, thereby affecting its true energy pattern. It is best to trust the body and let it do what it knows best.

Do magnets work? Of course they can, temporarily. Using a crutch when a solution is available is not all that positive though, for those who are looking for long-term solutions. What if you forget to wear the magnet, what then?

Q - Are the affects of Bowen hypnotic in nature?

No. There is no auto or self-suggestion used. The Moves are simply performed on the body and the body does all the work.

Q – What can I do to enhance and accelerate my healing processes?

Active participation in your session by following your practitioner's instructions always proves to be the best course.

Q – I just had a recent injury. Could Bowen help?

Yes! Bowen often offers its most impressive results in addressing recent injuries. The faster Bowen is applied to an injury, the quicker and more powerful the recovery can be. Bowen applied moments after an injury has occurred helps the body get and stay out of shock and bypass many unnecessary pain and inflammation reactions allowing the body to go directly and focus on healing.

Q – What can I do to help the process between sessions?

You're on to something here! Bowen can give you the best most lasting results when health-robbing habits are stopped and fresh health-generating ones are taken on.

The following suggestions help greatly, particularly during the course of your sessions.

[*__Note: These suggestions do not replace any advice or instructions given you from your medical professional.__*]

- **Walk.** Spend as much time walking as you reasonably can. 15 - 30 minutes per day minimum. If you are unable to do this, take two or three short walks. We're talking about a leisurely stroll here, not a race. It should be easy and enjoyable. **Take your water with you and drink it!** Walking also has many great benefits. It involves no danger of strain or injury.

   Gentle walking activates the lymphatic "pumps" in the body, helping it to rid itself of waste and toxins more efficiently. Increased respiration aids in this process, too.

   Ideally, Bowen will release chemical stressors in the body, and walking gets them to move out much faster and helps to improve body functions, while stimulating your body at a much higher level.

- **Make it a "be kind to yourself"/easy day on the day of your Bowen session.** No heavy exercise or lifting on the day of session is definitely best. Because you finally feel better, this definitely is not the time to begin a new rigorous exercise, stretching, or Yoga program. Stretching is very helpful, I must add. You may feel an unfamiliar burst of energy on the day of your session or for many days thereafter. **It is crucial that you give your body the time and space that it needs to internalize the session you have received for deeper level repair, nervous system reintegration, and healing**. Don't blow it!

- **Drink lots of water.** Distilled water is best, purified water second. Distilled water will absorb the toxins kicked up by your body. Drink distilled water for a few days after your session to enhance the elimination effects of Bowen. Drink the purest water you can find. Every body function relies on proper hydration. **How much is enough?** According to some experts, drink one-half your body weight in ounces daily. (i.e. 150 lbs ÷ 2 = 75 ounces) This may take a bit to get used to and start it all in one day if you haven't been drinking water. Regulate your electrolytes if you are exercising.

- **Move around**. On the day of your Bowen session, after you have received it, it is especially important to move around every thirty minutes or so. Use a timer if you must, to remind you.

- **If you feel like sleeping – By all means, go ahead and sleep!** Evidently your body is in need of the rest.

- **Avoid temperature extremes.** No hot baths, showers, or Jacuzzi's. No ice packs. No heating pads. Warm showers or baths do well. You may also use Arnica Montana, Traumed®, Traumeel®, or other homeopathic formulas, natural, herbal, or essential oils.

- **If you are tender, sore, or have some discomfort, take a warm** Epsom salt or apple cider vinegar bath to help soothe and relax you. Use aspirin or ibuprofen only if you must.

Chapter 20

Final Note

Bowen is the whisper heard by the innermost core of the body that "Awakens the Doctor and healing within you!..."

This book has presented Bowen as a consistent and remarkable results-oriented approach to optimal health, which can effectively be used to assist healing the body and mind, unveil the spirit from within, and induce IntraPersonal Metamorphosis. The methods used in its application to help the body reset its healing mechanisms have been depicted in a simple and forthright manner. The cases herein have presented a broad spectrum of the body, mind, and spiritual aspects that Bowen has been able to address, but in no way contain the entire diversity of work this approach encompasses. Any result received by an individual case shared within this book is not any kind of guarantee of any result that you can or may experience. Individual results vary.

> The significance and importance of this work must not be underestimated. The substantial, long-term effects of the work accomplished in a few Bowen sessions are obvious; the need for this therapy in the world, tremendous.

The findings have presented an extremely strong argument for the healing capacity of the body, and the impact that Bowen sessions have on greatly enhancing this capacity through removal of the blockages, whether physical, mental, or emotional.

The non-invasive characteristics and simplicity of Bowen can be used to cover and address a wide range of applications for various health-related issues. Its high level of effectiveness in nearly every case proves the validity of the work. The profound benefits experienced by those who have received Bowen to influence the restoration of their body's own ability to reset itself, supports nature's own standard of using the body's own wisdom to heal itself.

The magnitude of this simple approach is revealing itself in such a way that *it is and will continue to* revolutionize the healthcare industry as a whole, worldwide. The discovery of a therapeutic approach that can safely be applied to anyone, regardless of age or condition, that releases the blockages that commonly produce negative mental and emotional states, and simultaneously restores physical and spiritual well-being on a very consistent basis, solidifies the preferability of Bowen over many other forms of therapy.

The significance and importance of this work must not be underestimated. The substantial, long-term effects of the work accomplished in a few Bowen sessions are obvious; the need for this therapy in the world, tremendous.

In conclusion, Tom Bowen (1916-1982), the originator of this profound healing system, discovered a unique way to unlock the secrets of healing that have been hidden for thousands of years. He has broken the cryptic code of health that has baffled the best minds his world has to offer. His work has stayed consistent with the great healing mantras of the ancients that state, "Do no harm, true healing comes from the inside out, and let the body heal itself." It works alongside and in conjunction with the age-old teachings of doctors of mind/body and spiritual masters and again shatters the voices of Western medicine, which state, "If it doesn't work...try this. If that doesn't do it...do more or try this."

Bowen is unsurpassed in the effectiveness of the caring for individuals who on a consistent basis use Western or alternative and complimentary approaches. It stands firmly, first, and foremost as <u>the</u> number one leader in alternative healing methods for producing results. The vast range of applications for the body, mind, and spirit that Bowen can address is incredible. This preliminary volume will bring much encouragement, insight, and support to all those who have been searching for a remedy as advanced *and* simple as Bowen. ***Bowen simply bridges the gap between Western alternative healthcare.***

> ...challenges exist within the healthcare systems that are in crisis; the problem isn't that there are not enough doctors and nurses. ...the problem is that there are not enough qualified and highly skilled Bowen Practitioners to help with the ever-increasing load on the healthcare systems.

In the never-ending healthcare system dilemma that is prevalent in many countries, including the U.S. and Canada, and where the major challenges exist within these healthcare systems that are in crisis, the problem isn't that there are not enough doctors and nurses. In my view, the problem is that there are not enough qualified and highly skilled Bowen Practitioners to help with the ever-increasing load on the healthcare systems.

Modern medicine is very good at diagnosing and working with the extremes, when body is traumatized and weary, incapable of healing itself. In these instances it is wonderful at putting the body back on the stage and helps set the stage of healing. The truth remains that body actually does the healing itself. There is nothing outside it that can fully control it.

Designing a healthcare system around health and healing, not designing people's health around an outdated system, would save insurance companies hundreds of millions of dollars annually.

I never met the man, Tom Bowen, but my gratitude for this work that he spent his entire life developing and the difference it has made in saving my life will be shared from the heart as I play my part bringing Bowen to the world. I have chosen to pass along the gift of Life that was given to me.

Namaste'

Golden Rules of Health

---

1. Make healthy choices your first choice in everything you do.

   Stop putting poisons into the body
   Trade fast food for organic food

2. It takes 5 - 7 times the normal amount of nutrition to build and repair, as it does to maintain.

3. Eat lots of fresh, organic, raw foods daily. Eat as much raw food as possible.

4. Nothing heals in the human body in less than 3 months (except with Bowen). Then add one month for every year that you have been sick.

5. Practice moderation in all things.

6. Make peace with nature.

7. Live closer to Divinity.

8. Take responsibility for yourself and your health.

9. Exercise regularly the rest of your life.

10. Learn, understand, and practice Herring's law of cure.

All cure starts from within out, from the head down, and in the reverse order as the symptoms have appeared. ~ Herrings Law of Cure ~

Bowen is soon to be a common household word for natural health and healing.

If you'd like to share your testimonial of what Bowen has done for you please e-mail it to testimonial@bowenhealingsystem.com

For those who would like to make a financial contribution to either the Foundation for Bowen Studies or Foundation for Bowen Research please contact foundation@bowenhealingsystem.com

Appendix

Tennis Elbow – a named condition of inflammation of the elbow due to overuse or improper use - Common in those who use their arms and hands playing tennis, golf, baseball, etc., or working in a manner where they use repetitive hand and arm motions.

Repetitive Strain Injury (RSI) – a named condition for wrist and hand discomfort or pain caused by consecutive hours of repetitive work such as data entry (keyboard and mouse), food preparation, factory or food processing worker, store cashier, and so forth.

Whiplash: Automobile and sports accident victims commonly experience whiplash – a condition caused by the head and neck being suddenly and sharply snapped (like a whip being cracked). When this happens, sprains (slight muscle tears and stretching of nerves) occur in the cervical spine (neck) region. This can cause injury to radiate down to and affect the coccyx region (tailbone). The sprain(s) also stretch the ligaments and smaller and medium sized muscles in the cervical region.

Commonly, whiplash produces fever, swelling, and minor hemorrhages. Whiplash sufferers can also experience stiff neck, shoulders, upper, middle and lower back, numbness in the arms and hands, and ringing in the ears. This also includes TMJ problems, a feeling of disconnectedness, lack of clarity, sluggishness, and arm and leg pains that persist days after the injury. These time-release effects occur as a result of the sprains received and their influence on the nerves that lead from the cervical spine. Whiplash often leads to chronic aches and pains and many other conditions. These long-term ramifications commonly occur because of the severity of the injury and trauma pattern(s) held in the body.

Resources

www.bowenhealingsystem.com

www.bowtech.com

CONCUSSION

www.airsip.com

Treatment of ADD/ADHD
Bowen Hands/ The Newsletter of Bowen Therapy Academy of Australia Volume 7 No. 4 Issue No. 27 p.8

Treatment of the Aged
Bowen Hands/ The Newsletter of Bowen Therapy Academy of Australia Volume 6 No. 3 Issue No. 22 p. 23
Bowen Hands/ The Newsletter of Bowen Therapy Academy of Australia Volume 6 No. 3 Issue No. 22 p. 27

AIDS
Bowen Hands / The Journal of Bowen Therapy Academy of Australia Volume 11 No. 1 Issue No. 40 p. 14-15

Treatment of Asthma
Bowen Hands/ The Newsletter of Bowen Therapy Academy of Australia Volume 6 No. 3 Issue No. 22 p. 22
Bowen Hands/ The Newsletter of Bowen Therapy Academy of Australia Volume 7 No. 4 Issue No. 27 p.21

Treatment of Injuries from Automobile Accidents
Bowen Hands/ The Newsletter of Bowen Therapy Academy of Australia Volume 6 No. 3 Issue No. 22 p. 25

Treatment of Back Pain
Bowen Hands / The Journal of Bowen Therapy Academy of Australia Volume 11 No. 1 Issue No. 40 p. 21
Bowen Hands / The Journal of Bowen Therapy Academy of Australia Volume 12 No. 1 Issue No. 44 p. 19-20
Severe Back Pain
Bowen Hands / The Journal of Bowen Therapy Academy of Australia Volume 12
No. 3 Issue No. 46 p. 13

Treatment of Bedwetting
Bowen Hands/ The Newsletter of Bowen Therapy Academy of Australia Volume 9 No. 1 Issue No. 32 p.23

Treatment of Carpal Tunnel Syndrome
Bowen Hands/ The Newsletter of Bowen Therapy Academy of Australia Volume 9
No. 1 Issue No. 32 p.22
Bowen Hands / The Journal of Bowen Therapy Academy of Australia Volume 11 No. 1 Issue No. 40 p. 15

Treatment of Cerebral Palsy
Bowen Hands/ The Newsletter of Bowen Therapy Academy of Australia Volume 7 No. 4 Issue No. 27 p.10

Treatment of Chronic Pain
Bowen Hands/ The Newsletter of Bowen Therapy Academy of Australia Volume 6 No. 3 Issue No. 22 p. 10-11
Bowen Hands/ The Newsletter of Bowen Therapy Academy of Australia Volume 6 No. 3 Issue No. 22 p. 14
Bowen Hands/ The Newsletter of Bowen Therapy Academy of Australia Volume 9 No. 1 Issue No. 32 p.8
Bowen Hands/ The Journal of Bowen Therapy Academy of Australia Volume 12 No. 1 Issue No. 44 p. 27
Bowen Hands / The Journal of Bowen Therapy Academy of Australia Volume 11 No. 1 Issue No. 40 p. 21

Treatment of Chronic Fatigue
Bowen Hands/ The Newsletter of Bowen Therapy Academy of Australia Volume 6 No. 3 Issue No. 22 p. 15
Bowen Hands/ The Newsletter of Bowen Therapy Academy of Australia Volume 10 No. 1 Issue No. 36 p. 15

Treatment of Painful Menstrual Periods
Bowen Hands/ The Newsletter of Bowen Therapy Academy of Australia Volume 6 No. 3 Issue No. 22 p. 14

Treatment of Severe Acute Pain
Bowen Hands/ The Newsletter of Bowen Therapy Academy of Australia Volume 7 No. 4 Issue No. 27 p.23

Treatment of Sciatica
Bowen Hands/ The Newsletter of Bowen Therapy Academy of Australia Volume 6 No. 4 Issue No. 23 p. 16

Treatment of Sinus
Bowen Hands/ The Newsletter of Bowen Therapy Academy of Australia Volume 6 No. 3 Issue No. 22 p. 14

Treatment of Spinal Stenosis
Bowen Hands/ The Newsletter of Bowen Therapy Academy of Australia Volume 9 No. 1 Issue No. 32 p.5-7

Sports and Bowen
Bowen Hands / The Journal of Bowen Therapy Academy of Australia Volume 11 No. 3 Issue No. 42 p. 26

Treatment of Clients who have suffered a stroke
Bowen Hands/ The Newsletter of Bowen Therapy Academy of Australia Volume 10 No. 1 Issue No. 36 p. 18

Treatment of TIC - Douloureux
Bowen Hands/ The Journal of Bowen Therapy Academy of Australia Volume 12 No. 1 Issue No. 44 p. 25-26

Treatment of TMJ
Bowen Hands/ The Newsletter of Bowen Therapy Academy of Australia Volume 6 No. 3 Issue No. 22 p. 25
Bowen Hands/ The Newsletter of Bowen Therapy Academy of Australia Volume 10 No. 1 Issue No. 36 p.5-6, 10-11

Weight Management
Bowen Hands/ The Journal of Bowen Therapy Academy of Australia Volume 11 No. 1 Issue No. 40 p.18-19
Bowen Hands/ The Journal of Bowen Therapy Academy of Australia Volume 10 No. 2 Issue No. 37 p.8

Treatment by Medical Doctors who are Bowen Practitioners
Bowen Hands/ The Newsletter of Bowen Therapy Academy of Australia Volume 6 No. 3 Issue No. 22 p. 8
PIONEERING MEDICAL OPTIONS

Treatment by Chiropractors who are Bowen Practitioners
Bowen Hands/ The Newsletter of Bowen Therapy Academy of Australia Volume 6 No. 3 Issue No. 22 p. 13

Bowen for Nurses
Bowen Hands / The Journal of Bowen Therapy Academy of Australia
June 2003 p. 6-7
Bowen Hands / The Journal of Bowen Therapy Academy of Australia Volume 13
No. 3 Issue No. 46 p. 7

Bowen and Midwifery
Bowen Hands/ The Journal of Bowen Therapy Academy of Australia Volume 10 No. 2 Issue No. 37 p.5-6
Bowen Hands/ The Newsletter of Bowen Therapy Academy of Australia Volume 10 No. 1 Issue No. 36 p.12-13

Rick Minnery / European Conference Notes - Cypress
          Australian Conference Notes - Geelong

_____

Bowen – Animals and Pets

Equine Muscle Release Technique ~ EMRT

Bowen Hands/ The Newsletter of Bowen Therapy Academy of Australia Volume 9 No. 1 Issue No. 32 p.20-21
Bowen Hands/ The Newsletter of Bowen Therapy Academy of Australia Volume 10 No. 1 Issue No. 36 p. 14-15
Bowen Hands/ The Journal of Bowen Therapy Academy of Australia Volume 10 No. 2 Issue No. 37 p.14-15
Bowen Hands/ The Newsletter of Bowen Therapy Academy of Australia Volume 10 No. 1 Issue No. 36 p. 16
Bowen Hands / The Newsletter of Bowen Therapy Academy of Australia Volume 6 No. 1 Issue No. 20 p. 6-7
Bowen Hands / The Journal of Bowen Therapy Academy of Australia Volume 11 No. 2 Issue No. 41 p. 14-15
Bowen Hands / The Journal of Bowen Therapy Academy of Australia Volume 12 No. 4 Issue No. 47 p. 11
Bowen Hands / The Newsletter of Bowen Therapy Academy of Australia Volume 9 No. 1 Issue No. 32 p.20-21
Bowen Hands / The Journal of Bowen Therapy Academy of Australia Volume 11 No. 1 Issue No. 40 p. 20
Bowen Hands / The Journal of Bowen Therapy Academy of Australia Volume 12 No. 1 Issue No. 44 p. 22
Bowen Hands / The Journal of Bowen Therapy Academy of Australia Volume 12 No. 1 Issue No. 44 p. 15-16
Bowen Hands / The Journal of Bowen Therapy Academy of Australia Volume 11 No. 3 Issue No. 42 p. 10
Bowen Hands / The Journal of Bowen Therapy Academy of Australia Volume 11 No. 3 Issue No. 42 p. 32

Bowen and Animals
Bowen Hands / The Journal of Bowen Therapy Academy of Australia Volume 12 No. 3 Issue No. 46 p. 20
Bowen Hands / The Journal of Bowen Therapy Academy of Australia Volume 11 No. 1 Issue No. 40 p. 23
Bowen Hands / The Journal of Bowen Therapy Academy of Australia
June 2003 p. 13

Touch Balancing – Bowen for Animals
Bowen Hands / The Journal of Bowen Therapy Academy of Australia Volume 11 No. 3 Issue No. 42 p. 24-25

CCMRT (Cat and Canine Muscle Release Technique)
Bowen Hands / The Journal of Bowen Therapy Academy of Australia Volume 12 No. 1 Issue No. 44 p. 21

Other

Distance Healing
Bowen Hands / The Journal of Bowen Therapy Academy of Australia Volume 12 No. 3 Issue No. 46 p. 21

Milton Albrecht
Bowen Hands / The Journal of Bowen Therapy Academy of Australia Volume 12 No. 1 Issue No. 44 p.13

The Gentlest, Most Effective Pain Therapy Ever – *Second Opinion* **article submission**
Bowen Hands / The Journal of Bowen Therapy Academy of Australia Volume 12 No. 3 Issue No. 46 p. 5-6

UP TO DATE ARTICLES

For up-to-date current articles that have been written by healthcare professionals and Bowen practitioners regarding Bowen, visit **www.bowenhealingsystem.com**

OTHER REFERENCES

A Report to the National Institutes of Health on Alternative Medical Systems and Practices in the United States 1992
ALTERNATIVE MEDICINE EXPANDING MEDICAL HORIZONS Washington D.C.
US Government

ADVANCE for Physical Therapists & PT assistants
BOWEN
October 22, 2001 pp. 35-37 Dan Amato, RRT, RBT, RBTI

Archterberg, J. 1985
IMAGERY IN HEALING Boston
Shambhala

Achterberg J., Lawlis, F. 1982
IMAGERY AND HEALTH INTERVENTIONS
Topics in Clinical Nursing pp. 55-60

Becker, Dr. Robert O.
THE BODY ELECTRIC

Benson, Herbert 1975
THE RELAXATION RESPONSE New York:
William Morrow and Company

Burmeister, Alice and Monte, Tom 1997
THE TOUCH OF HEALING New York:
Bantam Books

Borysenko, Joan 1987
MINDING THE BODY, MENDING THE MIND New York:
Bantam Books

Brennan, Barbara Ann 1988
HANDS OF LIGHT New York:
Bantam Books

Childre, D.L. 1995)
FREEZEFRAME FAST ACTION STRESS RELIEF: A SCIENTIFICALLY PROVEN TECHNIQUE Boulder, Co
Planetary Publications

Chopra, Deepak 1990
QUANTUM HEALING New York:
Bantam Books

Darkik, I. 1996
"The origin of disease and health heart waves"
CYCLES

Evans, Julie October 1999
    PREVENTION pp.125
    Prevention Magazine

Everly, G.S. & Benson, H. 1989
    DISORDERS OF AROUSAL AND THE RELAXATION RESPONSE
    PSYCHOSOM pp. 15-21

Fischer, K. Brent D.C. August 2003
    WATER VS.COKE
    FYI - E-Mail

Gerber, R. 2000
    VIBRATIONAL MEDICINE FOR THE 21ST CENTURY   New York
    Harper Collins

Greenspan, FS, & Stewler, GJ 1997
    BASIC AND CLINICAL ENDOCRINOLOGY Stamford, CT
    Appelton and Lange

Hassmen, P. Koivula, N. & Hansson, T. 1998
    PERCEPT MOTOR SKILLS

Houk, James Charles, Jr.   1963
    A MATHEMATICAL MODEL OF THE STRETCH REFLEX IN HUMAN MUSCLE SYSTEMS
    Masters Thesis
    Massachusetts Institute of Technology (MIT)

Jacob, S. & Francone, C. 1989
    ELEMENTS OF ANATOMY AND PHYSIOLOGY 2nd Ed. Philadelphia
    W. B. Saunders

Johnson, Sharlene K. December 2004
    "Stay-Healthy Secrets of Alternative Doctors"
    FRESH THINKING - Health

Karigulla, S. and Kunz, D. 1989
    THE CHAKRAS AND THE HUMAN ENERGY FIELDS   Wheaton, IL
    Theosophical Publishing House

Kenner, C., Achterberg J. 1984
    NONPHARMACOLOGIC PAIN RELIEF FOR BURN PATIENTS Bethesda, MD
    National Institute of Health

Krieger, D. 1993
    ACCEPTING YOUR POWER TO HEAL   Santa Fe, NM
    Bear and Co.

Kunz, Dora, and Erik Peper 1982
    "Fields and Their Clinical Implications"
    THE AMERICAN THEOSOPHIST December

Leja, A. 1989

Mattimoe, Craig NT, RBT
  ACCELERATED RECOVERY
  AIRSIP.com

McLaren, Karla   1998
  YOUR AURAS & YOUR CHAKRAS   York Beach, Maine
  Samuel Weiser, Inc.

Newsweek, people….
  THE GREAT BACK DEBATE
  (www.msnbc.com/id/4767783/)

Maltz, M. 1987
  MAGIC POWER OF SELF-IMAGE PSYCHOLOGY New York
  Prentice Hall

McCarrol, J. 1996
  CLINICAL SPORTS MEDICINE.
  Jan 15 p. 1-17

McNamara, Rita J. 1998
  ENERGETIC BODYWORK   York Beach, Maine
  Samuel Weiser, Inc.

Migeon, CJ, & Lanes, RL
  PEDATRIC ENDOCRINLOGY   A CLINICAL GUIDE
  Second Edition   New York, New York
   Marcel Dekker, Inc.

Montoyama 1984
  A biophysical elucidation of the meridian and Ki-energy
  INTERNATIONAL ASSOCIATION FOR RELIGION AND PARAPSYCHOLOGY 7:1

Nicohlson, N, & Storms, C, & Ponds, R, & Sulon, J 1997

  Salivary Cortisol Levels and Stress Reactivity in Human Aging

  GERONTOLOGY

Oschman, J.L. 2000

  ENERGY MEDICINE THE SCIENTIFIC BASIS New York:

  Churchill Livingstone

Oz, MD, Dr. Mehemet   2003
  Healing With An Open Mind – a surgeon learns to trust the wisdom of other medical traditions
  PARADE
  30 November, p.27-28

Rossi, E. & Cheek D. 1988

  MIND-BODY THERAPY New York

  Norton

Rossi, E. 1986
    THE PSYCHOBIOLOGY OF MIND-BODY HEALING   New York:
    Norton

Rousselot, Patrik, P.T. ~ Novey, Donald, et al. 2000
    CLINICIAN'S COMPLETE REFERENCE TO COMPLEMENTARY AND   ALTERNATIVE MEDICINE
St. Louis:
    Mosby

Rowen, MD. Dr. Robert Jay   Atlanta, Georgia
    SECOND OPINION Vol. XIII, No. 7
    Second Opinion Publishing

Song, L. Z., Schwartz, G.E., and Russek, L.G. 1998
    "Heart-focused attention and heart-brain synchronization: energetic and physiological mechanisms"
    ALTERNATIVE THERAPY HEALTH MEDICINE Vol 4 p. 44-52, 54-60, 62

Stacey, Michelle July 2004
    "Need a tune-up?"
    bodywise
    O THE OPRAH MAGAZINE p.98

    Suinn, R.M. 1985
    "Imagery Rehearsal application to performance enhancement"
    BEHAVIOR THERAPIST 155-159

Task Force of the European Society of Cardiology and North American Society for Pacing and Electrophysiology 1996

    "Heart Rate Variability: Standard Measurement, Physiological Interpretation, and Clinical Use"

    EUROPEAN HEART JOURNAL April pp.151-179

Tusek, D. and Cwynar, R. 2000

    " Strategies for implementing a guided imagery program to enhance patient experience"

    AACN CLINICAL ISSUES 11 68-76

Weil, MD. Dr. Andrew 1995
    SPONTANEOUS HEALING New York
    Fawcett Columbine

Williams, Dottie 1998
    MIND, BODY, AND SOUL
    Bullfinch Press

Wise, A. 1995
    HIGH PERFORMANCE MIND New York
    G.P. Putnam's Sons

January-February 2005
    UTNE Periodical   Minneapolis:
    LENS Publishing Co. Inc.

NATURAL STANDARD

An organization that produces scientifically based reviews of complementary and alternative medicine (CAM) topics
www.naturalstandard.com

NATIONAL CENTER FOR COMPLEMENTARY AND ALTERNATIVE MEDICINE (NCCAM)
A division of the U.S. Department of Health & Human Services dedicated to research
www.nccam.nih.gov

Bowen Scientific Studies and Research

Research on the following topics and other various links can be found on www.bowenhealingsystem.com

BUNIONS
>Lambeth, B.

CARPAL TUNNEL SYNDROME
>Sheedy, G.

CHRONIC LOWER BACK PAIN
>Rayment, J.

FROZEN SHOULDER
>1. Carter, B.
>2. Kinnear, H. and Baker, J.

HEART RATE VARIANCE
>Whitaker, J., Gilliam, P., Seba, D.

MIGRAINES
>Ariffe, N.

PSYCHOPHYSIOLOGICAL EFFECTS
>Pritchard, A.

RESTLESS LEG SYNDROME
>Biorac, M.

WELLBEING
>Rayment, J.

Carter B. 2001
>"A pilot study to evaluate the effectiveness of Bowen technique in the management of clients with frozen shoulder"
>COMPLEMENTARY THERAPY MEDICINE December pp. 208-215

Carter B. 2002
>"Clients' experience of frozen shoulder and its treatment with Bowen technique" COMPLEMENTARY THERAPIES IN NURSING & MIDWIFERY AUGUST PP. 204-210

Long, L, & Huntley, A, & Ernst, E.
>Which complementary and alternative therapies benefit which conditions? A survey of the opinions of 223 professional organizations. Complement Therapy Med 2001;Sep, 9(3):178-185.